ton Mercury.

(To be continued Weekly.   Price Two-pence.)

Scheffer, Brother of our
oing back to Paris with the
been held on the Difpatches
t ago.   The King's Mini-
irected to give the Reafons
add to the Declarations it

All the Regiments have
eadinefs to take the Field at
s a Talk of forming a Camp
ital, and and another in

L Y.
Arrival of a Courier from
en to fill all the Magazines
Account the Court has pro
G.
dron which has been equip-
ort is now ready, and will
, in order to cruize on the

fron Berlin, that his Pruffian
ful at Algiers, for the Ad-
ubjects, and that M. Lutens
Gt.
g to the laft Advices from
Month twelve Corfairs, and
have lately taken two rich
om the Havannah.——The
ve of frefh Troubles in Italy,
pleated, and two new Regi-

ng it is confidently afferted,
g of Sardinia is compleating
his Garrifons in the Novar-
in it : On the Contrary,
here is generally a Circular
mpleat their Regiments, yet
; and in Novarra there is
s there ufed to be commonly

A N Y.
has fent Orders to M.

the North, and alfo from Spain and Italy ; but their Difpatches
are kept very fecret.   Expreffes alfo arrive frequently from
London, and the Court appears very well fatisfied with the
Marquefs de Mirepoix's Difpatches relating to the Affairs of
the North, as his Excellency fends a Confirmation of the Britifh
Miniftry's fincere Defire to do all that lies in their Power to
prevent Hoftilities between the Swedes and the Ruffians, efpe-
cially fince the King of Pruffia has declar'd to the Courts of
London, Vienna, and Peterfburgh, that he will affift Sweden,
in cafe fhe be attack d by Ruffia.   As for the Sincerity of the
Britifh Miniftry in this Affair, we don't in the leaft doubt it,
but very much queftion their Succefs. L.

Paris, April 10.   We received Letters which advife, that
on the 3d of this Month there has been about Orleans and
Blois a very hard Froft, which it was apprehended had done
great Damage to the Fruit-Trees and Vines.   G.

F L A N D R E S.

Bruffels, April 13.   They write from Oftend, Ghent,
Bruges, Calais, and other Places, as well in Flanders as on the
Coafts of France, that there daily arrive a great Number of
Englifh Families, who retire thither to avoid the terrible Earth-
quake with which they imagine they are threaten'd in England
the 15th or 16th of this Month. Wh.

Bergen-op-Zoom, April 13.   Yefterday at Noon all the
Soldiers in this Garrifon were drawn out to receive the Prince
Stadtholder, who arrived here about Three in the Afternoon,
to the great Joy of the Inhabitants.   His Royal Highnefs was
immediately faluted by a general Difcharge of all the Cannon
on the Ramparts, and foon after complimented by the Magi-
ftrates in a Body.   Laft Night and this Day his Highnefs has
been vifiting all the Fortifications of this Place. Gt.

H O L L A N D.

Hague, April 17.   The States of Holland have publifhed
an Ordonnance, by which they lay a Duty of one Duyt per
Sheet upon all Pamphlets, News Papers, and other Periodical
Pi   inted in this Province, and double that Tax upon
a   ted in Foreign Parts, and
j   exempt from this Duty fuch
                            e Hebrew, Greek, or Latin
                          that all Works, (even the
                          he real Name of the Printer,
and the   where they are printed, fhall be feized by the Col-

News from the

English Countryside

WILLIAM FAULKNER.

*Newsman to the Manchester Times and Cheshire
Examiner.*

THE MARY EVANS PICTURE LIBRARY

News from the English Countryside
1750 - 1850

Clifford Morsley

Harrap London

To Georgina
my wife
and our daughters
Penelope and Judith

First published in Great Britain 1979
by GEORGE G. HARRAP & CO. LTD
182–184 High Holborn, London WC1V 7AX

© *Clifford Morsley* 1979

ISBN 0 245 53453 9

Designed by Robert Wheeler

Filmset by Woolaston Parker Ltd, Leicester
Printed by William Clowes and Sons Ltd, Beccles
Bound by Western Book Company Ltd, Maesteg

Contents

Introduction *page 7*

1750-59   11

1760-69   39

1770-79   69

1780-89   95

1790-99   125

1800-09 *page 149*

1810-19   181

1820-29   213

1830-39   241

1840-50   279

Indexes   314

The vignettes in the text are taken from the History of British Birds *and the* General History of Quadrupeds *by the great British engraver Thomas Bewick (1753–1828)*

The front and rear endpapers are reproduced by permission of The British Library

Introduction

Lord Macaulay declared that 'the only true history of a country is to be found in its newspapers'. There is little doubt that he was thinking particularly of outstanding national events—parliamentary struggles, military campaigns and the like—as reported in the well-known dailies and weeklies available in his own lifetime. I have read through over a hundred years of newspapers (1750–1850) for news stories from the market towns, the villages and the hamlets of England from the later part of the reign of George II until the early Victorian era. As a result, I am very sure that they contain much of the true history of rural life in the eighteenth and nineteenth centuries.

In this book national events are covered to show how much, or how little, they influenced the life of the *countryman* and his family. But most of the reports in this collection—mainly from provincial newspapers—are of happenings which concerned only a fairly limited area. One of the earliest gives advice on 'How to Perplex a Witch', and ninety-two years later there is an account of a man who claimed to have been the victim of a spell cast by his mother-in-law. In between are records that include murder and smuggling, dire distress and old customs—and some good country humour as well.

As to the historical 'backcloth' to these news stories, I think that firstly it is of some value to remember that many of the first readers of the earlier ones were people who had very recent recollections of 'the '45', when the Young Pretender made his abortive attempt to win back the throne of his grandfather, James II. Indeed, several of them could recall the death of Queen Anne, last of the Stuart monarchs, in 1714. But in 1750 the Hanoverian dynasty was firmly established, and George II had been king for twenty-two years. William Pitt, later Earl of Chatham, was a leading Minister; in 1756 he was to become Secretary of State, and was the architect of Britain's victories in the Seven Years War.

In October 1760, at the beginning of the second decade covered in these pages (1760–9), George III came to the throne, and in 1763 the Seven Years War ended with the Peace of Paris. The years immediately following were of great significance in what we know to-day as the Industrial Revolution. Of even greater concern to those whose way of life was chronicled in the country newspapers was the Agricultural Revolution, which owed much to the crop-rotation ideas of Viscount ('Turnip') Townshend in the earlier part of the century, and to the machinery developed from Jethro Tull's seed-drill (1701). For small farmers and labourers, however, it was a far from prosperous time. Under the Enclosure Acts of the latter eighteenth century a great many of them lost their farms and common land to wealthy men, and were compelled to look for work in the industrial towns. Those who remained in the familiar villages toiled under conditions which led to rick-burning and riots. In the 1770s a large number of these unhappy and hungry men joined the smugglers. Their illicit trade was mainly in tea and brandy; the papers abounded in stories of desperate affrays in which soldiers met up with 'free-traders' in gangs of a hundred or more. Several of the stories from 1775 have a martial flavour, for the reason that this year saw the outbreak of the War of American Independence, which came to an end with the Treaty of Versailles in 1783.

In 1784 there was a major domestic development of particular importance to those who lived in the country areas and had the inclination or need—and the money—to visit the towns and cities. In that year the first mail-coaches took to the roads, in succession to the springless stage-coaches which had creaked over broken-down and ill-kept highways that became hazardous on the slightest approach of bad weather, and were quagmires in heavy rain. The mail-coaches travelled on a system of much-improved 'turnpike' roads that had been started in the 1770s. Much more exciting were the exploits of M. Lunardi, who flew over England in a balloon in 1784, five years before the start of the French Revolution.

The French revolutionaries had been much influenced by the War of American Independence, for volunteers from France who had served with George Washington craved political freedom for their own country, and the success of the American colonists had greatly encouraged them in their plans to obtain it. The French Revolution began in July 1789, with the fall of the Bastille, and in January 1793 the French beheaded their king, Louis XVI. The English newspapers recorded that there was little sympathy for such revolutionary activities among the subjects of George III. It will be seen that in the towns and villages of England there were meetings in support of 'King and Constitution', at which there was also a great amount of beer-drinking.

In February 1793 the French declared war on Britain; it was to continue, with brief intermissions, until Napoleon was defeated at Waterloo in 1815. As a result of the war the people of Britain were for the first time subjected to an Income Tax, levied on all with an annual income above £60. The Younger Pitt's proposals for the tax were agreed in December 1798. Those whose means were far below the £60 limit suffered in a more tangible manner. It will be seen that in the summer of 1800 *The Times* reported potato riots; these were due to bad harvests which made famine and starvation real possibilities. In 1800 the price of wheat increased to the alarming price of 134 shillings per quarter, and in 1801 there was a further increase of 22 shillings. A quartern loaf of bread cost two shillings, which put it far beyond the purses of the labouring classes.

In 1803 the war came very close to home with the threat of imminent invasion, as Napoleon's fleet gathered at Boulogne. At least one of the many news stories about plans to repel the French can surely rank with the most evocative of reports of present-day war correspondents:

> The Beacons are establishing at Canterbury, Shorn Cliff, Barham, Isle of Thanet, Shottenden, Hythe. . . . which, beginning from Canterbury . . . will be successively fired at the near approach or actual landing of the enemy . . . on which signal everyone is to assemble at his known place of rendezvous.

In that same issue of the *Kentish Herald* is the news that Mr Pitt had visited the coast to inspect the defences as Lord Warden of the Cinque Ports. In another autumn nearly 140 years later, Winston Churchill, also Lord Warden, was to make similar inspections as the country prepared to defend itself against invasion by a German army.

When peace came again it was accompanied by a Corn Law (1815) which together with bad harvests provided a very tragic aftermath to a war which had lasted over twenty years. 'Distresses in Staffordshire', recorded in *The Times* in August 1816, exemplified conditions in many other parts of the country at a time when the Corn Law had the effect of raising the price of a loaf of bread to the equivalent of a labourer's wage for a whole day's work. These were further privations and hardships, which were to have a culmination in the Agrarian Revolution of 1830, when the fields of England were set ablaze by men who rallied to the cry of 'Bread or Blood' and carried tricolour flags.

In the year of the farmworkers' rebellion George IV died at Windsor Castle on 26 June. The short reign of William IV, almost exactly seven years, saw the final stages of the battle for parliamentary reform which resulted in the Reform Bill of 1832. It also included the introduction of the Poor Law Amendment Act of 1834. While the former had little immediate influence on the enfranchisement of the poor—the latter was the source of the harrowing workhouse stories—based on fact—in which Victorian novelists seemed to take particular delight.

Victoria became Queen in 1837, in the early years of the railways. At the time of her coronation, and again in 1840, when she was married, hundreds of villages celebrated in the fashion of 'loyal and patriotic Welwyn' as reported in the *Hertford and Bedford Reformer.* The beef and plum-pudding distributed on such occasions were much enjoyed by families which existed on a wage of nine shillings per week (in some parts of Dorset, as little as seven shillings). Happily, in the closing years of the period covered by this book an appreciable and stable reduction in the price of a loaf of bread was made possible through the Repeal of the Corn Laws in 1846, after years of agitation by the Anti-Corn-Law League (formed in 1838).

In the earlier part of this introduction I mentioned that people who read the earlier stories in this book when they first appeared in the newspapers could remember the death of Queen Anne in 1714. Some who read the reports of 1850 as they came off the press in that year were still alive in 1914, and read of the outbreak of the Kaiser's war.

Headlines in early newspapers were very much of a rarity. A village occurrence was generally included in a single, unheaded paragraph in a column of snippets from several other parishes. When such items were given some sort of grouping later on, a general classification was used, often just 'Country Matters', or 'Country Affairs'. Because of this most of the headlines in this book are of my own making. Those used by a newspaper's own editorial staff are marked by an asterisk.

I am grateful for the courteous assistance of members of the staff of the British Museum Newspaper Library over a very considerable period. I acknowledge, too, the kindness of the people I approached in my research for notes which give background information for some of the stories. They include the present-day occupiers of some of the inns and other buildings referred to in the old newspapers.

CLIFFORD MORSLEY

1750-59

A TURNSPIT DOG
The dog is seen at work in the wheel.

1750

A Wedding Breakfast

On the 7th. instant was married at Rothbury in Northumberland, Mr. William Donkin, a considerable Farmer of Tossin in that County, to Miss Eleanor Shotton, an agreeable young Gentlewoman of the same Place. The Entertainment on this occasion was very grand, there being provided no less than 120 Quarters of Lamb, 44 Quarters of Veal, 20 Quarters of Mutton, a great Quantity of Beef, 12 Hams with a suitable Number of Chickens &c, which was concluded with eight Half Anchors of Brandy made into Punch, 12 Dozen of Cyder, a great many Gallons of Wine, and 90 Bushels of Malt brew'd into Beer. The Company consisted of 450 Gentlemen and Ladies, who were diverted with the Music of 25 Fidlers and Pipers, and the whole was concluded with the utmost Order and Unanimity.

The Northampton Mercury
25 June 1750

A Royal Treat

Bristol, July 14
Yesterday their Royal Highnesses, the Prince and Princess of Wales, with their eldest Daughter, Princess Augusta, attended by some of the Nobility, came in Wherries about five miles down the River, and dined in Publick, under two Tents, in a large Mead near the River Side, where Abundance of Country People resorted, and to whom his Royal Highness gave several Hogsheads of Beer, which were brought in a Cart from the Handsome Landladies. A Band of Musicians attended the whole time.

The Northampton Mercury
30 July 1750

❀ *This particular Prince of Wales was 'Poor Fred', eldest son of George II. The site of this picnic, on the banks of the Avon, was a meadow at Saltford, a few miles from Bristol. 'Poor Fred', who died in the following year, was the father of George III.*

A Turnspit Dog

Bristol

Last week a Turnspit Dog, at Mr. Roberts's, at the Crown, without Lawfords Gate, being mad, bit the following Persons, viz. Mr. Bearcroft's Maid Servant, Mrs. Dyer, a Midwife, and the Drawer of the said Publick-House; and also several Dogs. On Wednesday the above persons were dipp'd in the Salt Water at the New-passage. The Dog was kill'd as soon as discovered to be mad.

> The Northampton Mercury
> 30 July 1750

❁ *Turnspit dogs were used in the kitchens of many inns and large private houses. They were put into an iron wheel connected to a roasting jack, and turned the wheel with the weight of their bodies. Dr Caius, founder of Caius College, Cambridge, and the renowned English writer on dogs, declared that they 'so diligently look to their business, that no drudge nor scullion can do the feat more cunningly'.*

Smuggled Tea

Bristol, September 22

We had last Week the following melancholly Account from Dover: A Gentleman having Purchased a Pound of Bohea Tea from a Smuggler, brought it to his wife, who looking on it found it mix'd with an Herb, nearly resembling the Tea Leaf; and suspecting it might be of a pernicious Quality, carried it to an Apothecary in the Neighbourhood, who not understanding the Herb mix'd with it, pounded some and gave it to a Dog, which was immediately seized with Convulsions, and the Day following died. Diligent Search is making after the Smuggler, but 'tis feared he is got quite off; all the Account that can be learnt of him since is that he belongs to a large Gang in the West.

> The Northampton Mercury
> 1 October 1750

❁ *Bohea was a black China tea, and at this time would have been a choice variety. By the end of the nineteenth century, however, the description identified a poor-quality black tea.*

Threat to burn Luton

Whereas the Revd. Mr. Barnard, Vicar of Luton, in Bedfordshire, received a Letter by the General Post, not dated, signed L. D. threatening to burn the Town of Luton, and as many Farm-Houses, Barns, Ricks of Corn and Hay, as he can, and also to poison all the Cattle, Grass, Hay and Water, if he refused to collect, or cause to be collected from the Parishioners, by the Parish Officers, the sum of Five Pounds, and leave it under the Figures of the 31 Mile Stone in the Road leading from Luton to St. Alban's—For the better discovering and bringing to Justice, the Person, or Persons concerned in writing the said Letter, we the Churchwardens of Luton aforesaid, for ourselves and Successors, do hereby promise a Reward of Twenty Pounds to any Person or Persons (except the Person who actually wrote the said Letter) who shall discover one or more Accomplice or Accomplices therein, so that he, she, or they, may be apprehended and convicted thereof.

Joseph Freeman ⎱ Churchwardens
John Surry ⎰

And as a further encouragement, the inhabitants of Luton aforesaid do promise to make all the interest they can to obtain his Majesty's most Gracious Pardon for any such Accomplice who shall make the aforesaid Discovery. They will likewise be entitled to the Reward the Government has allowed in these Cases.

The Northampton Mercury
31 December 1750

1751

Fatal End to a Witch Hunt

Last Monday the following most extraordinary Affair happened at Tring, in Hertfordshire; some of the Country People having entertain'd an Opinion that an old Man and Woman in that Town were a Wizard and a Witch, on Account of several Cattle dying of the present Contagion, great Numbers assembled, some on Horseback and others on foot, and went in a Body and proclaimed them as such in three different Market-Towns, and about Four in the Afternoon return'd to Tring, and demanded the supposed Wizard and Witch, whom the inhabitants had sent to the

Workhouse for Security; which the enraged populace being informed of, went thither, and being refused Admittance, they pull'd down the greatest part of the Workhouse and a House adjacent; but the Master, in the mean while, having convey'd them to the Vestry of the Church, they afterwards assembled there, obliging the Master of the Workhouse to go with them; they took them out by Violence, and carried them two Miles from the Town, where they bound her Hands and Feet, and after beating her in a cruel and barbarous Manner, threw her into a Pond of Water, where she perish'd; the old Man was likewise treated in the same Manner, but fortunately happen'd to survive this Cruelty. Several persons are since taken and committed to Custody, for so inhuman a Proceeding; and an Enquiry is order'd to be made by Mr. Atkins, Coroner of the County, into the Affair, and a Jury of Gentlemen summoned to attend at Tring on the Occasion.

The Northampton Mercury
29 April 1751

The Inhuman Transaction at Tring

The following being a more circumstantial Account of the inhuman Transaction at Tring in Hertfordshire, than what was mentioned in our Last ... we presume that our readers will not be displeased at its being inserted. A Person who keeps a Publick-House had given out he was bewitched by one Osborne and his Wife (inoffensive People of the age of 60 years and upwards) and had it Cried at several Market Towns, that they were to be tried by Ducking on Monday the 22nd., when about Noon, a great Concourse of people appeared in the Town. The Officers of the Parish had privately removed the Poor old Couple, in the dead Time of the Night, to a Place of Safety. The Mob demanded these unhappy Wretches at the Workhouse, but on being acquainted they were not there, they pulled down the Pales and Walls, broke all the Windows, and demolished a Part of the House. After searching the Chimnies and Ceilings without Effect, they seized the Governor, hawled him down to the Stream, and declared they would drown him, and fire the whole Town, unless they delivered up those poor Creatures in to their Hand. The Mob ran up and down the Town with straw in their Hands and were going to put their Threats into Execution, had they not been delivered up. These miserable Creatures were now dragged two Miles, strip stark naked, their Thumbs tied to their Toes, and in this shameful Manner, were thrown into a muddy Stream. After much Ducking and ill usage, the poor old Woman was thrown quite naked on the Bank, almost choaked with mud and expired in a few Minutes, being kicked and beat with sticks even after she was dead. To add to their barbarity they put the dead Witch (as they called her) in Bed with her Husband, and tied them together. Last Thursday Joseph Atkinson, Esq., Coroner for the County of Hertford, sat on the Body of the poor Woman, while the following persons were brought in guilty of Wilful Murder, viz. Thomas Mason, William Myatt, Richard Grice, Richard Wadley, James Froudham, John Sprouting, John May, Adam Curling and Francis Meadows, besides twenty others, whose Names are unknown.

The Northampton Mercury
6 May 1751

❀ *Ruth Osborne is said to have acquired a reputation as a witch through an incident that took place six years earlier, in 1745, when Charles Stuart was still enjoying some triumphs in his march towards London. Begging some milk from a farmer named Butterfield and getting a firm refusal, she apparently voiced the hope that the Pretender would soon be at Tring and take away Butterfield's cattle. Because of an illness and other misfortunes which followed soon afterwards, the farmer became convinced that Ruth Osborne had put a spell on him, and he arranged for a wise woman, or white witch, from Northamptonshire to take counter-measures. On her orders, six men armed with pitchforks were put on a day and night guard at the Butterfield home. To prevent their being bewitched in turn, she gave them charms to hang round their necks. It was when Butterfield continued to suffer misfortune that he and his friends decided on more direct action against the unlucky Mrs Osborne. It was on their instructions that the town criers of Hemel Hempstead, Leighton Buzzard and Winslow made the following announcement on market day in their towns: 'This is to give notice that on Monday next a man and woman are to be publicly ducked at Tring, in this county, for their wicked crimes.'*

Defeating the Wreckers

Extract of a Letter from Bridport, May 1
Yesterday sail'd from hence the Reine Gabrielle, John le Bratte, Commander, from Morlaix, laden with above 100 Hogsheads of Honey, from Dunkirk. The said Ship was on the 25th. March last, in a violent Storm, drove ashore on our Beach, but all the Hands were saved. The Captain, on his coming on shore, was recommended to Robert Fowler Coade, Esq. a considerable Merchant of Lyme-Regis, and accordingly applied to him for Assistance, and by the Care and Directions of this

Gentleman, the said Ship was got off the Beach, and brought safe again into the Harbour, with little Damage, which was soon repair'd, and the whole Cargo sav'd and reshipped entire, without the least Embezzlement from the Country People, tho' they came down in large Numbers to the beach the Night the Vessell was stranded, in Hopes of making a Prey of both Ship and Cargo. But by the Courage and Vigilance of Mr. Brown, Officer of the Town, and others he call'd to his Assistance, their barbarous Design was frustrated. Tho' the Cargo was *Honey*, they found it would be a *sour* Jobb to pilfer any, and therefore soon dispersed.

The Northampton Mercury
13 May 1751

Arrangements for Execution

Hertford, August 17
Last Tuesday, in the Afternoon a second Reprieve arriv'd here for Thomas Colley, who was to have been executed on this Day, for the Murder of Ruth Osborne, as a witch, on the 22nd. of April last, in a Pond called Marlston-Mere, in the Parish of Tring, and appointing his Execution to be on Saturday, the 24th. instant. He is to be carried from thence to Marlston-Green, where the Murder was committed (which is near 30 miles) and there hang'd on a Gibbet to be erected for that purpose, and afterwards hung in Chains on the said Gibbet. The People in that part of the Country, still continuing so infatuated as to believe the old Woman was a Witch, and that the Man is to be hang'd wrongfully, threaten to rescue him, but a large Guard of the Royal Regiment of Horse Blues is order'd to attend the Execution. The Farmers &c. in the Neighbourhood of Tring are also so silly as to suppose the Husband of the poor Creature deceas'd to be a Wizard and notwithstanding he is able and willing to work, they will not employ him; and he is now provided for by the Parish. He was extreamly ill-treated at the same Time with his Wife, but, being of a hearty constitution, survived.

The Northampton Mercury
26 August 1751

Death and Declaration

Last Friday, about Ten in the Morning, Thomas Colley, condemn'd for the Murder of Ruth Osborne, as a supposed witch, received the Sacrament at Hertford, administer'd to him by the Rev. Edward Bouchier, when he signed the following Declaration of his Faith, relating to Witchcraft; which he desired might be carried to the Place of Execution and was there

publicly read, at his earnest Request, just before he was turn'd off, by the
Rev. Mr. Randall, Minister of Tring, who attended him in his last
Moments. Friday night he was lodg'd in St. Alban's Gaol; and at Five the
next morning was put into a One-Horse Chaise, with the Executioner,
and conducted thro' Corner Hall, over Bexmore, thro' Berkhamstead and
Tring, by the Sheriff and his Officers, and a Guard of the Regiment of
Horse Blue, who join'd with another Party that met them at
Berkhamstead, in all 108, and seven Officers, with two Trumpets (the
Procession being slow, solemn and moving) who convey'd him to a place
called Gubbclutt Cross, the People above Marlston-Mere having
petitioned he might not hang so near their Houses, and came to the Place
of Execution about Eleven and, after about half an Hour spent in Prayer,
he was executed, and immediately after hung up in Chains on the same
Gibbet he was hang'd on. He behaved very penitently, but said very little.
The Populace were so affrighted at the Sight of the Soldiers, that they
durst not come near, but stood at a great Distance, scarce 100 coming to
the Place, and those chiefly Women and Children. Not but that there
were many Thousands who stood at a great Distance from the Soldiers as
they passed by different Places and, no doubt, would have obstructed the
Execution, had they not been intimidated, by insisting that it was a hard
Case to hang a Man for destroying a wicked old Woman that had done so
much Damage by her Witchcraft. A very odd Accident happened in Tring
Town, which was that just as the Prisoner's Wife and Daughters were
permitted to speak to him, one of the Trooper's Pistols went off,
occasioned by his Handkerchief evidently getting into the Holster, which
he pulling out drew the Trigger, and the Ball went into the Ground, but
no other damage ensued than putting the Corps in some Disorder, it
being at first imagined to have been fired out of a Window.

The declaration of Thomas Colley

Good People!

I beseech you all to take Warning by an unhappy man's suffering that
you be not deluded into so absurd and wicked a conceit as to believe there
are any such Beings on Earth as Witches.

It was that foolish and vain Imagination, heightened and inflam'd by
the Strength of Liquor, which prompted me to be instrumental (with
others as mad-brained as myself) in the horrid and barbarous Murder of
Ruth Osborne, the supposed witch, for which I am now so deservedly to
suffer Death.

I am fully convinced of my former Error and with the Sincerity of a
dying Man, declare that I do not believe there is such a Thing in Being as a
Witch, and pray that none of you, thro' a contrary Persuasion, may

hereafter be induced to think you have a Right in any Shape to persecute, much less endanger, the Life of a Fellow Creature.

I beg of you all to pray to God to forgive me, and to wash clean my polluted Soul in the Blood of Jesus Christ, my Saviour and Redeemer: So exhorteth you all, the dying

Thomas Colley.

The Northampton Mercury
2 September 1751

❀ *Ruth Osborne met her death in a pond at what is now known as the Gabblecote cross-roads at Tring. A part of the gibbet used at Colley's execution was still to be seen near by, in the village of Wilstone, nearly two hundred years later. In the nineteen-twenties it served a far less gruesome purpose, as a bracket for a horse-trough in the blacksmith's shop.*

Death of a Beggar

Bristol

Last Saturday was 7-night, a ragged beggar came to a Public House in Puckle-Church in Gloucestershire, to ask Charity of some countrymen who were drinking there, who told him, in a joaking manner, they used to hang all Beggars and would hang him; he told them he was not fit to die; but they taking hold of him, he begg'd they would do him no harm; however they got a Rope, put it about his Neck, and drew him up to a Bacon Rack, and bid him cry Bacon; to which they hung him so long, that he seem'd without Life, his tongue extending from his Mouth, so let him fall again, and perceiving they had carried their Folly too far, and being frightened with the Apprehension of what might ensue, carried the Beggar to a neighbouring Field, and laid him under a Hay-Rick for dead. He recovering his senses, and making mournful groans, a Woman heard him, and upon approaching the Hay-Rick, the poor Man gave her instruction by signs, how he came in that Condition, and pointed to the House where he receiv'd the Injury, and died soon after.

The Northampton Mercury
25 November 1751

❀ *'Last Saturday was 7-night' indicated that the beggar was killed 'last Saturday week'. Generally the newspapers of the time did not use the numeral, but referred to 'se-nnight' or 'seven-night'.*

1752

❀ *1752 was a year that lost eleven of its days, for it was then that Britain adopted the Gregorian Calendar as observed widely on the Continent since the sixteenth century. Under an Act of 1751 for 'Changing the Style', the 2nd of September came and went as usual, but the next day was not 3 September, but 14 September.*

The change was a drastic one, and in many ways similar to another great domestic change in Britain over two hundred years later, when shillings and pence were abandoned in favour of decimal currency. It was greeted with suspicion, misgiving and, in some areas, open hostility. Protestants thought that the acceptance of Pope Gregory's calendar was something in the nature of a Popish plot. A great many of the uneducated felt that they were being defrauded of eleven days of life, and statesmen and parliamentarians were frequently barracked with shouts of 'Give us back our eleven days!'

Understandably, there was very real bewilderment about Fair Days and Festivals. It will be seen that while some of the country folk agreed to go along with the new-fangled idea, others felt they had good reason for ignoring it. In 1752 and for many years afterwards their annual jollifications were not held on 25 December, but on 'Old Christmas Day' (5 January), eleven days later.

Jack and Joan's Fair

NOTICE is hereby given That the Fair at Canterbury (commonly called Jack and Joan's Fair) which used to be kept on St. Michael, will be kept this year on the 10th. Day of October, old Michaelmas Day.

The Kentish Post
Wednesday, 26 August, to Saturday, 29 August, 1752

❀ *'St. Michael' was, of course, Michaelmas Day, 29 September.*

Several Witches and Wizards in Suffolk

By a letter from Woodbridge in Suffolk we learn that the Country People about Aspal-Stonham and that Neighbourhood, are still so full of Ignorance and Superstition that they imagine there are several Witches and Wizards in that Neighbourhood; and that they have tied up two or three old People in Sheets, with Cords round their Middles, and flung them into the Rivers, to see if they could save themselves; but whether the cords held them up, or Providence supported the poor Wretches, it's certain they got safe on shore. This has confirm'd their Opinion; and to them they attribute their Loss of Cattle, bad Harvest &c. and insist that these poor Wretches shall be tried by the Church Bible, whether they are Witches or no: for if Witches the Bible will turn round and not weigh them down, and such idle Stuff; but the Clergy in that neighbourhood are too wise to listen to them, or suffer such nonsensical Trials. It's strange People should so soon forget the Execution at Tring in Hertfordshire on this very Account, or forget the Act of Parliament against Witchcraft is repealed.

The Kentish Post
Saturday, 16 September, to Wednesday, 20 September, 1752

❁ *Under the 'Act of Parliament against Witchcraft', many who practised the black art were hanged, for witchcraft was a capital offence. As late as 1716 a woman and her daughter—a child of nine—had been executed after being found guilty of selling their souls to the Devil. But sixteen years before that terrible affair at Tring, prosecutions for witchcraft and sorcery were brought to an end by the Witchcraft Act of 1735. Nevertheless, despite the warning that their witch-baiting was unlawful, the folk of the Stonham Aspal area (the* Kentish Post *got the name wrong) were still ducking old crones almost to the end of the century. In 1795 an old woman was 'swum' in the pond at Stanningfield, Suffolk, about twenty miles from Stonham. And there is no doubt that witches continued to be 'perplexed' by recipes such as the one below, long after the Act of 1735 came into force.*

How to perplex a Witch

The following was taken from an old Collection of Receipts written when the laws of our Country admitted of Witches and punishing them; and which was looked upon by the serious of that Age as a very effectual one:

To perplex or kill a Witch

Take a new Pipkin, and two or three Quarts of the Party's Urine that is bewitched, and put into the urine a Foul's Heart new killed, with three Needles stuck lengthways in it, and a great many crooked Pinnes, all up and down in the Heart; also the Parings of the Bewitched's Finger and Toe Nails, with a little Lock of his Hair taken from a little above the Neck Hole, with some of the Bewitched's Blood being warme taken from him, and all these put into the Urine, and boyle it gently away over the Fire. And if you do mistrust any one, if you send to see them, you will find them naked, and their skin turned black, and in most horrid Torments, as you are boyling these things, and if you boyle it all away you will kill her.

The Kentish Post
Saturday, 18 November, to Wednesday, 22 November, 1752

1753

Old Christmas Day

Bristol, January 6
Yesterday being Old Christmas Day, the same was obstinately observed by our Country People in general, so that it being Market-Day (according to the Order of our Magistrates) there were but few at market, who embraced the Opportunity of raising their Butter to Nine-pence or Ten-pence a Pound.

The Salisbury Journal
15 January 1753

'New Christmas Day is Wrong'

Southampton, January 12
On the 25th. of last Month, many people went into the New Forest to observe whether the Oak (which is said to blow every Christmas Day) conform'd to the New-Style, or not, but finding no Buds or any Appearance of green Leaves, came away greatly dissatisfied with the Alteration of the Day: And on Friday last, being old Christmas, they went again, and to their great Joy found the Oak blown, and several branches almost covered with green Leaves; some of which they brought away with them. This Circumstance has served to convince Abundantly that the new Christmas-Day is wrong, and they are henceforth determined to keep only the old.

The Salisbury Journal
15 January 1753

❀ *There was also convincing proof from Glastonbury that the change in style should never have been allowed. The* Gentleman's Magazine *for January 1753 related that although the famous thorn failed to blossom on 25 December (new style), it 'blowed as usual' eleven days later.*

A Gruesome End for Chimney-sweep's Boy

Bristol
Last week a young Lad who had lately run away from his Master, a Chimney-Sweeper, in this City, went to ask for Employment in a Gentleman's House the other Side of the Passage; just as he entered the back Part of the House, a Pack of Hounds fell upon him, and tore his Bowels quite out before any Assistance could be got.

The Oxford Journal
8 September 1753

1754

Skeleton found on Durnford Downs

Salisbury, April 15

On Wednesday last, as some labourers were levelling a small Barrow on Durnford Downs, near this City, they found a human Skeleton lying on the left side, in a stooping Posture. It was covered with very large flint Stones, not above two Feet below the surface of the Earth; the Jaws and Teeth were perfectly sound. It is remarkable that about twenty years ago, two small Urns of ordinary clay and rude workmanship, were taken out of the same Barrow, about three Feet on the left Side of the above Skeleton; and not above two Yards distant was found a human Trunk with a Dart in it, which Urns and Dart are in the Possession of a Member of the Royal Society, who was at Little Durnford when they were dug up. The Antiquaries are desired to account for the Bodies of some and the Ashes of others being buried together in the same Tumulus.

The Oxford Journal
20 April 1754

A Flogging at the Whipping-post

Yesterday three Men and a Woman received a Flogging at the Whipping-post here, for endeavouring to impose the most notorious Falsehoods on our Magistrates, which afterwards they confessed were so. One of the Men had, or pretended to have, no Tongue; another had really but one Arm and the third had a wither'd left Hand. This is mentioned to caution the charitable Credulous not to be imposed on by such daring Imposters, one of whom threatened to fire the Town. They had Women and Children belonging to the Gang, to the amount of above Twenty.

The Oxford Journal
29 June 1754

Altering the Milestone

Worcester

A few days since, as a Gentleman and his servant were travelling between Bromsgrove and Birmingham, they observed a mischevious fellow *amusing* himself in erasing the Figures out of one of the Mile Stones, and they reprimanding him for it, he gave them very fancy language; whereupon they seized him, and taking him to a House near the Place, borrowed some strong Cording, with which they bound him Hand and Foot, and then carried him back to the Stone, to which they fastened him, with a Label pinn'd to his Skirts, denoting the Crime he had been guilty of, and desiring the first Person that should happen to come by, to horsewhip him, and set him at Liberty; soon after another Gentleman came by; who released the Fellow, after disciplining him according to the Request of the other Gentleman.

The Oxford Journal
7 September 1754

Harvest Frolic led to Murder

On Saturday Night, the 31st. past, a bloody murder was committed in the Parish of Lipput, near Honiton, in the County of Devon, by one Henry Bishop on the body of Hannah his wife. The particulars whereof are related as follows: Several labourers were reaping in a Field in the Parish of Lipput, among whom was this Henry Bishop, whose deceased Wife, with other Women, was also there binding Sheaves. One of the Men (as usual in Harvest), often saluted the Women, and sometimes indiscretely threw Bishop's Wife on the Ground; which was not very pleasing to him, who conceited he was wronged in the tender Part. After the Labour of the Day was ended, the Women went to their respective Homes, and Bishop soon after repaired to his, where finding his Wife asleep, her Head resting on a Table, he instantly drew his Knife, and cut her Throat from Ear to Ear. Struck with horror at his Guilt he ran to a Neighbour (one George Bradley) crying out "What shall I do? What shall I do? I shall be hanged! I have killed my Wife!" Adding that if he could plunge a knife two inches into John Pulman's heart, he should be content and easy. The People amazed at his outcry and Behaviour, presently ran to his House, where they found the deceased murder'd, as he said; which through the Astonishment they were at first in, they neglected to do. But it was then too late, for during their absence he fled. However he was the night after taken, and this Day brought to High Gaol. The Coroner's Inquest have brought it in Wilful Murder by the Hands of the Husband. A second Account says that he failed in his first Attempt to cut her Throat and in a Scuffle which ensued she got a wound on her Thumb; and that he gave her several wounds over her face 'ere he could accomplish his Design of cutting her Throat.

The Oxford Journal
14 September 1754

A Marriage Bonus

Newcastle, October 19
Thursday se'nnight, at the great Sheep Fair held at Wooler, ten neighbouring unmarried Gentlemen being in Company together, a Proposal was made for entering into a Subscription of one hundred Guineas each, to be given to the first man married, which was unanimously agreed to, and which, it is hoped, will spur on the Batchelors, and hasten the young men to be happy.

The Oxford Journal
2 November 1754

1755

An Early Cuckoo

Extract of a letter from Biddestone in Wiltshire
At this Place, three Times in December last, the Cuckoo was seen and heard to cry by more than Forty People. And on Sunday last he was again heard by several, who then looked after and found him. We conclude nothing particular from it, but:

"It may well be understood
To mean our Place but little Good"

The Oxford Journal
18 January 1755

❀ *There are many superstitions about the cuckoo in country lore, and many beliefs fixed a definite date for its first appearance each year—21 April. When this report appeared, on the day they first heard the cuckoo, Shropshire labourers were entitled to take the rest of the day off and toast the bird in 'cuckoo ale'. This story also proves that letters about early cuckoos did not originate in correspondence to the Editor of* The Times, *which did not make its own first appearance until thirty years later—in 1788.*

Smugglers' Victory

They write from Mountbay that on Friday se'nnight a Gang of Smugglers, after having beat the Officers of the Customs and Excise, came in Triumph thro' Marazion, in a Body of at least sixty or eighty Men, and horses loaded; and as a Signal of Victory, rang out the Chapel Bell, which so alarmed the Inhabitants, supposing it a Signal of Fire, they were in the utmost Consternation.

The Oxford Journal
8 February 1755

The Man-Midwife of Bristol

The Man-Midwife of Bristol is dead, who, about three weeks ago, was called up at midnight to deliver a Lady about six Miles off; and when he came to the Outside of the Temple Gate, was blinded by the Messenger with a handkerchief, 'till he arrived at the place, where he was shown into a magnificent Room, richly furnished, in which was the Lady lying on a Couch, with her face covered, whom he soon delivered, was well rewarded, and afterwards carried back blind-folded, 'till he came again to Temple-Gate. 'Tis supposed he never recovered the Fright he was in upon this Occasion.

The Oxford Journal
29 March 1755

Female Press Gang

Taunton, April 16
Three merry Girls in Cornwall lately dressed themselves in Men's Cloaths, and put Cockades in their Hats, pretending to be a Press Gang, and had the boldness to go under this Disguise to Denny-bowl Quarry, where there were near sixty Men at work, who all run away as fast as their Leggs could carry them, as soon as these disguised Females came in Sight, tho' they had just before been boasting that if a Press Gang came they would bury them in the Rubbish.

The Oxford Journal
26 April 1755

Buried at Crossroads

On the 6th. instant, an elderly man hanged himself with his handkerchief, at Linkincehorn, in Cornwall, which he fastened to a small Hedge Oak, and was found almost on his knees, from whence it was judged he was fully bent to execute the dreadful Resolution. The Coroner's Inquest brought in the verdict, Felo de se. He was buried at Kesbrook Cross and a Stake driven through his Body.

The Western Flying Post
23 June 1755

❀ *Suicides were denied a resting-place in consecrated ground. The purpose of the stake in the heart had its origin in days when it was thought it would prevent the dead man or woman arising after nightfall to haunt the neighbourhood. Similarly, the grave was at a cross-roads to confuse the ghost about the way he should take to get back to familiar places on earth.*

'Young White Eyes', the Smuggler

On Tuesday Night an out-law'd Smuggler, known by the name of Young White Eyes, who lately returned from France, where he had been for several years, was surprised by a Party of Dragoons at a little Alehouse near Benacre in Suffolk and taken after a smart Engagement, in which he was so terribly wounded that it is thought he cannot recover. There was £500 Reward for apprehending him.

The Bath Advertiser
6 December 1755

❀ *For obvious reasons, in their smuggling activities men were known by names far different from those which they received at the font. 'Young White Eyes' came from Hadleigh in Essex; from Diss in Norfolk was a smuggler called 'Ill Will' and another was known as 'Curse Mother'. In 1751 'The Young Papist' had been captured at the Blue Boar at Oulton in Suffolk.*

1756

The London Coach

January 3

This is to give Notice That the Two-Days Flying Machine, which goes from the Swan, in West-gate Street, Bath, and puts up at the Talbot Inn, near the New-Church in the Strand, London, will set out on Monday next and again on the Friday following, and will carry Passengers for Eighteen-Shillings each, and those on the Outside at Ten.

This Machine goes three Times every Fortnight, Monday and Friday one Week, and on Wednesday the next Week.

Performed by Timothy Thomas.

The Bath Advertiser
3 January 1756

An Invasion Alarm

A few Days ago eight or ten Sail of foreign Ships appeared off at Sea near Alnmouth, which being taken for Frenchmen, the People there assembled in great numbers along the Shore, armed with rusty Swords, Spits, Pitchforks &c., vowing to give them Battle if they attempted to land. The Ships hovered about without making any such Attempt, and the people made Fires along the Coast, and lay under Arms 'till next Morning, when a small Boat was despatched to them, to ask in the King's Name, who they were and what they wanted. They detained the Boatmen, which gave the People stronger suspicions than ever; however a Messenger came shortly after to acquaint them that the Vessels were Dutchmen, and the Boatmen kept to pilot them to Shields, on which the People who had shewn so much of the laudable Spirit of antient Britons dispersed and returned Home.

The Bath Advertiser
3 April 1756

❈ *The danger of invasion by the French was a very real one. Britain was engaged in the Seven Years War (1756–63), united with Frederick of Prussia against France and her allies. She was ill-prepared for an attack on her own shores.*

Desperate Deed to evade Naval Service

Last week several Men were impress'd at Bromsgrove for his Majesty's Service, one of whom (a lusty able-body'd Fellow) in Hopes the Regulating Officer would deem him an useless Hand, chopt off one of his Fingers, and desparately wounded another. Notwithstanding this, the Officer accepted him, presuming he was still a Match for any Frenchman.

The Bath Advertiser
24 April 1756

Resisting the Press Gang

Last Sunday Morning as Jacob Sparrow of Studley-Green, near Calne, was in Bed, a Press-Gang broke into his House to impress him, when he submitted to go with them, and dressed himself accordingly, but they threatening to bind him, he refused, and told them he would not be bound and would stab whoever should attempt it; when William Watts, Junr. seizing him behind, he with a short knife stab'd him to the Heart dead on the Spot. Sparrow is committed by Justice Hungerford to Jail.

The Bath Advertiser
24 April 1756

❀*In time of war the Press Gangs were permitted to take for the King's Navy all men with experience of life afloat. As well as 'impressing' seafaring men—former Navy men and merchant seamen—they could also compel the services of those whose knowledge of the water was limited to river boats. Ship's carpenters who had left the sea many years previously were just as liable for forcible recruitment as gunners who had been ashore for only a few weeks.*

1757

Robinson Cruso—Upholsterer

Lynn Regis, April
Robinson Cruso, Upholster and Auctioneer, In the High Street, near the Tuesday-Market-Place, has always a neat assortment of Beds ready-made,

in the newest Fashion, as Lindseys, Cheyneys, Harrateens, Marines, and Checks, some of them ready standing: Paper-Machee Ornaments for Cielings, Chimney, Stair-Cases &c. India Paper Hangings, and great Variety of Common Paper Hangings, and all other sorts of Upholstry. Goods as cheap as in London. Wanted, an APPRENTICE. A sober Lad of Good Character, will be taken on reasonable Terms.

The Ipswich Journal
9 April 1757

❈ *Is there any link between the Lynn 'Upholster' and auctioneer and the Robinson Crusoe of Daniel Defoe's famous book? A connection does seem quite likely, for Defoe visited Lynn Regis—now more generally known as King's Lynn, in Norfolk—and mentioned it in his book* A Tour through the Whole Island of Great Britain. *An additional reason for thinking he borrowed from King's Lynn this somewhat unusual name for his book is the fact that the title of one edition included the surname without a final 'e'. It was called* The Life and Strange Surprising Adventures of Robeson Cruso, Marriner.

The firm which advertised for an apprentice in 1757 continues to-day as Cruso & Wilkin, auctioneers and estate agents, of Tuesday Market Place, King's Lynn.

People die for Want of Bread

We have an Account from Cumberland that Corn is so scarce that People actually die for Want of Bread, and that a poor Widow and two Children, after living some time on Grain and Bran were found dead one Morning; the Children had Straw in their Mouths ... It was thought that the stopping of the Malt Distillery for a Time would have reduced the Price of Corn; but this, it seemed, was an Oversight, for while the Distillers stand still at home, they are very industrious in the Corn-Markets, buying up large Stocks of Grain, in order to resume their Business at the Expiration of the Prohibition: So that we cannot but humbly presume the Prohibition ought to have extended to their buying any Corn, as well as their extracting Spirits from it.

The London Evening Post
quoted in The Ipswich Journal
16 April 1757

Distress among Poor Families

We are informed that a poor Woman in Buckinghamshire, with nine Children, and big with a Tenth, was so far distressed as not to have had, for some Days, any kind of Sustenance, either for herself or Family. A Person accidentally giving her Six-pence, she bought a Calf's Pluck to make into Broth; but while she was gone out to get a few Sticks, the Children fastened on it, raw as it was, and eat it up every Bit, Gullet and all, before their Mother's Return. ... 'Tis inconceivable to what Distresses many poor Families are reduced, insomuch that many of them have never had, for several Months, any other Food than Grains and Salt, or boiled Horse-Beans, the Consequences of which, in all Probability, will be a Distemper amongst them, which, like a Pestilence, will sweep away Thousands. How much, therefore, does it behove every Magistrate to exert himself for their timely Relief, and avert as much as in him lies, this impending Evil.

The London Evening Post
quoted in The Ipswich Journal
28 May 1757

Sudden End to Sermon

We hear from Herefordshire, that by the late high Winds and Rain on Sunday se'nnight, the Tower of the Minster Church in the Town of Kingsland, is entirely beat down; but what is very remarkable, the Rev. Mr. Davis was in the Middle of His Sermon, and there was a large Congregation, yet nobody was killed; several were very much hurt in attempting to get away, besides being terribly frighted.

The Ipswich Journal
27 August 1757

Rapacious Rats

A certain Farmer, near Stratford in Essex, who was possessed of a very large Quantity of Wheat, some of which he has sold at Eighteen and some at Twenty Pounds a Load, at length refused to part with any more under Twenty-two Pounds a Load, but the Price falling he was forced to break into his Stacks, and out of about Eighty Load, found near One-third of it destroyed by Rats.

The Ipswich Journal
17 December 1757

1758

Robert Twigger of Hadleigh

Robert Twigger At Hadleigh in Suffolk Draws Sun-Dials, paints Alter-Pieces in Churches, writes the Creed, the Lord's Prayer, and Command-ments in the neatest Manner, draws Scripture Sentences upon the Walls, with beautiful Margins round the frame. He has lately beautified Hadleigh and Hitcham Churches. Any Gentlemen, Church Wardens &c. who will please to employ him, shall meet with entire Satisfaction, and the Favour gratefully acknowledged, by their humble servant.

Robert Twigger.

The Ipswich Journal
11 February 1758

Inoculation

The following extraordinary Notice appeared in the Oxford Journal of Saturday last—February 11th, 1758:

I George Ridley near Stroud in the County of Gloster Broadweaver at the desier of peeple hereabout do give Nautis That I have inockilated these too Seazons past between 2 and 300 for the Smale Pox and but too or three of them died. A Mainey people be a feard of the thing but eviath it is No More than Scrattin a bit of a haul in their Yarm A pushin in a peece of Skraped rag dipt in Sum of the Pocky Matter of a Child under the distemper—That every Body in the Nashon may be sarved I will God Willin Undertake to Inockillat them with the pervizer they will take too Purges before hand and loose a little blud away, for half a Crown a head; and I will be bould to say Noo body goes beyond me. N.B. Poor Volk at a shillin a head but all Must pay for the Purgin.

The Ipswich Journal
4 March 1758

❁ *Inoculation against smallpox in Britain owed much to the famous Lady Mary Wortley Montague. She learned of it while living in Turkey in 1717, and did a great deal to get it accepted in this country, against strong opposition. (Inoculation, with a weak form of the smallpox virus, is to be distinguished from vaccination, with the cowpox or vaccinia virus, introduced by Jenner in 1796.) George*

Ridley, the humble Gloucestershire weaver, was inoculating in his neighbourhood only four years after the treatment was finally recommended by the College of Physicians. A further seventeen years were to pass before the opening of the first dispensary for free inoculation of poor people in London.

The Giant Chestnut

At the seat of Lord Ducie at Tetworth in Gloucestershire there is now growing an English Chestnut, which measures 51 feet about, at the Height of six Feet above the Ground. The Tree divides itself at the Crown into three Limbs, one of which measures 28 Feet and a Half in the Girt, and five Foot above the Crown of the Tree. The soil is a soft Clay, somewhat loomy. The Situation is the North-West Side of a Hill. The Tree was stiled in King John's Time, the Great, or Old Chestnut-Tree at Tetworth, so it is supposed to be now above 1000 Years Old.

The London Chronicle
quoted in The Ipswich Journal
9 September 1758

Opposition to Militia Act

We have had some disturbance last week at a Justices meeting at Dunchurch, to put the Militia Act in execution. The Constables were to give in a list of the inhabitants to serve as militia men. On which several of the people of the neighbouring towns assembled, and would do something, tho' they did not know what. They demanded the lists from each town, and the Justices were obliged to consent to let them have them; nay, some were so riotous as to burst into the room among the justices, and took the lists by force. But after they had taken them they went off without further violence; and the gentlemen went to dinner pretty quietly. After dinner, some of the rioters came again, and burst into the room a second time, when the gentlemen took to their pistols, and seized two of the ringleaders, and a third they took in the street; the rest dispersed. Two of the three, however, were rescued at Coventry, in their way to Warwick goal, but the third was committed without any riot.

We shall have another meeting soon; the gentlemen are determined to get the better of them. Our town was very quiet, but Lawford took their list from their constable, and their is a substantial man bound over to the assize for being concerned.

The Leeds Intelligencer
10 October 1758

❀ *This report was from Dunchurch in Warwickshire. Under the*
Militia Act (1757) the men required for service were selected by
ballot. They were not required to serve with the Regular Army,
but enlisted for local defence duties.

Fortune-teller in Pillory

Last Tuesday, at the Sessions held at Newbury, came on the Trial of
Elizabeth Stevens, otherwise Dame Cryer, a noted Fortune-teller for
several years past, being prosecuted by one Mondy, of the Parish of
Kingsclere, for having charged him with robbing his Father of some
Household Goods and a Gammon of Bacon, the Father upon losing these
Things having applied to the said Fortune-teller for information
concerning them. She was tried by a Special Jury, and being found Guilty,
was sentenced be imprisoned for twelve Months and to stand four Times
in the Pillory within the time of her imprisonment.

The Ipswich Journal
16 December 1758

1759

The Parson-General

A few days ago died at Clowbent in Lancashire, in the 87th. year of his
Age, the Rev. Mr. James Wood, commonly called General Wood, on
Account of his training a Hundred of his Hearers, going at the Head of
them himself and hazarding his Life in opposing the Rebels in 1745.

The Ipswich Journal
10 March 1759

❀ *When Parson Wood raised his band of parishioners to fight the*
rebels, Prince Charles Edward Stuart, the 'Young Pretender', was
on his victorious way through Lancashire to Derby, at the head of

six thousand Highlanders. He was totally defeated in the following
April.

Entertainment for Ripley Worthies

At an Entertainment given by the Master of the Talbot Inn, at Riply, in
Surry, on Shrove Tuesday last, to Twelve of his Neighbours, Inhabitants
of the said Parish, and who lived within Five Hundred Yards distance, the
Age of the whole amounted to One Thousand and Eighteen years. What
is most remarkable, one of the Company is the Mother of twelve
Children, the youngest of whom is Sixty. She has within the Fortnight
walked to Guildford and back again (which is twelve miles) in one Day.
Another has worked as a Journeyman with his Master (a Shoemaker, who
dined with him) forty-nine years. They all enjoyed their Senses and not
one made use of a Crutch.

The Manchester Mercury
13 March 1759

❀ *The Talbot Inn, established in 1453, is on the main London to*
Portsmouth road. Many famous people have broken their journey
at this old coaching inn on their way to the coast. Almost exactly
two years before the Shrove Tuesday party for old parishioners,
Admiral Byng stayed there en route for Portsmouth and execution.
He was shot for negligence on 14 March 1757, on the
quarterdeck of the Monarque. *Lord Nelson and Lady Hamilton*
were frequent guests at 'The Talbot' in later years. Visitors can use
seats which they often occupied there, and see Lady Hamilton's
spinning wheel.

Lightning destroys Great Billing Steeple

... soon after Divine Service, the Steeple of Great Billing Church, near
Northampton, was knock'd down|by a Flash of Lightning, and some of the
Stones whirl'd into the Air at such astonishing Force, as to be carried to a
considerable Distance. One of a very large Size ploughed up the Ground
in Mr. Blackwell's Garden, like a Cannon Ball, bounded from the Place
where it first fell with great Violence, and was carried several hundred
yards further. Many of the Pews in the church were shivered to Pieces,
and the sulphureous Smell was so powerful that scarcely any body could
bear to go near the Church, which is so much shatter'd that it is thought
the whole Fabric must be entirely rebuilt.

The Ipswich Journal
21 April 1759

Helping the Enemy

On Thursday last William Scullard, a Collar-Maker at Liphook in Surry, was brought before the Justices assembled at the Quarter-Sessions at Guildford, charged with acting as a Guide and providing Horses to aid and assist two French Officers of Distinction, who were Prisoners of War, to facilitate their Escape. After Examination, the Court ordered him into Custody until a Messenger was despatched and returned from Liphook. On Saturday he was re-examined before Joseph Shaw, Esq., who committed him to the New Gaol at Southwark. Scullard is a reputed smuggler and can talk French; and had in his Custody a List of all the Cross-Roads from Liphook round by Dorking to London.

The Ipswich Journal
21 July 1759

1760-69

LEAVING THE VILLAGE
The Enclosure Acts compelled many poor people to leave the country for the towns.

1760

Accident at Chuckers

In a Letter from a Gentleman in the West of England we are informed of the following remarkable Occurence, which happened in Avon, a small village in Devonshire. As one John Wilson, an old labouring Man of that Place, was lying on a Bench fast asleep, some boys being at play with Chuckers, and the old Man's Mouth being open, one of them chucked one directly into his Mouth, which waking him, and him not being aware of it, stuck in his Throat, and choaked him before any Assistance could be procured. He was upwards of 90 years of Age and never had any Sickness.

The Ipswich Journal
22 March 1760

❀ 'Chucks', 'chuckstones' or 'chuckers' was an outdoor version of the game of 'Pitch and Toss'. The 'chucker' thrown into the old man's mouth would have been a small stone, or pebble.

A Homing Cow

Last week a Cow was sent from Cold Harbour, near Urickham, in Kent, to East Sheen, in Surry (a distance of about 15 miles, thro' bye Roads, across a very close Country, in which above a dozen Gates must have been opened) and put up in a well fenced Field, from which she broke out the next Night and found her way back to her old Pasture at Cold Harbour. An odd instance of sagacity in a Species of the brute Creation that is scarce supposed to have any.

Jopson's Coventry Mercury
5 May 1760

Fire from Cow's Belly

A morning Paper of this Day has the following Paragraph. On the 17th. of March an extraordinary Phoenomenon happened at Stanton-Drew, one mile from Pensford, and which, as it is a certain Truth, may employ the Minds of the curious Enquirers into Nature. Farmer Cadwallin of this Place, had a cow died in Calving, and opening her to take out the Fat, a Fire issued out of the Belley of the Cow, and burnt the Hair of his Face and

Eye-Brows, and some of the Hair of his Head, a Servant Made standing by had her Handkerchief about her Neck burnt in several Holes, and the Flames continued burning in the Cow for several Minutes after being opened.

Jopson's Coventry Mercury
5 May 1760

Great Storm at Littleport

On Monday the 19th. instant, in the Afternoon, there was the greatest Storm of Hail, attended with Thunder and Lightning, that hath been known in the Memory of Man, at Littleport in the Isle of Ely; some of the Hail-Stones measured three Inches about and the Ground was covered more than six inches deep on the Level; the Storm entirely destroyed a large Field of Hemp, except one Corner, so that it has been ploughed and sown again; the Fruit Trees appear as in the Fall of the Leaf, the Ground being covered with Leaves &c. Some of the Stones that lay in a North Aspect were measured on Thursday afternoon, and were then two Inches and a Half.

General Evening Post
quoted in
The Ipswich Journal
7 June 1760

Horse died in 100 Miles Race

Worcester, June 5
The Chaise-Horse, which was engaged to go 100 Miles in 11 Hours on the Road from this City towards Gloucester, started on last Tuesday Morning at Two o'Clock, and in the first five Hours went 56 Miles, but when the poor abused Creature had completed about 84 Miles, in due Time, he dropt down and died almost directly. Thus was the Life of one of the most useful Animals amongst us most scandously sacrificed for the Purposes of mere *Gambling*, and whoever seriously reflects on Abuses of this Nature, cannot but Condemn and detest the merciless, wicked Promoters of them.

General Evening Post
quoted in the Ipswich Journal
21 June 1760

1761

Stag captured in Public House

A few days ago a stag was turned out in Long-Leat Park, by Lord Weymouth and some other Gentlemen, which shewed fine Sport for some Miles; when taking the Turnpike Road he ran into Frome, and Making into a Publick-House, the Sign of the Waggon and Horses, took Shelter in the Cellar, where he was pursued, and taken alive under a Butt of Stale Beer.

The Ipswich Journal
24 January 1761

Poisoned Tea

Corfe Castle, Dorset, March 4
On Saturday last a remarkable incident happened at Mr. H. Strickland's at Chadwell Farm, near this Town; as he and his Family, consisting of a Wife and five Children were drinking Tea in the Afternoon, he observed, after drinking two or three Dishes, that the Tea looked of a darker Colour than usual and had no flavour in it, upon which, after various surmises of what could be the Reason, the Kettle was examined, wherein, to their great astonishment, they found a large Toad, boiled to that Degree that the legs were separated from Body; upon this alarming Circumstance, they all seemed greatly indisposed, concluding themselves poisoned, and sent directly for a Apothecary, who very prudently gave each of them a large dose of Sallard Oil, which both purged and vomitted them plentifully, and they all now seem out of Danger.

Jopson's Coventry Mercury
16 March 1761

Odd Method of Robbing

Bath, April 30
Last Thursday a very odd method of robbing was made use of. A villian drest in women's apparel lay down in the high road between Tetbury and Cirencester in the county of Gloucester. A gentleman riding by, the supposed woman begged of him to alight and help her on her feet, saying

she had been just robbed, and otherwise ill-treated, and that if he would be so kind as to raise her off the ground she would endeavour to crawl to the next village. The compassionate gentleman readily alighted to lend her his assistance, when the pretended woman started up, and presenting a pistol, cried *D--n your blood! deliver all your money this instant, or I'll blow your brains out.* So unexpected a salutation filled the gentleman with astonishment; he gave her seven pounds five shillings and the villian likewise took from him his watch. He then threw off his woman's disguise, mounted the gentleman's horse and rode off.

The Leeds Intelligencer
12 May 1761

1762

'No' at the Altar

We have received the following humourous Account of a Wedding at Northleach in this County: A young Girl of about 20 Years of Age having sworn a Child upon an old Man of 60, a warrant was granted for apprehending him, and he was taken into Custody, when it was put to his choice, whether he would go to Gaol, or marry the Girl. The poor old Fellow, after a long Deliberation, determined on the latter, and so to Church they went, escorted by the Parish Officers and a numerous Company of Attendants. The Man went through the several Parts of the Ceremony with tolerable *Resignation*, and the Girl performed her Part with Propriety enough 'till she came to these Words, *Wilt thou have this Man to be thy wedded Husband?* to which she answered, No! and on being asked a Second Time replied *I won't!* and immediately took to her heels, and ran out of the Church, to the great Joy of the Bridegroom and the Entertainment of the Spectators.

The Glocester Journal
23 March 1762

Man and Horse stung to Death

We hear from Iver, a village near Uxbridge, that as one Carter, a Carpenter, was driving a Horse to draw a Piece of Timber, coming near some Bee-Hives, the Horse kicking, threw down One of them, when the

Bees fastened on him, and the Horse continually kicking threw down
Three more of the Hives: upon which all the Bees fixing upon the Man
and Horse stung them to Death. The Man had his Son with him who
saved his Life by running to a Hedge and thrusting his Head into it.

The Glocester Journal
2 August 1762

Strangled by Sheep

On Tuesday in the afternoon a man was found strangled in a field near
Mitcham, with the hind legs of a sheep tied, which went a-cross his neck.
He had stole the sheep, and in order to carry it away, had tied the hind legs
to put over his head, but in resting it upon a gate, it is supposed, by the
sheep's springing, the feet slipped over his face and strangled him; for
they were found fast together; the sheep hanging on one side, and the
man dead on the other side.

The Glocester Journal
27 December 1762

1763

A Fair on the Ice

Stamford, January 20
On Thursday a sheep was roasted upon the river at Peterborough, and a
kind of fair held with all manner of stalls, &c. on the ice. On Tuesday five
hundred weight was drawn up the river on a sledge from Wisbich to
Peterborough, which is 21 miles, by three men who skated, and were
fastened to it by ropes.

The Leeds Intelligencer
1 February 1763

Centenarian's Promise

A few days since died at Prestbury in this county, Mrs. Blocksum, aged 103. It is remarkable of the old Lady that she taught children to read for several years after she lost her sight and retained her mental faculties 'till within three days of her death. She used frequently to say that she should rise again a few days after her death and therefore declared that her coffin lid should be taken off when she was interred, which was performed agreeable to her request. If the old woman should be as good as her word, our readers may depend upon hearing of it.

The Glocester Journal
28 February 1763

Bathing at Aldeburgh

At Aldeburgh in Suffolk are neat and commodious BATHS (with private Dressing-Rooms for both Sexes) whose near situation to the main Ocean furnishes them with Sea Water, which Constantly flows through the same in its utmost Purity and Strength. And for the convenience of those who choose Bathing in the real Ocean there is a curious MACHINE that, by the Assistance of a Single Person, may be run into the Sea to any Depth proper for Bathing.

N.B. Proper Lodgings and other suitable Accommodations may be had by applying to Mr. Levet, Surgeon there.

The Ipswich Journal
21 May 1763

✿ *In these twentieth-century days visitors are drawn to Aldeburgh because of the Aldeburgh Festival founded by Benjamin Britten in 1948. Britten's opera 'Peter Grimes', about a rascally Aldeburgh fisherman, is based on an incident in a poem by George Crabbe (1754–1832). As he was born at Aldeburgh, and grew up there, Crabbe would certainly have seen the 'commodious baths' and the 'curious machine' advertised in 1763.*

A Sad Time for Cyder

Ledbury in Gloucestershire, July 16
A procession was made through the principal parts of this town by the servants of the Cyder Merchants, Coopers, Farmers, and some poor labourers with numbers of poor people, the day the Cyder Act took place, in the following manner, viz. A man, with a drum covered with black crape, beating the dead march, drum sticks reverted; two mutes, with crape hatbands and black cloaks; an empty barrel upon a bier, carried by six poor Farmers, dressed in Cyder hair cloths, with hair cloths covering the barrel, and a gauging stick in the bung hole, and the pall of hair cloths, supported by six others in black; two men, the one on the right, with an empty can upon his head covered with crape, upon the top of which was a branch of an Apple-tree, with Apples thereon, covered also with crape; the other on the left in black, with the tools on his shoulder necessary to be made use of in felling of trees; and in the rear a number of poor objects, with Apples in their bosoms covered with crape. The bells were rung muffled all the day; and every face expressed a sympathetic sorrow for the impending ruin that awaits this country.

The Leeds Intelligencer
26 July 1763

✸ *The Cider Act was introduced by a Government led by George III's favourite, Lord Bute. It imposed a tax at the rate of four shillings a hogshead (fifty gallons), and was a measure to reduce the National Debt, now at a very high figure because of the Seven Years War. As well as being very unpopular with the fruit-farmers and their workpeople because of the threat to employment and profits, it was hated generally as an infringement of civil liberties. This was because it required excise officers to investigate the affairs of every apple-grower in the country. And these were days in which there was growing concern about the despotic attitudes of the new King, who had succeeded to the throne in 1760.*

The opposition to the Cider Tax and to Lord Bute personally was so great that the Prime Minister—long uneasy—felt compelled to resign, and he left office as the Act came into effect. It was not repealed until three years later.

As will be seen from a report in Adams Weekly Courant *in April 1766, the people who were appropriately sad in 1763 were just as demonstrative in the other direction when good times returned.*

In Hereford there is a tangible reminder of the Act in a museum belonging to a firm which still makes cider thereabouts. It is a cider mug bearing the inscription 'No Liberty—No Excise'.

Death at Windmill

On Friday last an Inquisition was taken at Long-Buckby, by Mr. William Jackson, Surgeon of this Town, and one of the Coroners for the County, on view of the Body of one Edward Low, who being at work in a Wind-Mill, the Mill, by a violent Storm of Wind, was on Thursday in the Afternoon, blown down, when one of the Stones fell upon him, and crushed him to Death. The Jury brought in their Verdict. Accidental Death.

> The Northampton Mercury
> 5 December 1763

The Great Mr Benjamin Bower

Salisbury, December 10

Tuesday, the 29th. ult., died at His House at Holt, near Winburn, Dorset, the great Mr. Benjamin Bower, so called from his enormous Size, which it's supposed he exceeded any man in England since the great Bright, of Malden, in Essex, who weighing 43 st. and an Half was 9 st. 3 lb. heavier than Mr. Bower, who weighed only 34 st. 4 lb. Notwithstanding his amazing bulk, he was a lively, active man, and travelled to and from London in a Stage-Coach, but a few days before his Death, which was occasionned, so we hear, by his drinking a Gallon of Cyder at an Inn on the Road to keep off a Fit of the Gout, which he apprehended as coming upon him. So large was his Corpse, that Part of the Wall of the Room where he died was obliged to be taken down to get it out, and no Hearse being wide enough to admit the Coffin, it was placed on the Carriage in the Room of the Hearse, which was taken off, and so carried to the place of Interment.

> The Northampton Mercury
> 19 December 1763

1764

A Shepherd for 90 Years

Reading, January 28

Last year died at Basingstoke one William Taylor, aged 102, as appears by the Register, in the Parish Church of Basingstoke aforesaid; he was strong and healthy till a few days before his Death, and is said to have followed the Business of a Shepherd upwards of 90 years.

The Northampton Mercury
6 February 1764

The New Seed-plough

A few days ago was finished at York, a newly-invented seed-plough, firm, but not heavy, going on two wheels, to be drawn by one or two horses occasionally, which is intended to make three seed-furrows at once, at any distance from each other, and to sow any sort of seed, and to cover it at the same time, with great expedition and exactness, pursuant to the notice thrown out by the Society in London for the encouragement of Husbandry.

The Leeds Intelligencer
5 June 1764

'Butcher' Cumberland entertains

On Saturday about twelve o'clock, his Royal Highness the Duke of Cumberland entertained a company with the following Diversion; a stag was inclosed by toils in his Royal Highness's paddock at Windsor, and one of his tigers let loose at him: the tiger attempted to seize the stag by the haunch, but was beat off by his horns; a second time he offered at his throat, and the stag tossed him off again; a third time the tiger offered to seize him, but the stag threw him a considerable distance, and then followed him, upon which the tiger turned tail, and run under the toil into the forest, among a herd of deer, one of which he seized and killed him in a moment. Two Indians pursued him, and whilst sucking the blood, they threw over his head a sort of hood which blinded him; they then put a collar round his neck; with chains, and after feeding him with part of the deer, led him away. The motions of the tiger were something like those of a cat, creeping slowly on the ground till within reach of the prey, and then, by a spring, leaping at it.

The Leeds Intelligencer
10 July 1764

❀ *Perhaps it is hardly necessary to add that this Duke of Cumberland was 'The Butcher', who had earned this name because of his cruel treatment of the Highlanders after the battle of Culloden (16 April 1746). He was the second surviving son of George II, and died the year after this Windsor 'entertainment'.*

'Toils' were traps or snares. The stag was apparently trapped in a 'toil' or cage of strong netting.

A Yorkshire 'Character'

On Sunday, the 15th. ult., died, in the 125th. year of his age, George Kirton, of Oxnop-Hall, near Reeth, in this County, Esq. A Gentleman more remarkable for Fox-hunting than the remarkable Mr. Draper, for after following the chase on horseback till he was upwards of 80, so great was his desire for the diversion that (till he was one hundred years old) he regularly attended the unkenneling the fox in his single-horse-chair. And as a proof that length of days are not always entailed on a life of temperence and sobriety, he was an instance to the contrary, for no man, even to within ten years of his death, made freer with the bottle. ...

The Leeds Intelligencer
7 August 1764

Intelligence Extraordinary

Cambridge, August 9
We hear from Huntingdon that at the races there last week, a certain noble Lord, who tho' placed in one of the highest offices of state, has condescended to put himself upon a level with the meanest of his Majesty's subjects, entertained a company of foreigners and friends, by way of filling up some vacant hours not destined to the circus, with the following truly polite and classical amusements. *First, The Hunting of the Hen*, performed by a set of men with their hands muffled, the first that pulled a feather to be declared the victor, and to have the Hen, for a reward. Secondly, *A Diving Match*, enacted thus: a shilling, or other piece of money, was placed at the bottom of a tub of water, to be dived for by men with their hands tied behind them (if the competitors had large heads of hair, so much the better), the person who could first bring it up in his mouth to have it for his pains. Thirdly *A Race by Men tied up in Sacks*: What an improvement upon this last diversion would it be to have it performed by a set of our hobbling University Doctors, properly secured up in their congregational robes, which are so particularly fitted for this purpose! May one not hope if ever a person of his L——p's taste should gain a proper degree of influence amongst us to see this hint put into practice?

The Leeds Intelligencer
21 August 1764

Invitation to Bowmen

To all GENTLEMEN ARCHERS of the LONG BOW that on THURSDAY the Eleventh of October next, the GOLDEN ARROW will be shot for at Darlington; the Dinner will be at Widow Heslop's, the sign of the Three Tuns, where the Favour of your Company will greatly oblige, Gentlemen,

Your very humble servants,
Robert Hall, Captain
Geo. Bickerby, Lieutenant

The Newcastle Chronicle
20 October 1764

Watch found in Pike

Littleport (Isle of Ely), December 17
About ten days ago a very large pike was caught in the River Ouse, which weigh'd upwards of 28 pounds, and was sold to a gentleman in the neighbourhood for one guinea. As the cook maid was gutting the fish, she found, to her great astonishment, a watch with a black ribbon and two steel seals annext, in the body of the pike; the gentleman's butler upon opening the watch, found the maker's name, Thomas Cranefield, Burnham, Norfolk. Upon a strict enquiry it appears that the said watch was sold to a gentleman's servant, who was unfortunately drowned about six weeks ago in his way to Cambridge, between this place and South-Ferry. The watch is still in the possession of Mr. John Roberts, at the Cross-Keys in Littleport for the inspection of the public.

The Newcastle Chronicle
29 December 1764

1765

Strange Death after Cock-fight

Worcester, June 27
We hear that on Friday se'nnight at a Cocking at Norton Waste, near Alcester, a Man that had a Cock to fight against another, said, with an Imprecation, *that if his Cock was killed he would die also.* It so happened that his Cock was killed, and the Man did not survive many minutes.

The Oxford Journal
29 June 1765

Foot-Ball Play at West Haddon

West Haddon, Northamptonshire, July 27
This is to give notice to all Gentlemen Gamesters and Well-Wishers to
the Cause now in Hand That there will be a FOOT-BALL PLAY in the
Fields of Haddon aforesaid, on Thursday the 1st. day of August, for a
Prize of considerable Value, and another good prize to be play'd for on
Friday the 2nd. ...
All Gentlemen Players are desired to appear at any of the Public Houses
in Haddon aforesaid each Day between the Hours of Ten and Twelve in
the Forenoon, where they will be joyfully received; and kindly entertained
&c.

The Northampton Mercury
29 July 1765

❋ *Football in the eighteenth century was by no means the eleven-a-
side soccer, or Rugby football, as played in the twentieth century. It
called for much larger teams, and these often played for many
hours over the commons and meadows of an entire village.
Sometimes all the married men challenged the bachelors, and quite
frequently all the able-bodied men of one parish played against all
those in the adjoining one. But succeeding issues of the*
Northampton Mercury *make it clear that this advertisement was
really an invitation to something far more serious than a 'foot-ball
play'.*

Tumult at Football Match

Northampton
We hear from West Haddon, in this County, that on Thursday and Friday
last, a great number of People being assembled there in order to play a
Foot-Ball Match, soon after many formed themselves into a tumultuous
Mob, and pulled up and burnt the Fences designed for the Inclosure of
that Field, and did other considerable Damage, many of whom are since
taken up for the same by a Party of General Mordaunt's Dragoons sent
from this Town.

The Northampton Mercury
5 August 1765

Death in Harvest Field

Bristol
Last week an unfortunate Affair happened at Clerton, near Wincanton, in
the County of Somerset. Some Men being reaping in a Field, two of them

disagreeing, one struck the other with his Reaping-Hook, and cut off two of his Fingers, on which the wounded Man ripped up the other's belly, so that his Bowels came out and he died on the Spot.

The Oxford Journal
17 August 1765

West Haddon Rioters

Whereas Francis Botterell, of East-Haddon, in the County of Northampton, Wool-Comber, stands charged upon Oath before John Bateman, Esq., one of his Majesty's Justices of the Peace for the said County, with preparing and causing to be published in the Northampton Mercury of the 29th. July last, an Advertisement, inviting Persons to West-Haddon aforesaid, on the 1st. of August following, for the purpose of a pretended FOOT-BALL MATCH, in consequence of which a great Number of Persons assembled on the said 1st. of August, at West-Haddon aforesaid, in a very riotous Manner, and tore up and destroyed great Part of the INCLOSURES of the Common Field of the said Parish (which had been made in pursuance of an Act of Parliament obtained for that Purpose) and burnt and destroyed large Quantities of Posts and Rails, which had been made into Stacks by the Proprietor of the said Field for the purpose of the said INCLOSURE: and whereas it has appeared by Information upon Oath, laid before the said Mr. Bateman, that John Fisher the Younger, of West Haddon aforesaid, Weaver, did, with several other Persons not yet taken, contribute to the Expence of inserting the said Advertisement, and Warrants have been accordingly filed for apprehending the said several Persons, but they, having absconded, are not yet taken. Now, for the better and more effectual Discovery of and bringing to Justice, the said Francis Botterell and John Fisher the Younger, the Proprietors of the said Fields of West Haddon do hereby promise a Reward of TWENTY POUNDS to be paid to any person or Persons who shall apprehend, or cause to be apprehended, the said Francis Botterell and John Fisher the Younger, or either of them; such Reward of TWENTY POUNDS to be paid by Mr. William Caldecott, of Rugby, in the County of Warwick, upon the Commitment of each of them, the said Francis Botterell and John Fisher the Younger, to any of his Majesty's Gaols.

I do hereby undertake to pay the above Reward.

Wm. Caldecott

The said Francis Botterell is about 40 years of Age, about five Feet eight Inches high, wears his own dark strait Hair, and has a thin, long, sallow visage.

The said John Fisher the Younger is about 30 Years of Age, about five Feet nine inches high, wears his own light-brown Hair, rather curling at the Neck, and has a long thin visage and pale Complexion.

The Northampton Mercury
19 August 1765

❀ *The riot at West Haddon was one of many that took place at this time, particularly in the Midlands and the South of England. They were to become increasingly frequent, with the introduction of much-improved farming methods, as the century wore on. The 'open-strip' farming which had allowed villagers, for hundreds of years, to cultivate small areas of land within large open fields disappeared through Enclosure Acts. These permitted landowners to divide up the land and enclose it in fields of a size more appropriate to the new agricultural developments. They involved too the disappearance of much common-land previously used by all villagers who had a need for it. Many of the men who had cultivated small holdings of land in the open fields were unable to continue farming under the new arrangements, and because of this were reduced to penury. The enclosures in individual villages each required a separate parliamentary act until the passing of a General Enclosure Act in the early years of the nineteenth century.*

The 'footballers' of West Haddon knew that the passing of the Enclosure Act for their 'Common Field' would bring them very real hardship. Their endeavours to keep the land, like scores of similar efforts elsewhere, had no chance of lasting success, although they might delay the loss of the field for a short while, and perhaps defer similar enclosures thereabouts.

1766

Divine Vengeance

We have an account of a very extraordinary instance of Divine vengeance
that happened about a week ago at Chalford in this county. One Richard
Parsons, a young man of that place, was playing at cards, and he most
prophanely wished his flesh might rot and his eyes never shut, if he did
not win the next game. When he was going to bed, he observed a black
spot upon his leg, from which a mortification began, and immediately
spread all over his body, so that he died in a day or two, his flesh being
quite rotten; nor could his eyes be shut, notwithstanding all the efforts of
his friends to close them. The truth of this fact is attested by many of the
neighbours who were with him.

The Glocester Journal
quoted in Adams Weekly Courant
25 March 1766

Repeal of the Cider Act

Gloucester, April 21
They write from Hereford that on Monday last, upon the arrival of the
news that the bill for the repeal of the Cyder Act had received the Royal
Assent, that city gave the strongest testimony of its joy and gratitude
which could possibly be expressed. At noon the populace were
entertained in the market-place with two hogsheads of Cyder, and in the
evening the town was universally illuminated. Grand exhibitions of
fireworks were made at the cross and on the Castle-hill, whilst bonfires
blazed in every street, and on the eminences within five miles of the city.
At Exeter, Honiton and other Places, the inhabitants made as great
rejoicings on the same account.

Adams Weekly Courant
29 April 1766

✸ *This story is in happy contrast to the mournful proceedings at
Ledbury three years earlier, when the Cider Act was introduced
(see extract from the* Leeds Intelligencer—*26 July 1763).*

Protest at Newbury

We hear from Newbury that on Thursday last a great number of poor people assembled in the market-place during the time of the market on account of the rise of wheat, when they ripped open the sacks and scattered all the corn about, took butter, meat, cheese and bacon out of the shops, and threw it into the streets, and so intimidated the Bakers that they immediately fell their bread 2d. in the peck loaf, and promised next week to lower it still cheaper. From Newbury they proceeded to Shaw Mill, where they threw the flour into the river, broke the windows of the house, and did other considerable damage there, as well as at several other mills, to the amount of near £1,000. A poor man, whose name was Parker, one of the mob, was killed, who has left a wife and five children; another man had his arm broke, but we do not hear of any other accidents.

Adams Weekly Courant
19 August 1766

Mills destroyed by Riotous Poor

Sherborne, August 11
Saturday last the inhabitants of this town bought wheat by a contribution, and sold it out to the poor at 7s. per bushel, which is about 3s. under the market price; and it is proposed to continue it every market day till the harvest.

The poor, we hear, have pulled down the bunting mills at Cullompton, Bradnish, Tiverton, Silferton, &c. In most places they behaved remarkably well, taking only corn, and leaving the value of it in money at a moderate price. It is the general opinion that bunting mills are one chief cause of the high price of wheat, and therefore the interposition of the legislature in it seems highly necessary.

On Friday the price of wheat was raised so high in the market at Barnstaple that the poor, who are in the utmost distress, joined in a body and compelled the Farmers to sell it at 5s. per bushel. Some of the Farmers refusing to take the money, the poor were honest enough to tie it up carefully for them in their sacks; and as soon as they had taken at a lower price sufficient to supply their necessities, they dispersed, leaving the Farmers to make what price they could of other people.

Adams Weekly Courant
19 August 1766

Mob Action for Cheaper Butter

Gloucester, September 8

We are told in letters from Birmingham, that Tuesday se'nnight the mob went into the market, and took the butter baskets from the country people, who had raised the price of that necessity to 10d. per pound, and sold the same for 7d, the money for which they returned to the uttermost farthing; after this they assured the country people that they would pursue the same measures every market day, unless they would conform to the above reasonable price, which they have since complied with.

Adams Weekly Courant
16 September 1766

Bread Riots

Great Colton, Warwickshire

A mob has rose here consisting of upwards of 1,000 Men, who divide themselves into Gangs of 3 or 400 each, and continue traversing from one Market Town to another, doing incredible mischief wherever they come; the Reason they alledge for their assembling in the manner is the Farmers sending their new Corn to Bristol for exportation, which has raised its price to Eight Shillings per bushel and through this iniquitous Practice the Bakers sell only three pound four ounces of bread for sixpence. In their route they visited Alcester Market, where they committed no very great outrages; from thence they proceeded to Kidderminster, where the soldiers being under arms (having heard of their approach) fired at them and killed eight persons upon the spot, but we have not heard which side got the better. Intelligence has been received here that the Birmingham Gang went to Stratford, well armed with iron caps on their Heads; stopping all the wheat they met in their route, and disposing of it at their own prices. If some speedy method is not found out to relieve the Distresses of the people, there is no knowing where this will end.

Adams Weekly Courant
14 October 1766

Trouble at Trowbridge

It having been represented to the King, that on the 1st. instant the following threatening letter was thrown into the House of William Bell, of Trowbridge in Wilts. viz.

To J. Cock, In Duck Street, Troge
Trobridge and Bradford, Dam you Long Jack and you Bel as I

understand you are Going to takeing up some of the mob wick the first man that is taken up dam us if we dont be Revenge of you and all your Effects be Longing to You; so I would have you take care what you are going upon and consider for the Best, and before worst come of it, for it is but a short time you Both have to Live if you go any further in this ofair so I will Rest till you hear further of us so I am you Savt. flams is hot and hell is hoter.

And that on the 4th. instant, in the Evening, a Hay-Rick of the said Mr. Bell's, contigous to Trowbridge, was set on Fire, and one Half thereof consumed, or spoiled; His Majesty has promised his most gracious Pardon to any of them (except the Person who wrote the letter, or fired the Rick) who shall discover his or her accomplices.

Adams Weekly Courant
21 October 1766

1767

Ravens kill Man on Christmas Day

Liverpool
We are informed from Bristol that, on the 25th. of last month, one Dodridge, a Blacksmith, of Bridgewater, in contempt of that day, went out a shooting. On Pallet Hill he espied a large flight of old ravens, fired and killed two, which so exasperated the rest, that they immediately descended upon him, and plied their bills and claws so dexteriously about his head and face that notwithstanding all possible care was taken of him, he died last Monday. This may appear strange, but our correspondent assures us it is absolute fact.

Adams Weekly Courant
20 January 1767

Sheep saved by Rum

Whitehaven
A Farmer near Innerdale going in search of some sheep which were missing during the severe snow, in order to arm himself against the inclemency of the weather, took with him a bottle of rum, and a small glass; some of the sheep seeming just dying with the cold, it immediately occurred to him that as spirits were a cordial to the human species, they

might act in a similar manner upon animals; whereupon he gave every one a little of the rum mixed with water, which instantly revived them. To those that appeared least affected, he gave none. He got all that had taken the rum safe home, but the rest died by the way.

Adams Weekly Courant
17 February 1767

An Interrupted Wedding

Newcastle, April 18
Last week a Country Girl, after the due Publication of Banns at Kirbysteven, fixed the happy Day, which being come, the Company advanced in good Order towards the Church, but upon entering it, the Bride was perceived to steal off, and being immediately pursued was soon overtaken and asked the Reason of her Behaviour, who frankly told them that an old Man, the preceding Night, had promised to marry her, and as he was worth Forty or Fifty Pounds more than the other, she was resolved to have him, though she preferred the Youth, in Point of Love, to all Men in the World. However, by the interposition of some friends and a neighbouring Gentleman, she was prevailed upon, though with some Reluctance, to marry the Youth.

The Oxford Journal
25 April 1767

An Appeal from the Poor

The following laconick address was found, on Sunday Morning last, posted to one of the Doors of Ombersley Church in this County, viz.

The Gentlemen of this Parish are desired to consider the Poor, to raise poor Workmen's Wages, or lower the Price of Corn, for poor Men have worked a long while with dry Bread, and not Half a Belliful of that, so that they can hardly do a Day's Work that have a Family of Children: A poor Person cannot have a Sixpenny Loaf of Bread without Sixpence to pay for it, which make poor Children cry for Bread, and we have none to give them. This makes poor Mothers Hearts to ache.

The Oxford Journal
8 May 1767

A Busy Midwife

Salisbury, June 1
On Sunday, the 24th. of May, died Mrs. Mary Hopkins, of Wilton, in this
County, widow; a person well practised in the art of midwifry, and who,
during the space of forty-five years last past, delivered upwards of 10,000
women, with the greatest success, and is therefore greatly lamented by all
who knew her.

Adams Weekly Courant
9 June 1767

1768

Deer runs with Hounds

We hear that Marmaduke Craddock, Esq., of Gainford, near Darlington,
in the Bishopric of Durham, has a sorrel male deer, three years old, which
runs in company with his Hounds, when they hunt with Hare or Fox and
will be foremost when he pleases, skipping and showing his apish tricks,
and is so familiar and well-known to the dogs, that they never attempt to
seize or molest him.

The Chelmsford and Colchester Chronicle
26 February 1768

A Long-lived Couple

From Alford in Cheshire we learn that one Edward Parker and his wife
are now living in a cottage near that place, whose ages make 218 years, the
man being 112 and the woman 106 years old.

The Chelmsford and Colchester Chronicle
18 March 1768

Celebrating a Re-election

Bury, April 7
On Thursday last Sir Thomas Charles Bunbury, Bart. kept open house at
his seat near this town, on the occasion of his being re-elected to
represent the County in Parliament. A large Ox was roasted whole, and
several barrels of strong beer given to the populace. During the

distribution of the ox, one man, by the violent pressure of the crowd, was forced upon a tenter hook, by which his body was torn in a dangerous manner; another received a violent stab under his ribs; and a third was beaten down, and the wheel of the beer cart went over him, but they are all likely to recover.

The Chelmsford and Colchester Chronicle
8 April 1768

❀ *Tenterhooks were nails with hooked ends and used for stretching wet or damp cloth to a frame called a 'tenter', so that it might keep its shape when drying out. This story suggests that sacking or similar material on tenters was used in an unsuccessful endeavour to close off the roasting area and serve out the meat in an orderly fashion. It indicates too why we say nowadays that a person is 'on tenterhooks' when 'stretched' with anxiety or suspense.*

Stolen Pigeon Pie and Queen Cakes

Cambridge
On Saturday night the house of Mr. Lawrence at Chesterton, near this town, was broke open by some hungry villians, who struck a light, and regaled themselves with pigeon-pye, twelve queen-cakes, and several bottles of liquor, after which they broke a tea-chest, and stole a pair of tea-tongs, leaving a number of spoons that were marked, and carried away a new bridle and saddle.

The Chelmsford and Colchester Chronicle
8 August 1768

Panic at Church

On Sunday morning a fire broke out in the kitchen of Mr. Chapman's house at Springfield mill near this town. A person being immediately despatched to procure assistance, entered our church in the time of divine service, and whispered the accident to the clerk, who left his pew with an apparent precipitation, and immediately ordered the engines to be drawn out, without mentioning for what purpose they were wanted. This circumstance immediately alarmed the congregation; their conjectures were various, but the generality imagined the church to be on fire. It is impossible to describe the confusion that ensued by the violent thronging towards the doors. Hats and gloves were left: caps, aprons and ruffles bore the sad marks of terror and affright. Some women actually fainted away: others fell over the graves in the churchyard, lamenting their children in an agony of distraction. Their terrors, however, soon subsided on being informed where the fire really was. In the mean time, every possible assistance was sent to the Mill, and such spirit and activity exerted as cannot be sufficiently commended. In about an hour the fire was got under, and a fine mill (on which upwards of £600 had been expended in improvements) and the greatest part of a handsome brick-fronted house was happily saved, with most of the furniture, &c. The damage was not so considerable as was dreaded, tho' the inside of the back part of the house was entirely consumed. The Surveyor to the Royal Exchange Assurance Office has since examined the premises, and paid the party assured for the damages sustained.

The Chelmsford and Colchester Chronicle
19 August 1768

Ass on Church Steeple

Hexham, September 10
Saturday sennight, at night a number of Grovers, at Alston, in a frolic got a potter's ass, and having tied all legs together, put it into a box which the workmen used to take up mortar in, hoisted him up to the top of the steeple of the new church building there, and left him. In the morning the ass set up a-braying, which greatly alarmed all the town and neighbourhood, and terribly affrighted many of the common people, who could not be dissuaded but that some evil spirit had taken possession of the church.

The Chelmsford and Colchester Chronicle
16 September 1768

Three Wives in Seven Weeks

A farmer at Harlestone in Wiltshire buried a wife on the 1st. of September, on the 8th. he married a second, who dying on the 4th. of this month, he took a third partner to his arms on Wednesday last.

London Evening Post
quoted in The Chelmsford and Colchester Chronicle
21 October 1768

1769

Wood for Widows

Last week fifty loads of wood was cut down in Epping Forest by the order of the Earl of Tylney, and distributed to fifty poor widows of the parish of Barking, according to annual custom.

Kentish Gazette
Wednesday, 4 January to Saturday, 7 January, 1769

Four Dead at Poorhouse

Extract of a Letter from D—— Herts. January 23

The following melancholy tale is perfectly true. I write not from report, but the evidence of my own eyes, and what adds to the concern I feel is that the dismal scene happened in our own parish, and almost within a gun shot of my house.

My servant informed me this morning that a man, his wife and three children had perished for want in one of the poor houses! and that the floor of their wretched hovel was covered with their naked and emaciated carcasses! Scarce able to believe him, I went to the place, where, in a hovel of one room only, the gabel end of which lay quite broke open, and exposed to the severity of the weather, and a window frame at the other unglazed and uncovered, I saw four of the emaciated dead bodies, lying upon a little straw quite naked, for they had neither clothes nor covering when alive! The third child (about eleven years old) is yet living, but unable to stand, or give any account how long his father and mother, brother and sister, had been dead, although otherwise sensible.

Upon enquiry, I am informed they were taken ill on Saturday three weeks, that they had no relief that they knew of till Thursday was se'nnight, when one of the people called overseers of the poor came and left them half a crown. The poor wretches, however, seemed then to be too far gone, unable, or too tired with their wretched condition, to wish for food or life, for they only desired a faggot and a candle to be bought, which faggot, candle, and part of the change of the half crown was, or was pretended to be, found in the house, and likewise a piece of bread. It was found, however, by the same overseer who relieved them with it. I will only add to this sad relation that several poor of this parish are in almost as wretched a condition, and to desire some humane, learned man in the law to inform me, by a letter directed to P.T. at Mr. Davis's, Bookseller, in

Piccadilly, what steps are to be taken to bring the authors of these people's death to punishment, if it should appear any have been accessary and to satisfy such who either out of curiosity or humanity may enquire, may be informed with my name, by enquiry as above.

The Kentish Gazette
Wednesday, 25 January, to Saturday, 28 January, 1769

No Fire for Ten Days

D——, Herts
It appeared upon the examination of witnesses examined on oath relative to the death of the four persons found dead in the Poor-house here, as mentioned in our paper of Saturday last, that no fire had been seen in the house for upwards of ten days previous to their being found dead. One of the witnesses said that about ten days ago she saw the poor woman, with a kettle, attempt to fetch some water from a puddle near her door, but that after filling it, she fell down, left the kettle, and crawled on all-fours again to her wretched habitation.

The Kentish Gazette
Saturday, 28 January, to Wednesday, 1 February, 1769

Terrible Conditions in Hertfordshire Parish

Extract of a letter from D——Herts
I have this day visited the poor Houses in this Parish, and I do assure you all that has been said before, relative to the Dead and the Living, is infinitely short of what the Poor here suffer. In one House, not 50 yards from that in which the four Persons were lately found dead, I saw the surviving child of that Family, and eight other human Beings almost perished to Death. Their Hole, for it cannot be called a House, a Hovel, nor a Hut, has neither Coverings, Sides, nor Ends, but is exposed on every Side to the Inclemency of the Weather! and though the People who compose this tragic scene have some pecuniary Relief from the Parish, as well as what have been sent from Mr. Hoare's for that Purpose, I think they must perish for want of Fire and a better House. A neighbouring clergyman, at my earnest Request, attended me to this Place, who pronounced it infinitely worse than his or any imagination could have conceived.

The Ipswich Journal
18 February 1769

✹ *The overseers who so badly neglected their responsibilities were parish officials whose appointments originated in the Poor Relief Act of 1601. The funds of such officers came from a Poor Rate charged on property-owners in the parish, and were to be used solely for people who really belonged there. There was nothing for newcomers, or visitors.*

From an article in the winter edition of The Countryman *for 1951, written by Mr Robert Trow-Smith, I found that the parish disguised as D—— in the newspaper reports was Datchworth, about three miles from Welwyn, and that the poorhouse was one maintained by vestry funds. The four who died were James Eaves, who had been out of work for many months, his wife Susannah, and their daughters, Susannah and Sarah. The bodies were discovered by a shepherd boy, who looked through a hole in the wall when his flock sheltered by the house from the snow.*

The people of Datchworth kept away from the poorhouse because of the quite baseless suggestion that the Eaves family was suffering from gaol distemper; none of them had at any time been in prison. When the Eaves's eldest son, Philip, had visited them after they had received the half-crown, he had begged the overseers to grant them further relief. One of them had replied, 'Send them relief? Send them a halter! Let them die and be damned.'

The man who reported this dreadful affair to the Kentish Gazette, *under the initials P.T., was Philip Thicknesse, a retired army officer, who unsuccessfully tried to get the overseers—they were also Datchworth's churchwardens—brought to trial for neglect.*

The bodies of James and Susannah Eaves and their two children were taken to Datchworth churchyard in two long wooden boxes, which served as coffins. They were borne there on a farm wagon by night and buried in the light of a lantern. William, the boy who survived, had become demented through his experiences in the poorhouse, and was an imbecile for the rest of his life.

There is a tradition in Datchworth that in the years since 1769 a ghostly farm wagon, bearing two boxes covered by straw, has often been seen lumbering towards Datchworth church on a winter's night.

Man dug up Dead Wife

We hear that on Sunday, the 26th. of February, one John Mitchel, of Pulham in Dorsetshire, labourer, buried his wife, and being reflected on by his neighbours for ill usage towards her, on the next day he had her dug up and opening the coffin, took her in his arms, kissed her three or four times, and desired if ever he did her any ill, that she would then discover it to the spectators, which were many, then put her into the grave again, and went home satisfied.

The Kentish Gazette
Wednesday, 15 March, to Saturday, 18 March, 1769

Susannah Lott—Death by Burning

On Wednesday came on the trial of Susannah Lott, for the murder of her husband, John Lott, of Hythe in this County; after a long hearing she was found guilty and condemned to be drawn upon a hurdle on Friday, the 21st., to the usual place of execution and there to be burnt 'till she was dead. At the same time, Benjamin Buss, convicted also of the murder of the said John Lott, was condemned to be hanged and his body to be afterwards delivered to the Surgeon, to be dissected and anatomized. The behaviour of Mrs. Lott, during her confinement, had been serious, decent and resign'd. She was convicted principally on her own declaration, and the confession she sign'd soon after her husband was poisoned. She was much affected during the whole of her trial, particularly at the time of her child being brought into court to be suckled, which was twice repeated in the course of the trial, in order, it was supposed, to excite the compassion of the jury; and at the time of her receiving sentence, so great was the agonies she seemed to suffer, she drew tears from almost every body present, since when, with becoming fortitude and composure, she has borne her fate, and prepared herself for execution.

Benjamin Buss behaved with an insolent indifference, till the verdict was found against him, when he instantly changed colour, and in the utmost agony, falling down on his knees, begg'd the mercy of the court.

The Kentish Gazette
Wednesday, 19 July, to Saturday, 22 July, 1769

Execution of Mrs Lott

On Friday last, a few minutes before twelve o'clock at noon, Susannah Lott and Benjamin Buss were taken from the gaol in order to be executed pursuant to their sentences (as mentioned in our last). Buss, dressed in black, was carried in a waggon drawn by four horses and attended by two or three Sheriffs Officers. Mrs. Lott, dressed in a suit of mourning she had for her husband, immediately followed on a hurdle drawn by four horses. In this manner they proceeded till they came to the place of execution, when Buss, after joining in a prayer with the Clergyman, was hanged on a gallows about one hundred yards from the place where Mrs. Lott was to be executed. When he had hung about fifteen minutes, the officers then proceeded to execute sentence on Mrs. Lott, who was particularly desirous that he should suffer before her.

A post about seven feet high, was fixed in the ground; it had a peg near the top, to which Mrs. Lott, standing on a stool, was fastened by the neck. When the stool was taken away, she hung about a quarter of an hour, till she was quite dead; a chain was then turned round her body, and properly fastened by staples to the post, when a large quantity of faggots being placed round her, and set on fire, the body was consumed to ashes. She was sensible of her crime, and died entirely penitent. The man did not betray any remarkable concern for his approaching end. It is computed there were 5,000 persons attending the execution.

> **The Kentish Gazette**
> Saturday, 22 July, to Wednesday, 26 July, 1769

❀ *In the eighteenth century murder of a husband was still deemed to be petty treason, and death by burning was the prescribed sentence under a law enacted by the Normans some seven hundred years previously. But Mrs Lott met her end under a modified practice which had been followed for many years before her execution—i.e. although told she would be 'burnt until you are dead', the prisoner was strangled well before the fire was started.*

Susannah Lott and Benjamin Buss were tried and executed at Maidstone.

Tragedy—and a Wedding

Last week two maid-servants at a gentleman's house near Coventry, being with child, one by the gardener, the other by the footman, agreed to hang themselves on a tree in a field adjoining to the house; and a person soon after passing that way, cut them down, when one of them was quite dead. The surviving girl has since married the gardener, and their master has settled £20 upon them for life.

> **The Kentish Gazette**
> Wednesday, 16 August, to Saturday, 19 August, 1769

A Nest of Thieves

There are not less than five hundred gypsies, vagrants and smugglers who have taken sanctuary in a wood between Guildford and Naphill. All the farmers and inhabitants thereabouts have suffered more or less from these rapacious vagabonds, who subsist chiefly by plundering people of their geese, fowls, ducks, or whatever may come in their way. Fourteen pieces of cannon, mounted upon carriages, set out on Saturday, by order of Lord Albermarle, who, together with the neighbouring gentlemen, are determined to dispossess, by force, this nest of thieves from preying upon the honest farmers.

The Kentish Gazette
Wednesday, 23 August, to Saturday, 26 August, 1769

One Mother—30 Children

We hear from Nottingham, that on Friday, the 11th. instant, Mrs. Melvin, of Bulwell, in that County, was safely delivered of a daughter, which is the 30th. time of her being with child. It is very remarkable that this good woman is now in the 45th. year of her age, and notwithstanding her having borne so many children, 17 of whom are living, she enjoys a good share of health and spirits.

The Kentish Gazette
Saturday, 26 August, to Wednesday, 30 August, 1769

1770-79

CRICKET IN THE EIGHTEENTH CENTURY
The first 'Laws of Cricket' were drawn up in 1744.

1770

'Bewitched' Animals

We hear from Ivinghoe (Buckinghamshire) that one Horse and two Sheep, belonging to a Farmer, in the Parish of Slapton, near that place, having died, the Farrier, who had them under his care, not having sufficient Skill to recover them, yet had the Sagacity to discover the cause of their Death, which he declared was owing to their being *bewitched* and named the Witch, a Widow about 55 Years old. This ridiculous Assertion made the poor Woman a Terror to her weak Neighbours, and very unhappy in herself, and as she was not conscious of being a *Witch*, was willing to undergo the usual Method of Trial; viz. by Water-Ordeal, and weighing against the Church-Bible, and a Miller in the Neighbourhood was pitched upon to perform the Ceremony. On the 18th. past, every Thing being got ready for the Trial, the poor Woman went to the Mill, where a great Number of People were assembled, in order to prove her Innocence, but the Miller recollecting the fatal Consequences of a similar Affair about 18 years ago,† declined performing it before so great a Concourse of Spectators, but promised that he would do so in private the first Opportunity.

†At Tring, where a poor Man and his Wife, accused of Witchcraft, were so cruelly used that the Woman died on the spot, and the Man was with Difficulty recovered; for which Offence one of the Ringleaders was executed, and his Body hanged in Chains.

The Northampton Mercury
2 July 1770

❁ *The murder of Ruth Osborne at Tring is covered earlier in this book by reports from the* Northampton Mercury *in 1751.*

Boy eats Cat

Cambridge
On Tuesday evening a country lad, about 16, for a trifling wager, ate, at a public house in this town, a leg of mutton which weighed near eight

pounds, besides a large quantity of bread, carrots, &c. The next night the cormorant devoured a whole cat smothered with onions.

Cambridge Chronicle
quoted in The British Chronicle
13 September 1770

Strangest 'Phaenomenon' within Living Memory

Birbeck Fell, September 23
The following circumstance, however improbable, may be depended upon as a matter of fact. A farmer's wife, in this neighbourhood, who attended duly to the milking of her cows morning and evening, observed for two or three mornings successively that her best cow was deficient in her usual quantities of milk; this made her suspect that some of her neighbours were not over honest, and communicating her suspicions to her husband, they resolved to watch all the succeeding night, which they did without making any discovery, till about sun-rising, when they observed the cow, on which they had their eyes fixed all the night, move towards a bush at some distance, in the pasture, and there to make a stand. Following her thither they observed a most enormous over-grown adder, or hag worm, crawl out of the root of the bush, and winding up one of the cow's hind legs, apply its mouth to one of the paps, and begin to suck, which she suffered it patiently to do, till the farmer attacked it with a cudgel, and ere it could recover its den, kill it. It measured upwards of four feet in length and its skin, stuffed, may be seen at the farmer's house. The whole is looked upon as the strangest phaenomenon that has been known within the memory of the oldest man living.

The British Chronicle
15 October 1770

Poachers' Paradise

Canterbury, December 19
A few days since, as some gentlemen were hunting in a wood near Malling, they suddenly discovered some smoak issue from a lump of bushes in the most remote part of a thick wood; and upon collecting a party together, they searched and found a cavern-like asylum, partly above and partly underground, and upon entering this temporary hovel discovered a man with a long beard employed in picking of fowls, and with a large tin kettle over a good fire, in which was a goose boiling. Several fowls and sacks, besides a great quantity of rosemary, sage, turnips and other things were found in the dwelling, which was furnished

with a couch, rugs and every conveniency for a small family. Upon his being discovered he impeached a gang of fowl stealers, three of whom were that evening apprehended, and with the hermit of the wood, committed by the Rev. Mr. Style to Maidstone Bridewell.

The Nottingham Journal
30 December 1770

1771

Death Premonition—and Preparations

Hereford
Last week died at Mr Davies's, of the Knapp, in the parish of Bridge, in this city, Mr Martin Bird, who formerly kept a tavern at Richmond, in Surrey. About a week before his death he ordered a coffin and shroud to be made, and likewise a certain number of hatbands to be brought for those that were to attend his funeral. He desired they might be brought for him to see, and after examining the coffin-lid he lay down in his bed and died about ten or twelve hours later.

The British Chronicle
3 January 1771

A Most Melancholy Accident

A letter from Long-Ledenham, on the Cliff-Row, Nottinghamshire, says: Last Thursday se'nnight a most Melancholy Accident happened at this Village; two Farmers went to a Neighbour's House to view a sick Calf, the Weather was then most intensely cold; while they were handling the Calf it went mad, and slaver'd on each of them; alarmed at this, they by Advice of Friends, set off to bathe in the Sea; but on the Tuesday following they were brought back dead in a Cart, to the Terror of the whole neighbourhood.

The Northampton Mercury
4 March 1771

❁ *The belief about cures by immersion in water was many hundreds*
of years old. In medieval times it was the custom to duck the
sufferers in the village pond, but by the eighteenth century sea-
water was considered to be necessary. As well as being ineffective
in March 1771, it will be seen from a later report that it was
equally unhelpful in the following November!

Women pull down Enclosure Fences

A letter from Burton-on-Trent, in Staffordshire, informs us that on
Friday the 31st. of last Month, several Women were taken up for
destroying the Fences for inclosing the Rewhay, a Common near that
Place, and brought to Burton, where they were examined before the
Justices, and Warrants made out for their Comittment to Stafford Gaol,
but the Populace getting Information of the Affair, immediately called to
Arms, and after a few Broadsides of Stones, Dirt, &c. being discharged at
the Persons who were conducting the Prisoners to Confinement, they
rescued the women from the Hands of the Officers, and took them away
in Triumph.

The Northampton Mercury
10 June 1771

New Salisbury–London Coach Service

The conveyance between SALISBURY and LONDON having been
found very inconvenient, on account of the carriages travelling all night,
it is presumed that a well-constructed plan, free from such inconvenience,
will be generally approved. The Ladies and Gentlemen of the City, Close
and Neighbourhood of Salisbury are therefore most respectfully
informed that:

A SALISBURY DILIGENCE

will set out every morning at five o'clock from the White Hart at
Salisbury, and at six from the Angel, behind St. Clements', London, by
way of Stockbridge, and will arrive at each of those Inns early the same
evening, as fresh horses will be taken at every stage, the same as with a
post-chaise.

To carry three passengers, at 3d. per mile each, and 14 lb. luggage; all
above 1d. per lb.

The proprietors will not be accountable for anything more than five
pounds value.

The carriages are quite new, elegant and Commodious, and as the
Proprietors are determined to make this conveyance as agreeable as

any method of travelling can be, they humbly hope for the favours of the public.

N.B. Drivers and turnpikes are paid by the Proprietors, and no stoppage on the road, but to change horses.

The Proprietors respectfully beg leave to return thanks to the public for those favours they have already received, and assure them nothing shall be wanting to deserve a continuance of their future preference and support.

The Salisbury and Winchester Journal
21 July 1771

Gander—75 Years Old

Worcester

We are assured that there is now alive, at Mr. Ross's, in the parish of Grimley, in this county, a gander which is seventy-five years old, and appears still in a very healthy state.

The British Chronicle
17 October 1771

Disappointed Sportsman

Last week died, at Hinton, in the parish of Peterchurch, Mr. Walter Delahay, descended from an ancient and good family in this county. His well-known abilities as a sportsman principally distinguished him, but a generous and social disposition endeared him to his acquaintance. It is remarkable that, for many years, he killed the first woodcock in the county, and it is thought that his death was occasioned by his having failed in that particular the last two seasons.

The British Chronicle
24 October 1771

Death from Dog-bite

A few days since a young man, in the neighbourhood of Bath, who had been bit by a mad dog, was conveyed to Pill, to be dipped in the sea, after strong instances of the hydrophobia had appeared. In a lucid interval before he reached Pill he declared his certainty of not being able to survive the dipping, and actually died immediately after he was put into the boat.

The British Chronicle
14 November 1771

1772

Soldiers defeated by Smugglers

Last week Mr. Harvey, Supervisor of Excise at Brentwood, received Information of a Party of smugglers being on the Road from Billericay towards Brentwood, with several Horse-Loads of Tea and other Smuggled Goods. He immediately applied to one Serjeant Lightfoot of the 34th. Regiment of Foot, now on a Recruiting Party and quartered at Brentwood, to assist him in making a Seizure of the same, who, together with three new Recruits, the Supervisor and three other Excise-Officers, armed with Pistols &c. went on Horseback between Twelve and One in the Morning towards Billericay to meet them; and about Three Quarters of a Mile beyond the Turnpike leading to Hutton met about 20 horses loaded, and as many Men well armed to attend them. They imprudently, without considering the Inequality of Number, fell on the Smugglers Sword in Hand, but were soon forced to give way, being overpowered; the Supervisor, Serjeant and Recruits behaved with Courage and Resolution, and had the others done the same, there doubtless would have been much Mischief done, if not Murder, on both sides. The Supervisor presented a Pistol at one of the Smugglers, who in a sneering manner bid him put it up as he would certainly come off the Worst if he went to that Work; but before he could make any Reply was knocked down. The Smugglers proceeded on their journey towards London, went through Brentwood in Triumph about Two, and were seen to go through Ilford about Four. One of the Smugglers received a violent Cut with a Sword on the side of his Head, which almost took off his Cheek; the Serjeant received six Wounds on his Head, one of which it is feared will prove mortal. The Supervisor is dangerously wounded and his Recovery is very doubtful; and one of the Recruits is likely to lose his Arm.

The Northampton Mercury
13 January 1772

❋ *These were the years in which smuggling by well-organized gangs was almost a nightly occurrence along the South Coast and the beaches of the East Anglican seaboard. Each year the Treasury was defrauded of enormous sums by the running of contraband goods—tobacco, tea and spirits. The smugglers were well-armed villains who worsted the 'Redcoats' and excise-officers very frequently.*

Poor take Corn intended for France

Woodbridge in Suffolk, March 20

It is impossible to describe the distresses of the Poor, in this part of the Country, for want of Bread Corn; it is not occasioned by a bad Harvest, for we had a very good one and well got in, and many Farmers have now two Years Crops by them, but they will not bring it to Market, saying they can make a greater Advantage of it by sending it to London; but it is strongly suspected that, instead thereof, it goes to feed our inveterate Enemies, the French, and three Days ago we were confirmed in our Opinion, by some Words let drop by a Sailor belonging to a vessel, which lay in a small Creek, within four miles of this Town, to take in Corn, that they were bound to Dunkirk; upon which a Number of People assembled, went to the Place where the Vessel lay, seized all the Wheat, which they divided amongst themselves, and then set Fire to the Vessel; had they not been in such a Hurry, they might have met with a larger Booty, as several waggons were on the Road, loaded with Corn, to put on board, and about a score of fine fat Sheep. The Master and Crew made off, and have not since been heard of.

The Northampton Mercury
6 April 1772

❀ *Out of fairness to the Suffolk farmers of the time perhaps it should be made clear we were not actually at war with our 'inveterate enemies' in 1772.*

Wagons stopped by the Hungry

Monday last three waggons loaded with corn and several cart loads of meal and flour were stopped at Colchester, by the manufacturers and poor inhabitants of that town, who declared they were in want of the common necessities of life, and as they could not be procured at a reasonable price, they were determined to redress so intolerable a grievance, be the consequence what it would; it was vain to remonstrate, the people were resolute, and a speedy compliance was absolutely necessary, after which little or no disturbance ensued; proper persons were appointed to measure the grain, &c. and sell it in small quantities to the poor, at the following prices, viz. wheat 4s.6d. meal 5s. and flour 6s. per bushel. Same day they stopped about 40 live bullocks, declaring they would kill and sell at three-pence per pound, as many as they had occasion for; however, they did not put this scheme in execution, but let them pass soon after unmolested; the carcase butchers, said they, are the sole cause of the high price of meat, let us not injure the fair dealer, but the moment any of their carts appear, 'twill be proper to welcome them into town, where they will doubtless meet with a warm and cordial reception; that very night, Mr. Hearn, waggoner of Stowmarket, received intelligence at Dedham, that if he went through Colchester he would be considered a carcase butcher, mal-treated, and his waggon pillaged; to prevent this he crossed the country, and went through Boxted, an obscure village about five miles from Colchester, intending to pass that town and come into the great road at Lexden-Heath; however, they were soon informed of his intention, and before the waggon arrived at Lexden-Heath, he was escorted by upwards of 40 people, who obliged him to drive immediately towards Colchester, but as the waggon went slow, and the guards were impatient, two horses were taken from a waggon they met on the road, and added to Mr. Hearn's; one of the mob rode postillion, they entered Colchester in triumph, and drove to the market-place, where a price was agreed upon and proper persons appointed to receive the money. 14 packs of veal and pork were taken out of the waggon and sold at the rate of threepence per pound.

The Chelmsford Chronicle
10 April 1772

Sextuplets at Bolsover

Northampton, August 10
The following is strictly true:
On the 2nd. of July last, the wife of John Charlesworth, who keeps the Cross Keys Inn at Bolsover, in Derbyshire, was safely delivered of three children. The good woman continued in tolerable health ten days, when she was delivered of a fourth child, and she was on the 22nd. of July seized in labour for the third time and brought two more children into the world. These six children, although very small, were perfectly well formed; four are dead, but a boy and a girl, with the mother, are likely to live.

The British Chronicle
13 August 1772

Serious Fire caused by Cruel Sport

On Friday the 23rd. of last Month, a melancholy affair happened at the Farm-House of Mr. Gammon, at Worbrough, in Oxfordshire. Some boys were unluckily playing with a Rat, which they contrived to set on fire; on which the Rat made towards the Barn, which was full of Corn. This was about five in the Evening and at Twelve at Night, a Fire broke out in the Barn, which entirely consumed the same, set fire to the Dwelling-House, and the Maid Servant, and two young Children perished in the Flames ere the Fire was discovered. Mrs. Gammon, who was brought to bed but the Day before, was with great difficulty saved from sharing the same Fate. The Flames continued very fierce till Four in the Morning, for want of proper Assistance. The Barns, Stables, Dwelling-House and several Outhouses were all consumed.

The Northampton Mercury
2 November 1772

1773

Public Whipping for killing Hare

Reading, January 30
Monday last, two young Men underwent a Flagellation at the Public Whipping-Post in our Market-Place, in consequence of an Order from a Justice of Peace, conformable to a late Amendment in the Game-Act, for killing a Hare. As the Act now stands, the offending Party must be punished (i.e. whipt) within three Days after his Commitment, and on the fourth he may bring an Appeal.

Adams Weekly Courant
9 February 1773

A Family of Sweeps

The following odd Circumstance, says a Correspondent, is strictly true! A Chimney-sweeper at a Village in Kent has seventeen Children, Sons, who all follow the Occupation of their Father.

Adams Weekly Courant
2 March 1773

The Nottinghamshire Giant

Nottingham, February 3
Last Sunday was interr'd at Sutton-Bonnington St. Ann's, in this County, Mr. Rice, Mason, aged 30, who lately died of a Consumption. He retained his Senses till within a few Minutes of his Death, when he desired his Mother to take away the Candle, it being troublesome to him, and bad her farewell; she calling the Family up, and going to see him, he expir'd soon

after. His Coffin was eight feet four Inches long, and sixteen inches deep, and was carried to the Church by eight of his Father's labourers, the Pall being supported by eight young Women of the Place. Upwards of 500 people were assembled on the Occasion; and a Sermon suited thereto was preached by the Rev. Mr. Whistler, who took his Text from Job XIV Ver i.ii.† The Grave was ten Feet long, and when the Coffin was in the Grave, three strong Stakes were driven on each side of the Coffin, and fastn'd over with Strong Bars of Iron fix'd thereto, in order to prevent any Person from taking up the Body, and the Earth rammed down as close as Hands could do it, for 'tis said a very eminent surgeon in London offer'd 300 Guineas for his Body when dead. This young Man, when living, was called the modern living Colossus, or the wonderful Nottinghamshire Giant. He increased annually (from his 14th. to his 20th. Year) near six inches in Height; he stood seven feet four Inches and a half high, without any Deception, and was justly esteemed a very extraordinary Curiosity, on Account of his prodigious Stature and proportionate Bulk, for his Hands and Limbs were equally gigantic with his Body. He was viewed three Times by their Majesties, and the Royal Family, at Richmond in Surry.

Adams Weekly Courant
2 March 1773

† *Man that is born of a woman is*
of few days and full of trouble.

He cometh forth like a flower, and is cut down:
he fleeth also as a shadow, and continueth not.

❀ *As the newspaper report did not compare Mr Rice with the 'great Mr Benjamin Bower' of Dorset (see* Northampton Mercury *report: December 1763), presumably he was more famed for his height than for his weight, and Mr Bower was the heavier man.*

Extraordinary Cricket Match

Wednesday last was played on Guildford Downs a very extraordinary Match at Cricket, between a Carpenter on one Side, and a Company of nine Taylors on the other, for a Quarter of Lamb and Cabbage, which was decided in favour of the Carpenter by 64 notches.

Adams Weekly Courant
3 August 1773

❀ *Although the single cricketer who took on nine others was victorious by 64 'notches' (runs), it will be agreed that the competition was hardly a fair one. The first 'Laws of Cricket' were drawn up in 1744; they were revised in 1755, and again in 1774.*

Wrestling at Carlisle

The great wrestling matches at Carlisle, on Wednesday and Thursday se'nnight were the means of assembling a vast concourse of people together. The competitors, nearly a hundred in number, were in general men of great bodily strength, with much science, both of which seemed to be exerted to the utmost. On Wednesday the chief prize of eight guineas was finely contested for between John Weightman and John Robson, and won by Weightman. Robson, the second best deserving, received two guineas. The same day, a match for one guinea, between two noted players, Graham and Liddle, was won by the former, who threw his antagonist three times successively (out of five). On Thursday the second prize of four guineas was wrestled for by the standing men of the previous day, which was gained by William Sands, of Whitehaven, throwing John Robley, in the last round. The prize for Youthful Wrestler was spiritedly contested for.

Such of the *Cockney Sportsmen* who took the field well provided with *cash*, have sent home a great deal of *game*—the others have had no success.

> The Weekly Register
> 12 October 1773

A Singular Parson

A few days since died at Christchurch, in the 92nd. year of his age, the Rev. Luke Imber, rector and vicar of North and South Shoebury, and one of his Majesty's justices of the peace for this county. A more singular character perhaps seldom occurs: though he possessed a genteel income, he for the most part affected the dress of the lowest indigence, and has often, by his acquaintance, been mistaken for a vagabond. At the age of eighty-three, he married a country girl of thirteen. In short his whole life was a continued series of oddities. He desired in his will that he might be buried in an old chest, which he had for some time kept by him for that purpose, and that the bearers should have each of them a pair of new shoes, and a pair of tanned leather gloves, which were given accordingly.

> The Chelmsford Chronicle
> 29 October 1773

New Way of scaring Crows

Extract of a Letter from Cowbridge, December 10
The following extraordinary Method of preventing Crows from eating the Corn after sown was tried by a Gentleman Farmer, not 20 miles from

this Town, and answered the End so well that other Farmers intend following the Method. He took a Cat and tied her by the Leg fast to a Stake in the field; no sooner was this done, but the Cat began crying, and so continued for two or three Days (being well fed Night and Morning) and not a Crow has been seen on the Field since.

Adams Weekly Courant
21 December 1773

1774

Recipe for 'Preserving Cattle'

We are informed from Saxmundham in Suffolk that the Distemper which lately broke out among the horned Cattle, and which so alarmed the County, is much abated, such effectual steps having been taken by every Farmer to prevent the Contagion from spreading that it is not doubted but a total stop will be put to it in a few days. . . .

The following RECEIPT was the means of preserving a great number of Cattle in George the Second's Reign, at a Farm in Yorkshire, where the Cattle in every adjacent place was ill, but not one in that Farm died:

Take Rue, Sage, Wormwood and Lavender, a handful of each, infuse them in a Gallon of White Wine Vinegar, in a Stone Pot covered close, set on Wormwood Ashes for four Days, after which strain the liquid through a fine Flannel, and put into Bottles well Corked; in every quart bottle put ¾ of an Ounce of Camphire, the Herbs the Liquor is made from set in a Tub in the Cow-house (the Cows are fond of the Smell) and every morning and night when the Cows come to be milked, dip a Sponge in the Liquid, and rub the Nostrils and Mouth of the Beast well.

The Norwich Mercury
28 May 1774

Bean-belly Jerry

On Monday a young Fellow, a Weaver, at Heigham, well-known by the Name of Bean-belly Jerry, undertook for the trifling Wager of 1s. to eat seven Pints (full Measure) of Windsor Beans, a loaf of Bread, Bacon, &c. The time allowed this Cormorant for eating this extraordinary Mess was three Quarters of an Hour, but he devoured it in the Space of forty Minutes, to the great astonishment of the Spectators.

The Norwich Mercury
13 August 1774

Highwayman killed by Coach Guard

Cambridge
On Thursday morning about Three o'Clock the Stamford Fly was attempted to be robbed near Stukely in Huntingdonshire, by a Single Highwayman, who ordered the coachman to stop, but the Guard, who travels with the Coach, told him to keep off, or he would shoot him; the Highwayman persisting in his Intention to rob the Coach the Guard fired a Blunderbuss and lodged two slugs in his Forehead. He was immediately put into the Basket of the Coach, where he lived but a few minutes, and before his death confessed he was the Person who robbed the Peterborough Stage about a fortnight ago. His Corpse was carried to Huntingdon, where it appeared he was a Horsekeeper belonging to the Cross-Keys Inn at that Place. He had no Fire-arms about him, but made use of a Candlestick instead of a Pistol.

The Norwich Mercury
17 September 1774

Contraband hidden in Sand

On Sunday morning the Yarmouth Excise Officers seized on the Denes to the Northward of the Town one hundred and eleven half-Ankers of Geneva, about 5 cwt. of Tea and Coffee, with some snuff and tobacco, which they conveyed to their Warehouse. The goods were concealed in a cave dug in the sand, and covered with a plank, within 150 yards of the sea.

The Norwich Mercury
1 October 1774

❀ *A half-anker was approximately four gallons. Geneva was gin—more generally that made in Holland.*

Saving a Bed

On Thursday last was married at Brompton, near Northallerton, Mr. Edward Clark, Widower, to Mrs. Ann Gibbins, Widow, both of the same

Place, whose ages together are upwards of 160 years. They have lived in the same House for some Time. and though no youthful vigour can have excited in them the Cause of performing the matrimonial Vow at Hymen's Altar, yet doubtless it is a lucky Thought to save the Trouble of making two beds, and to keep each other warm at this cold Season.

The York Courant
15 November 1774

1775

Roman Coins found in Field

A few days since as a Farmer at Morton-Banks, near Bingley (Tenant of Henry Wickham, Esq., of Cottingley-Hall) was making a Drain in a Field, he discovered a Copper Chest about 20 Inches below the surface, containing near 100 weight of Roman Silver Pieces, coined at 15 different Periods, some of which are as early a Date as Julius Caesar. They are about the size, but almost three times the Thickness of a Sixpence, and the Impressions are very perfect. There was also in the Chest a Silver Image about six inches long.

The York Courant
14 March 1775

Cure for Wasp Sting

As wasps are this Summer very numerous, it may be of some Utility to the Public to be informed that Onion Juice, gently swallowed, is a certain Remedy for the Sting of a Wasp in the Throat, an Accident that has been often known to prove fatal.

The Norwich Mercury
26 August 1775

Coach Passenger kills Footpad

Monday morning early the Norwich Coach was again stopped at the six mile Stone at Ilford by five footpads. An Excise Officer of this City, who was an outside Passenger, and had a brace of Pistols, discharged them both, and killed one of the villains on the Spot; the Guard being unwilling to fire, the Exciseman took his Carbine from him, fired it and broke the legs of another, who is in Custody.

The Norwich Mercury
9 December 1775

1776

Ten Feet of Snow in Essex

Billerica, Essex-January 18
The snow here affords the most amazing and melancholy scene ever known by the oldest man living, it being from six to ten feet deep in the roads, which renders them entirely impassable for carriages. The Rochford coach came in here on Saturday, but could get no further; neither that or the Billerica coach attempted to go either way till Wednesday, when both set out for London; the post boy came in here on Saturday and attempted to go to Rochford, but could not. About thirty men have been employed two days in cutting avenues through the snow in the several roads leading from this town.

The Chester Chronicle
29 January 1776

Caverns in the Snow

Canterbury, January 20
Our streets are, for horses and carriages, impassable; no mail has been received from London since that despatched on Saturday night last; we have several mails due from all parts of the coast, as no part of the country is yet sufficiently tracked to be passable with security, and nothing but the most extreme necessity for want of provisions would have opened a communication to many of the neighbouring villages, to which, in some places, caverns have been dug through the snow, arched over, as in coal-mines and chalk-pits.

The Chester Chronicle
29 January 1776

A Treasure Chest

Extract from a letter from Plymouth
The following extraordinary affair you may depend on as an absolute fact.
A poor man in this neighbourhood, who has a wife and several children,
being driven to great distress for firewood, was obliged to cut up (among
many more moveables) an old chest, which had lain in the house time
immemorial, when to his very great joy and relief a false bottom was
discovered by the jumping out of a piece of gold, which afforded him 240
pieces of coin of James the First, value from 22s. to 23s. each.

The Chester Chronicle
12 February 1776

Cow killed by Lady's Hat

Birmingham, September 26
A few days ago, as a lady was walking in a piece of ground contiguous to a
gentleman's seat not more than two miles from this place, a cow that was
feeding therein, mistaking her head-dress (from the variety of vegetables
that appeared thereon) for a kitchen garden, made hastily towards her
new pasture, which threw the lady into such a fright that, in making her
escape, she left behind her a great piece of the GRACEFUL furniture of
her head, which the cow greedily began devouring, when unluckily one of
the SPITS with which this LOVELY apparatus was kept together, stuck
in her throat and though every effort was tried to disengage it, the poor
creature died a few hours after in great agony. . . .

The Cumberland Pacquet
15 August 1776

Stone Coffins dug up at Acomb

York, October 16
About ten days ago, two stone coffins were dug up at Acomb, a village
near this place, which are supposed to have contained the ashes of Geta, a
son of the Emperor Severus (who was assasinated by his brother
Garacalla) and Papinian, that eminent civilian, who was also assasinated
for refusing to make an oration in favour of Geta's murderer. It has long
been supposed that they were buried nigh each other, South or S.E. of
Acomb village.

The Cumberland Pacquet
24 October 1776

1777

An Exchange of Brides

The following, however whimsical it may appear, is said to be a fact. Two young farmers, in the parish of Holmes Chapel, in Cheshire, being on the point of marriage, obtained, at the same time, licences for that purpose. But *intoxicated* either by the idea of their approaching nuptials, or by something more potent, each lover gave the name of the other's intended bride, in which manner the licences were executed. This error, as neither of the men could read, was not perceived until the day appointed to celebrate the nuptials, when it was discovered by the Clergyman. The mistake occasioned some little confusion, but the parties, wisely considering that long acquaintance and great previous caution cannot always ensure conjugal felicity—or, perhaps, that too great a degree of affection in that state frequently precludes a proper attention to the more important concerns of life—or, it may be, unwilling to disappoint their friends' expectations of seeing their weddings and partaking of the consequent cheer—they mutually agreed to be paired as the licences enjoined.

The Cumberland Pacquet
16 January 1777

Brandy at the Hunt

Last week there was the greatest concourse of people assembled at Wigton ever known—to see a Bag Fox turned down, it is computed the number of horse and foot amounting to near five thousand. Many assembled by six o'Clock in the morning, but it being a very hard frost, Reynard was not set down 'till near ten o'Clock. During the interval *Monsieur Coniac* was so very powerful that some were disappointed of the Chace, being obliged to be put to bed—and it may truly be said, no Fox Hunters ever set out with greater glee.

The Cumberland Chronicle
28 January 1777

❁ *A 'Bag Fox' was one taken along to the Meet and released there, as opposed to one found and roused by the Hunt after it had set off.*

The Taking of General Lee

The following advertisement was stuck on the Market-post at Tring in Hertfordshire on Friday se'nnight:

This is to give notis that Thursday next
will be helld a day of regoicin in commemoration
of the takin of General Lee when their will be a
sermint preached and other demonstrations of joye,
after which will be an nox roasted whole and
everery mark of festivity and bell ringing
imagenable whith a ball and cock fiting at night
in the hassembly room at the black Lyone.

> James Clinch
> Parish Clerk and Cryer
> Feb. 13, 1777.

> **Cumberland Chronicle**
> 25 February 1777

⊛ *Since 1775 Britain had been fighting against her Colonists in the American War of Independence, which continued until 1783. Charles Lee—a former officer in the British Army— became a revolutionary General. He had been taken prisoner by British dragoons who stormed his headquarters.*

Recruiting Parties at Fair

Lewes

At Shelmeston Fair on Friday last, great and small cattle sold remarkably well; sheep in general were bought for four and five shillings the head cheaper than they were at the above fair this time twelvemonth.

The Recruiting Parties quartered in this town were mighty industrious at the above fair; amongst the farmers' servants &c., many of whom the preceding evening in celebrating harvest home drank so plentifully that they presented themselves fair game to the recruiting Serjeants, who (very far from being lag in their pursuit) we hear enlisted six of them, but the next morning discharged five, on their paying smart money.

> **Sussex Weekly Advertiser**
> 22 September 1777

Whipping for Theft

Whitehaven

Last Thursday, at noon, Margaret Laidley was whipped at the Market-Cross in this town, for theft, pursuant to the Order of the Quarter Sessions held at Penrith on the 8th. instant. The novelty of a scene of this kind here, drew together several hundreds of people, who expressed their approbation of so public an example being made of such a notorious offender, she having been no less than eight different times in custody, in the course of a few years.

The Cumberland Chronicle
18 October 1777

Raven kills Fox

Last Tuesday morning a servant-girl, at Redhow in Lowswater, on entering the farm-yard, which is surrounded with buildings on all sides, observed a fox among the geese; she immediately informed her master of the circumstance, who came and placed her at the gate, with a stick in her hand, in order to cut off a retreat that way. Reynard being thus put to his shifts, and eager to avoid his enemies, jumped on the hog-stye, when a *Raven*, who had harboured on the farm for many years, flew at him with all his might and, after many hard struggles, with bloodshed on both sides, to the great astonishment of all present, the fox lost his life. What is very remarkable, the same fox had worried some of the geese on the Saturday before, in consequence of which the farmer has ordered they be shut up in the yard. Reynard, scorning to be outwitted, with a peculiar degree of sagacity, had hid himself in the cart-house, and, from circumstances which several of the family recollected, he had been there two days before he was discovered.

The Cumberland Chronicle
15 November 1777

133 years old—has had 13 Wives

There is now living at Broad Rush Common, in Devonshire, John Brookery, a farmer, who is in the 134th. year of his age and who has had thirteen wives.

The Bristol Journal
quoted in The Cumberland Chronicle
22 November 1777

'The Woman who stole the Yarn'

Last Saturday a woman was detected stealing 16 lb. of woollen yarn in Keswick Market. She was immediately led round the Market-place by the Bell-man, who, at intervals, proclaimed "This is the woman who stole the yarn". She was afterwards delivered up to the mob, who drove her a mile out of the town.

The Cumberland Chronicle
13 December 1777

Four Recruits from every Parish

A scheme is now under consideration for every parish in Great Britain to furnish four recruits for the army, which, it is said will raise above 50,000 men. They are to have a bounty, and to be discharged at the end of three years, as an inducement to their speedy entering.

The Chelmsford Chronicle
19 December 1777

1778

A Useful Suggestion

As a precaution against horse-stealing, a judicious correspondent recommends to the several parishes in the country, to furnish their blacksmiths with marking irons with the name of the parish, and then offer a liberal reward to all smiths who shall be instrumental in the recovery of horses that are stolen, which blacksmiths can readily guess at, by knowing from whence they came.

Sussex Weekly Advertiser
5 January 1778

Sheep wanted Twins

The following extraordinary circumstance it is said may be depended on as a fact:

A gentleman in Windsor Forest had a ewe which till heretofore always brought two lambs, but having only produced one this year, she violently attacked another ewe that had two lambs, and would not desist till she had seduced one of the young ones from its mother, which being effected, she returned to her own lamb and suckled them both with much seeming complacency and satisfaction.

The Cumberland Chronicle
11 April 1778

Man for Sale

A countryman at Windsor on Tuesday last offered himself to enlist to serve his Majesty, either in the Manchester volunteers, or the 25th. Regiment commanded by Lord George Lennox, now quartered in the environs of Windsor, and put himself up at a fair price to serve that Colonel who bid the most money. Lord George Lennox bid 45 guineas and the Colonel of the Manchester regiment gave 46, and he is now on his march with that regiment.

The Cumberland Chronicle
2 May 1778

'Gamesters' and 'Backsword'

On Friday the 19th. of June will be played for at Backsword, at Stow-on-the-Wold, Gloucestershire, a Purse of TEN GUINEAS, by nine or eleven a Side, to appear on the Stage in the Market Place, in Stow aforesaid, by Eleven o'Clock in the Forenoon; and in case no side by Twelve o'Clock. Half a Guinea will be given to each Man breaking a Head, and Half a Crown to each Man having his Head broken.
N.B. It is requested that all Gamesters will attend, as they will meet with great Encouragement; and if only one Side should appear, One Guinea will be allowed each Side to bear their Expenses.

The Glocester Journal
15 June 1778

❀ *The 'swords' for this game were stout ash sticks, with basket handles. The two contestants fought each other at a distance of not more than three feet. If one cried 'Hold', a minute's respite was allowed. The game was won by the first to 'break' his opponent's head, by drawing blood at any point an inch above the eyebrow.*

A detailed description of Backsword is given in Tom Brown's Schooldays. *The author, Thomas Hughes, wrote: 'If good men are*

*playing, the quickness of the returns is marvellous; you hear the
rattle like that a boy makes drawing his stick along palings, only
heavier. . . .'*

Press Gang Repelled

Last week a press gang from Blythe (with their Lieutenant) went to
Newbiggin to press some fishermen, when, to their great mortification,
and the unspeakable pleasure of many spectators, they were obliged to
retire from the village, with many demonstrations of an unkind
reception.

The Newcastle Chronicle
14 November 1778

1779

Many Miles to Market

There is now living in the City of Lincoln, a person who has travelled
upwards of 45,760 miles to and from Wragby Market, which is only 11
miles distant; but what appears still more extraordinary, he has not been
prevented by sickness, or any other cause, from attending every market
day during the last forty years.

The County Chronicle and Weekly Advertiser for Essex, Herts, Kent,
Surrey, Middlesex and Berks.
5 February 1779

Postboy robbed of Irish Mail

Oxford
Last Saturday night, about ten o'clock, the postboy, carrying the mail from
this city, was stopped in Hack-lane, near Long Compton, in his way to
Shipston-upon-Stour, Worcestershire, by two footpads with crepe over
their faces, who took from him the Irish mail, together with the inland
bags. The night being dark and foggy, the boy can give no other
description of the robbers, than they appeared to be little men. It seemed
that when he was first attacked the lad apprehended them to be drunken
fellows, and attempted to push them forward, 'till they produced pistols,

and with dreadful imprecations threatened to blow out his brains if he either resisted or moved one step further.

The Glocester Journal
1 March 1779

An Ancient Harvester

A few days since died at Irige-Hay, near Wirworth, in Derbyshire, James Simpson, commonly known by the name of Juggler, in the 114th. year of his age. He sheared corn last summer and could see nearly as well as ever he could in his life. He worked till about a week before his death.

The Chelmsford Chronicle
4 June 1779

An Offer of Service

To the Right Hon. Earl Nugent
My Lord,
   HEARING that you intend to propose opening a subscription and subscribing liberally towards raising men for the defence of this country in the case of an attack from the enemy, I have weighed the matter in my own mind coolly, and am firmly of opinion the speediest and most effectual way would be for the landowners to provide arms, and their tenants, sons and servants, within 20 miles of the sea coast, to learn the discipline two hours every day from six to eight o'clock; such as cannot afford to lose their time to be paid 2d. per hour, by the landlord or tradesman; there are old soldiers enough in the neighbourhood to learn us; and I think men that have property will make the best defence; therefore let the landlords in their proportion be the officers, the farmers serjeants and corporals; My Lord, I do assure you I have spoke to several spirited farmers who highly approve of this scheme; for my part I can raise 20 able men, and am ready to assist upon this plan, or any other better that your lordship may point out; and as your lordship has said you will do handsomely we expect to hear of some spirited offer.

A FARMER

The Chelmsford Chronicle
23 July 1779

❀ *The need for a large defence force in Britain became urgent when the French allied themselves with the Americans in 1778. Once again there was a real possibility of invasion.*

A Fine Cucumber

A cucumber was lately cut in the garden of Henry Shuttleworth, esq., of Great-Bowden, near Market Harborough, Leicestershire; which measured in length 31 inches, was three feet 11 inches over the middle, and weighed 60 lbs.

The Chelmsford Chronicle
20 October 1779

❀ *By comparison, the cucumbers we grow to-day are positively puny. The Guinness Book of Records (1979) gives the record United Kingdom weight for a garden-grown cucumber as 8lb. 4 oz. The record for one grown indoors is 11 lb. 6oz.*

1780-89

EVADING THE HORSE-TAX
A farmer rides his cow to Stockport Market.

1780

Wager at the Mill

Chelmsford

On Saturday last a bargain was made by Mr. Hamilton of Colchester with a miller in the neighbourhood of Ardleigh, seven miles from that town, for 30 quarters of Bran to be carried by a stage coach, with six horses, from the miller's house to the Stone's End, Colchester, in two hours, which, if Mr. Hamilton performed, he was to pay an under price for the bran, and if he carried 40 quarters he was to have it gratis. So great an improbability was it thought that many considerable wagers were laid; however, the 40 quarters (near six ton) were carried 20 minutes within the time, to the astonishment of hundreds of spectators. The load upon the coach made it more than 16 feet high, and several persons rode on it to balance the bulk.

The Newcastle Courant
15 January 1780

A Remarkable Large Ox

Last week a remarkable large ox was killed at Darlington, the tongue of which weighed 14 lb. and sold for a guinea. The whole of the animal, which is supposed to be the largest ever slaughtered in England, was sold at a shilling a pound.

The Norfolk Chronicle
15 January 1780

Smugglers rescue Contraband

Last Sunday as the people were going from Coatham to Kirkleatham church they were alarmed by the fire of a large gun from a smuggler at sea, which carried 24 guns, 9 and 12-pounders. The people saw about 70 or 80 of the crew coming from the ship in long boats, armed with blunderbusses, pistols, &c, in order to rescue a large seizure of liquors made at Redcar by the Whitby Officers, attended by four of the Cumberland militia. As soon as the smugglers landed they retook part of the seizure at Redcar and Coatham, and staved in the heads for the populace to drink and pursuing the carts &c. laden with the other part, they came up with them near Wilton, and seized the remainder, the officers and soldiers having expended all their rounds, but happily no lives were lost. They then staved three casks there, one in Wilton wood, and carried the remainder back.

The Newcastle Courant
19 February 1780

Cucumber wins Wager

Last week five tradesmen of Cambridge, being in company together, a wager was made that two of them outweighed the other three. As the odds seemed to be clearly in favour of the three, one of the two desired he might be weighed with a cucumber in his pocket, which being agreed to, he produced one from the garden of Mr. Smithson, Scholar's Cook of St. John's College, weighing 16 pounds, whereby he won the wager. This Cucumber is of a species never before grown in these parts, is of a deep green colour, very firm and would probably have been larger if planted early.

The Norfolk Chronicle
23 September 1780

Sixteen Children in Seventeen Years

The following circumstance is no less remarkable than true: A Shoemaker at Kirkoswald, in this county, has been married only 17 years, in which time he has had 16 children, 13 of them are now living and he is now in a fair way of having another, his wife being big with child. What adds to the curiosity of seeing them is that they are remarkable fine children, kept very neat and clean, much like each other, and so little space betwixt the birth of each other that it is with difficulty the neighbours discover them from one another.

The Newcastle Courant
25 November 1780

1781

Celebrations for Shrove Monday

Norwich
On Monday last, being Shrove Monday, a number of people from this city, and the adjacent villages, assembled at Thorpe, to be present at the rustic amusement of Bull-baiting. Next day a sheep was roasted whole on the river opposite Mr. Bore's house, but the weather proving unfavourable prevented many from partaking of the repast who otherwise intended it.

The Norfolk Chronicle
31 March 1781

❁ *Although not observed today, Shrove Monday used to mark the beginning of the pre-Lenten jollity. Another name for it was Collop Monday, when 'collops' of salted meat and eggs were eaten. On this day the children sang:*

Shrovetide is nigh at hand
And I be come a shroving;
Pray, dame, something,
An apple, or a dumpling.

Horse killed by Boar

Nottingham, May 12
On Thursday last, a Boar belonging to Mr. William Lowe, Innkeeper, in Newark, got into a Close and attacking a Horse belonging to Mr. Marshall, ripp'd up his Belly, so that he died soon after.

Adams Weekly Courant
15 May 1781

Poachers kill Keeper

Whereas in the night of Saturday, the 23rd, of December instant, Sixteen or Eighteen Poachers entered the Plantation at Blickling, belonging to the Earl of Buckingham, near adjoining to his Park, and in his own Occupation, where they shot 14 or 15 times, and on the Keepers being alarmed, and going there with their Assistants, the said Poachers threatened their Lives, swearing they would shoot them, and did violently assault and cruelly beat and wound them, with their Guns and Large Clubs, armed with Iron Spikes, insomuch that Jacob Blyth, one of the Keeper's Assistants, is since dead by the Wounds which he then received, and the life of James Gibbons, another of the Assistants, greatly despaired of, and others of such Assistants, most dangerously bruised and wounded.

For the discovery and bringing to Justice these violent and Inhuman Offenders, a REWARD OF ONE HUNDRED POUNDS is hereby offered to any Person or Persons who shall first make Discovery of them so as they may be prosecuted to Conviction, by applying to Mr. Robert Copeman, of Blickling.

ROBERT COPEMAN

N.B. One of the poachers appeared to be a tall stout Man, wore a long white Slop and had with him a rough coated light-coloured Water Spaniel.

N.B. It being supposed that some of these Poachers have Marks of Blows upon them it is therefore earnestly recommended to such Persons as live in a Neighbourhood where suspected Poachers usually dwell, to make Observation of such as may have received Blows, or any outward and visible Hurts, as the same may probably lead to the Discovery of the guilty Persons.

N.B. They left behind them a round Hat, with a pale Blue Lining, and very bloody, also the broken Stocks of two Guns.

The Norfolk Chronicle
29 December 1781

❀ *Blickling Hall is some 14 miles from Norwich. It was built in the seventeenth century, on the site of an earlier building which was a home of Anne Boleyn.*

1782

Recipe for Long Life

Tuesday, the 7th. instant, died at Wortham, near Diss, in the 103d. year of his age, Mr. Benjamin Parker, and was attended to the grave by a number of his children, grandchildren and great grandchildren; he was a strong, healthy man, and till within a few days of his death drank three pints of strong beer a day; he was never known to drink spirituous liquors, or tea, nor to smoak, take snuff, or chew tobacco; when pressed to take any of these idle things, as he called them, his saying was:

> Snuff, nor tobacco, gin, nor yet tea,
> A pot of good beer is the liquor for me.

The Norfolk Chronicle
16 February 1782

Ringing for Hats

On Tuesday, the 30th. of July, will be given to be Rung for, by Stephen Richards at Hurst Church, in the county of Berks, a set of good Plain Hats. Each company to provide an umpire, and the umpire of the winning set to be entitled to a hat. Each peal to continue 15 minutes, and no trial peal on the day of ringing; no man to ring, or be an umpire, but what dines. A good ordinary will be on the table at one o'clock, and to begin ringing at three. No Hurst man to ring, or be an umpire.

The Bowling is in good order—Coffee, Tea and Cheesecakes, as usual.

The Reading Mercury
24 June 1782

❀ *An 'ordinary' was a meal as usually served, as opposed to one specially prepared for the occasion. The contestants at Hurst probably enjoyed it at the village inn.*

A Berkshire Village 'Revel'

This is to give notice that Yattendon Revel will be kept as usual, on Wednesday, the 10th. of July, and for the encouragement of gentlemen gamesters and others, there will be given an exceeding good Gold-laced Hat of 27s. value, to be played for at Cudgels; the man that breaks most heads to have the prize; 2s. will be given to each man that positively breaks a head, for the first ten heads that are broke; the blood to run an inch, or to be deemed no head. ... To begin playing at three o'clock precisely.

Also will be given a very good Hat of 15s. value to be wrestled for; the man that throws most men to have the prize; no dispute about falls, but three go-downs.

Likewise an exceeding good Gold-laced Hat at 27s. value to be bowled for; ... the man that gets most pins at three bowls to have the prize. To begin bowling at one o'clock and end at nine.

Second Revel Day

On Thursday, the 11th., will be given Half-a-Guinea to be run for by Jack Asses, the best of three heats. No less than three will be allowed to start.

Also will be given a fine Holland Smock to be run for by women; the best of three heats; no less than three will be allowed to start. Likewise a Jingling Match by eleven blindfolded women, and one unmasked with bells, for a very good petticoat.

Also a gold-laced Hat of 27s. value to be played at Cudgels for by young gamesters, the same rules to be observed as on the first day.

Likewise an exceeding good Gold-laced Hat at 27s. value to be bowled for . . . the man that gets most pins to have the prize. To begin bowling at one o'clock and end at nine.

N.B. Stalls for people to put their goods on to be had at the Royal Oak, as usual.

The Reading Mercury
29 June 1782

❖ *A Jingling Match? In a ring formed by the spectators, the eleven blindfolded women would have tried to catch the twelfth, whose eyes would not have been covered. A bell would have been hung round her neck and her arms tied behind her back so that she could not prevent the 'jingling' as she ran about to evade capture. There was much fun and quite a few knocks at 'jingling' as eleven players collided with each other in their efforts to grab the twelfth and win a prize.*

Inhuman Treatment of Pauper

At the above Assizes, a Bill of Indictment for a Misdemeanour was found against a Parish Officer who in order to be rid of a Pauper put him into an open Cart at Eleven o'Clock at Night in the Month of January last, drove him Seventeen Miles from the Parish, and at Day-break left him exposed in the Highway. The poor Man was Fourscore Years of Age, very infirm, blind and helpless, and died within a Week after this Treatment. It seems the Overseer was the Youngest Man in the Parish, and in this matter obeyed the Directions of the Vestry Meeting, otherwise he would have been indicted for Murder. It is hoped that the Humanity and Self-Interest of Parishes will be alarmed and put upon their Guard by the unhappy and expensive Consequences of such inconsiderate and illegal Measures.

The Manchester Mercury
30 July 1782

❀ *The Assizes referred to in this report were held at Derby.*

Curate kills Schoolmaster in Duel

A letter from Derby, dated August 31, says:

Yesterday morning, a little after seven o'Clock, a Duel was fought in Spondon, near this town, between the Rev. Mr. B., curate of this Place, and Mr. Edward Taylor, the Schoolmaster, in which the latter was mortally wounded, and died this Afternoon, lamented by a numerous Acquaintance. Dr. H. attended the Deceased, but his Endeavours to extract the Ball proved ineffectual, it having entered the Body just under the lower Rib on the Right Side; Mr. B. is slightly wounded in the Arm and has absconded. The Coroner will sit upon the Body this Evening, and it is generally expected the Jury will bring in their Verdict, Manslaughter. It appears that the deceased and Mr. B. supped together the preceding Evening at a Gentleman's House in the village and both being rather elevated with liquor, a violent Altercation took place concerning a brisk gay Widow in the Neighbourhood, by whom it was said Mr. B. had been preferred, notwithstanding he has "a Wife and several children; which Circumstances Mr. T.—— commenting upon with great Freedom, and intimating that something of a criminal Nature had passed between the Parties, Mr. B. was so violently provoked at this Insinuation, that he threw a Decanter of Port Wine at Mr. T.——'s Head, which unexpected Salutation almost occasioned him instantly to retire from the Room, and upon Mr. B.——'s Return home, was presented with the fatal Challenge".

Another letter from Derby, dated Sept. 2, has the following article:

The inhabitants of Spondon, being completely dissatisfied with the Coroner's Decision respecting poor Taylor, he having brought it in Manslaughter, assembled together last Night in a tumultuous Manner, and being headed by the Usher of the deceased, assailed the Windows of the Widow B—— with Stones, Brickbats &c. and in a short Time totally demolished them, pulled down her elegant Palisades, Grecian Statue &c. and were proceeding to force open the Door of the Dwelling-house, in order to destroy the Furniture, when fortunately a Detachment of Soldiers arrived from Derby, who put a stop to the further Depredations.

The Widow decamped early in the Morning, for London, supposed to console with the Rev. Mr. B.—— on his unfortunate separation from a virtuous Wife and young Family.

The Manchester Mercury
10 September 1782

Died at 86—Grandparents still Living

On Thursday last was interred at Mottram-in-Longdendale, Martha Broadbent, aged 86 years, who had at the Time of her Death, a Father, Mother, Grandfather and Grandmother all living.

The Manchester Mercury
1 October 1782

1783

Buried in Unconsecrated Ground

On Saturday se'nnight, as some workmen were digging a foundation for some buildings in a paddock near Grantham, Lincolnshire, they discovered the entire skeleton of a man, over which lay a stone, with the following inscription:

Here lies the body of Zacharias Laxton,
deceased the 27th. of August, 1667, being
for his excommunication, denied the usual
place of burial.

The British Chronicle
19 June 1783

Funeral of Quadruplets

Yesterday se'nnight the four children of John Green, farmer, of Winscombe, of which his wife was delivered about thirteen days ago, were interred in the churchyard of that parish. They were all born alive, and lived some time, were perfect in every limb and feature, not less than the usual size, and so very much alike that they could scarcely be distinguished one from the other. They were all put in one coffin, and carried to the grave by six young women, dressed with such a propriety of elegant neatness as attracted the notice and gained the approbation of the numerous spectators who attended on the occasion.

The British Chronicle
19 June 1783

Valuable Coins found in Warwickshire Pit

A few days ago as three labourers were cleaning a Pit at Meridan in Warwickshire, they found near two hundred Guineas of Charles the Second. The Impression on both sides was very perfect and they weigh more than the current Coin of George the Third. The Men have large Families, and were prudent enough to keep the Discovery secret until they had got the whole out, and then divided it equally.

The Manchester Mercury
8 July 1783

Stolen Milk

On Thursday last was committed to the county gaol, Lavinian Chance, of the parish of Moccas, widow, charged on the oath of Thomas Lloyd, Bailiff to Sir George Cornewall, Bart, with having, on Friday morning, the 25th. ult., about two o'clock, feloniously milked the cows of Sir George and carried away the milk, from a field adjoining the copse near Moccas Church.

The British Chronicle
12 July 1783

Double Tragedy in Hayfield

A farmer near Linton, in Cambridgeshire, who had a young daughter, an infant in arms, of whom he was exceedingly fond, would not go into the hay field without her. Taking a fork to do something with his men, he laid the child down on his coat under a tree. Presently hearing her shriek, he ran and found a large viper had twined round her neck and bit her in the bosom; she died the same evening in great agonies, upon which the farmer went into the field and hung himself upon the tree under which the accident had happened.

The Nottingham Journal
26 July 1783

Seed-drill Triumphant

On Monday last were reaped two equal, but separate Crops of Wheat adjoining each other, belonging to Mr. Benjamin Johnson, of Top-of-Bank, near Manchester, and measured, while growing, by Mr. Thomas Wright, of Manchester, one of which said Crops of wheat was planted in November by the Rev. Mr. James Cooke's Patent Machine; the other was sown broad Cast the same day, when, to the astonishment of all the Reapers and a Number of Spectators, particularly Mr. Hudson, of Under Bank, Mr. Johnson of Top-of-Bank, Mr. Jer. Bramall, Mr. Robert Gregson, of Manchester, Mr. Fletcher, and the above Thomas Wright, the Crop planted by the above Machine (Straw and Grain together) was one fourth heavier than the crop sown broad Cast, and on Wednesday the 20th. instant, the above Crops were separately thrashed, when the Grain of the planted Crop weighed upwards of one third more than the Grain of the sown Crop. From the above Experiment there remains not a shadow of doubt, but the Land Occupier (however extravagant the Assertion may appear) has now an opportunity of being advantaged by the use of the above Machine and Labour saved, and better Crop, not less than from 5% to 6% of every Statute Acre planted as above by the said Machine, exclusive of very singular Advantages to be derived from the use of a new constructed Hand Hoe invented by the said James Cooke, whereby one Man will do the work of six or seven Men, in the same time, but more effectively.

The Manchester Mercury
26 August 1783

❈ *As well as superseding the age-old practice of broadcast sowing by hand, the seed-drill revolutionized farming by permitting the removal of weeds in a way quite impossible under the old method. Because the seed was now set out in straight and orderly rows, hoeing could be carried out with little or no damage to the crop.*

Cooke's machine was drawn by one horse on light land and two horses on heavy land. In the charge of a man or a boy it sowed eight acres (over three hectares) a day.

1784

Four Weddings—One Suit

A few days since was married at Thorney Abbey, in the Isle of Ely, Mr. John Broadway, to Miss Sarah Christian, both of Thornbury; as a proof of economy and neatness, Mr. Broadway has by him a complete suit of clothes, fresh and good, in which he was married to his first wife upwards of forty years past; he buried her and two others since, and is now married to a fourth, all of whom he attended to church in the same dress.

The British Chronicle
8 January 1784

A Careful Curate

The Rev. Mr. Mattison was curate of Patter Dale, in Westmorland, 60 years; his income for many years was £12 and never exceeded £18 a year. He married and lived comfortably, and had four children. He buried his mother, he married his father, and buried his father. He christened his wife, and published his own banns of marriage in the church; he christened and married all his own children and educated his son, so that he was a good scholar, and fit for the College; he lived to the age of 90 and died possessed of £1,000 and upwards. His son is now schoolmaster at Lowther in Westmorland.

The Cumberland Pacquet
quoted in The British Chronicle
5 February 1784

An Exploding Pestle

A few days ago, a Blacksmith of Elton, near Bingham, in this county, bought a piece of iron, about two Feet long and one inch and a half Diameter, supposed to be solid, which had been used as a Pestle, upwards of 60 years, but the Smith striking it on the Anvil, had his doubts and put it in the Fire to prove whether they were well Founded; it had not been long in that State before it went off with a great Explosion; he had just turned himself from the end of it, which in all Probability saved his Life, but was so near feeling its deadly Effects that a bit from within grazed his side, and lodged amongst the coals behind him, some of which were shattered to pieces. The above Piece of Iron was found in the year 1723 by some men digging in a field near that village; it was so well filled with dirt as to appear solid, nor was it supposed to have any concavity till the above Period, when it proved to be a Gun Barrel, of a small Bore, but great Strength, and of an old Construction. 'Tis very remarkable that the Powder should have retained its original Strength for so long a Time, as it appears the above Piece had been loaded above 100 years. Various are the Conjectures concerning the Time it lay buried in the Ground, but none can be formed with any degree of Certainty; several old people remember a few Swords and other warlike instruments being found near the same Place, from which it may be inferred they belong to some Persons that were slain in some of the civil Commotions with which this Kingdom was formerly embroiled.

The Nottingham Journal
7 February 1784

A Joke at the Gibbet

Glocester
Our assizes were concluded on Tuesday evening, when the number of criminals who received sentence of death were not less than fifteen, of whom the following were ordered for execution ... [these included] Henry Dunsdon and Thomas Dunsdon, natives of Fullbrook, near Burford, Oxfordshire, two desperate fellows who had long been a terror to the country where they lived. They were ordered to be executed on Friday and their bodies to be hanged in chains on Capslodge-Plain, near Whichwood Forest, the spot near which they had shot William Harding, who attempted to apprehend them. .... The morning of their execution they appeared very penitent. Henry was particularly free in acknowledging that a life so ill-spent as his could expect an exit no less miserable. He seemed a good deal affected that his body was to be hanged in chains so near his father's house. He endeavoured to exculpate his brother, as having been free from those villainies which marked his own condition, and endeavoured to keep up his brother's spirits to the last. The brother was lame of one leg, and when they were tying up, he exhorted him to be of good cheer. "Come Tom" said he "You have but one leg, but you have but a very little time to stand".

The Glocester Journal
2 August 1784

The New Mail Coach

August 11

The New Mail Coach has travelled with an expedition that has been really astonishing, having seldom exceeded thirteen hours in going or returning from London. It is made very light, carries four passengers and runs with a pair of horses, which exchange every six or eight miles; and as the bags at the different offices on the road are made up against its arrival, there is not the least delay. The guard rides with the coachman on the box, and the mail is deposited in the boot. By this means, the Inhabitants of this city and Bristol have the London letters a day earlier than usual.

The Glocester Journal
16 August 1784

Harvest-home

On Wednesday last a Harvest-home was celebrated at Hawkstone, the seat of Sir Richard Hill, Bart, which seemed to revive the idea of ancient English hospitality. Early in the afternoon Sir Richard's domestics and workmen were called to attend divine service in the chapel, for the purpose of offering up public thanksgiving to Divine Providence for a season distinguished by an uncommon profusion of the fruits of the earth, when part of the 65th. Psalm was sung, as being particularly adapted to the subject. After the service no less than two hundred workmen, reapers, &c. repaired to a regale, given them by Sir Richard and managed under the direction of his servants, consisting of five sheep, two of which were roasted whole, several pieces of beef pies, plumb puddings &c., when all was conducted with so much regularity, as happily to blend temperance and hospitality together, a union which it was so much to be wished, was always observed upon such occasions. Though the number of guests was so great, yet they behaved with the utmost decorum, and returned early to their respective families, without the least appearance of clamour, riot, or excess. The whole was concluded with three cheers of gratitude, and then the company went off highly delighted with the entertainment, and full of thankfulness to the amiable and hospitable founder of the feast.

The Nottingham Journal
9 October 1784

✸   *The part of the 65th. Psalm that was sung would have included the verse:*
   Thou crownest the year with thy goodness; and thy paths drop fatness.

Sunday School at Minchinhampton

Extract of a letter from Tetbury, November 10
I was last Sunday at Minchinhampton, and was highly pleased to observe
that the streets of that town, which, on this day especially used to be filled
with half starved naked little objects playing and lying about like so many
brutes, were now entirely free from them. I enquired how they had been
disposed of, and was desired to satisfy myself by taking a view of the
Sunday Schools, where I found 300 of these poor creatures sitting in great
order, and engaged, some in learning their letters, others spelling, others
reading the Testament, &c. The silence and good order that prevailed
astonished me. They all seemed very happy and contented. Of the
numbers assembled, I remarked 275, whom the benevolent people of the
parish had decently cloathed. What an honour to themselves and to their
country! I have great pleasure in acquainting you that the spirited
inhabitants of Tetbury have begun a very liberal subscription for
establishing a similar institution there, and under the guidance of our
worthy minister, we seem determined to follow an example which
promises great and permanent benefits to the rising generation of those
who form the bulk of the people.

The Glocester Journal
15 November 1784

❀ *There was no difficulty in getting support for Sunday Schools
through the Glo(u)cester Journal, for Robert Raikes (proprietor of
the paper, and son of the founder) was known as the 'first institutor
of Sunday Schools'. This report may well have been written by him.
The Glo(u)cester Journal is one of England's oldest newspapers. Its
souvenir edition of 1972, marking the 250th anniversary of the
paper, included a history of the Raikes family.*

1785

Evading the Horse Tax

On Saturday last the inhabitants of Wragby were much diverted by the
son of a farmer riding a bull instead of a horse. The farmer having entered
only one riding horse, and fearful of being made to pay a fine if he rode

one of the plow horses, and the son being very desirous to pay a visit along with his father we understand was the cause of the adventure. The bull performed the journey entirely to the satisfaction of the rider and all the spectators.

The Lincoln, Rutland and Stamford Mercury
14 January 1785

❀ *The farmer's son rode his unusual steed because of a tax on saddle and race horses that had been introduced by Pitt the Younger, who had become Prime Minister in December 1783. It was one of several measures to help reduce the National Debt at the conclusion of the war with the American colonies.*

Farmer killed by Fox-bite

About eleven months ago, William Knipe, a farmer near Kirby Stephen, was alarmed in bed by a noise in his byre, when he lighted a candle, went in and found one of his cows in a fierce contest with a fox. He attempted to seize the fox and received a very severe bite in his hand. After three weeks, the cow, some swine and several other animals which had been bitten by it, became mad, which alarmed him much; and he went to Ormskirk and took the medicine. Till Monday se'nnight he felt no inconvenience from the bite, when in Kirby Stephen market he complained of pain from the wounded hand, up to his shoulder, and went home. On that evening the Hydrophobia took place, which held him at intervals, and on the Thursday following he died raving mad.

The Lincoln, Rutland and Stamford Mercury
11 February 1785

A Farmer's Funeral

A few days since died, at Upper Yeldham Hall, in Essex, Mr. Hurrell, farmer and malster, aged 95. He ordered in his will that his body should be interred in one of his woods, be covered with one of his hair cloths he used to dry his malt on; and that six hedgers and ditchers should carry his corpse, six others be pall bearers and six more follow as mourners, all with their bills and hedging gloves; and likewise ordered a hogshead of old beer to be drank.

The Lincoln, Rutland and Stamford Mercury
18 February 1785

Liberating a Balloon

Mr. Cracknall was to have ascended with his balloon from Nottingham race-ground on Monday se'nnight, but, from some mismanagement, not being able to ascend with a child, the spectators (20, or 30,000) after patiently waiting from noon till seven in the evening, liberated the balloon, and burnt the apparatus belonging to it. The balloon passed over Nottingham towards Belvoir Vale.

The following account of a balloon was sent to the Publisher of this paper, in a letter dated July 8 and from the time of it being found, probably the same that was liberated from Nottingham.

"On Monday evening last at 3 minutes past 9 o'clock, an air balloon fell in the parish of Edlington, 3 miles from Horncastle in this county, about 18 miles East from Lincoln. From the villages over which it was seen to pass, it appeared to have taken an Easterly course from its first launching; there was a car affix'd to the bottom of the balloon, large enough to accommodate one or two persons, a yellow gilt shoe buckle with the tong twisted almost off was found in the car, but no ticket to mention the time or place from whence it was first launched. The balloon was about 16 feet high and 50 feet in circumference, had several bunches of grapes, flower-de-luces &c. painted on the outside. The car suspended by plated cords 10 feet below the balloon was ornamented with pink colour'd silk and blue fringe, and made of wicker work in the manner and shape of a cradle. The whole was entire when first found by Mr. Thomas Eblewhite, a farmer near the spot it fell".

The Lincoln, Rutland and Stamford Mercury
15 July 1785

A Barbarous Custom

Stamford

Monday last being our annual bull-running, the same was observed here with the usual celebrity—several men heated with liquor got tossed by the bull, and were most terribly hurt, while some others more sober had little better usage. What a pity it is so barbarous a custom is permitted to be continued, that has no one good purpose to recommend it, but is kept as an orgy of drunkenness and idleness to the manifest injury of many poor families, even tho' the men escape bodily hurt.

The Lincoln, Rutland and Stamford Mercury
18 November 1785

1786

Run Away

From his Master's Service on the 16th. of this instant, CHARLES SHEPHERD, Apprentice to Mr. John Bennet, Farmer, at Arnold, near Nottingham, he had on at the Time he left his Service, a brown coloured Coat, a Smock Frock, a dark coloured Waistcoat, good Leather Breeches, light grey yarn Stockings, new Pair of Shoes, an old round Hat, stands near 5 feet 7 inches high, and much marked with the small Pox.
Whoever will apprehend the said apprentice and will bring him to Master John Bennet, of Retford, or to WILLIAM BENNET, at Arnold, shall be handsomely rewarded, and reasonable charges.

The Nottingham Journal
28 January 1786

Strong Liquor found in Stackyard

A few days since, as some men were digging a hole in the stack yard of a very old building at Kenton, near Newcastle, a number of very old fashioned bottles were discovered at a small distance from the surface, containing different kinds of spiritous liquors, some of which were of an agreeable flavour, and of much strength. It is imagined they had been buried there in the rebellion of 1715, when the possessor of this house, on account of his attachment to the rebel cause, was obliged to flee, having concealed or carried off all his furniture and other property.

The Nottingham Journal
13 May 1786

A Very Sagacious Fox

A few days since a Man belonging to Mr. Fetton, of Booley, in Shropshire, observing a Number of Crows making a great Noise over an old Oak Tree, was induced to throw a Stone into it, when to his great Surprise, out jump'd a large Fox; the man immediately climbed up and found in a hollow Part of the Tree, no less than six young Foxes. But such was the sagacity of their Dame, that she came in the Night, and carried them all away. It appears she had inhabited the place some Time, for Mr. Corbet's Huntsman has remarked that whenever he had the Hounds that Way, they were sure to quest round the said Tree.

The Nottingham Journal
24 June 1786

Royal Excursion*

On Monday last, Woodstock, the ancient residence of Kings, exhibited a scene of festivity and joy which has seldom been equalled. Certain information having been received that their Majesties, with several of the Princesses and suite, were to pay a visit on that day to their Graces, the Duke and Duchess of Marlborough, the bells began ringing at an early hour, and a flag was displayed on the tower. The ardour of pleasing expectation was painted in every face; and every tongue was eloquent of congratulation on the occasion. On the approach of their Majesties to Woodstock, they were met by a joyful multitude, with flags streaming in the gale, drums beating and music playing. The Royal Family walked slowly along the street, appearing happy to indulge the numerous spectators with a sight to which they had been unaccustomed. No sooner had they entered the park, by the triumphal gate, than a discharge of six pieces of cannon announced their arrival; and this compliment was repeated at intervals during their stay and at their departure. Their Graces of Marlborough and family, having paid their respects to the Royal Visitors, conducted them to the Library, where breakfast was provided in all that splendour and taste which were worthy of the guests and the noble family they honoured with their presence, while a band of music, judiciously stationed, made the palace echo with melody. After breakfast their Majesties viewed some of the grand apartments, part of the gardens and pleasure grounds, and the King, in particular, expressed his satisfaction at the display of such beauty and magnificence, that seemed to flow from the irresistable impression they made on the Royal mind.

The apparent affability of their Majesties, and the happiness conspicuous in both the visitors and visited, gave the most entire pleasure to every spectator, and that the diffusion of joy might be universal, the gates of Blenheim were thrown open, by their Graces' condescension, and every person desirous, gratified with a sight of the august family.

About six o'clock the royal pair and attendants left Blenheim and returned to Nuneham. ...

The Nottingham Journal
26 August 1786

❀ *Among the ladies of their Household who accompanied George III and his queen to Blenheim Palace was the famous authoress and diarist Fanny Burney, Second Keeper of The Robes to Queen Charlotte. Nowadays, when it is open to the public, thousands of people from all over the world visit Blenheim Palace each year.*

Great Excitement at Landlord's Grave

Extract of a letter from Cowes, August 20

Some months ago the landlord of the Fountain Inn died, leaving behind a disconsolate widow, one daughter and a daughter-in-law, who were inconsolable for their good father. One evening last week as a person was walking about the church-yard, and happening to be near the tomb of the landlord, he heard a long and strong breathing, as of a person oppressed. He looked around, thinking somebody near him, but seeing no person, and hearing the same breathing again, he drew nearer to the tomb, when he distinctly heard the breathing in the tomb, as he thought, which surprised him so much that he ran into the town and declared that the landlord was not dead, for he had heard him very distinctly breathe. Curiosity drew to the churchyard an immense crowd of people, and the report having reached the Fountain, the widow and daughters were not a little surprised and were soon after flattered with the hope of seeing a beloved husband and father, by one of their acquaintances running to tell them that he was certainly yet alive, and was heard by everyone then in the churchyard to fetch his breath very long and heavy, as if wanting and struggling to get out. The feeling and transports of the widow are not to be described, and indeed hardly to be conceived. Pick axes and shovels were immediately ordered to remove the stones and earth, all Cowes attended, and the enraptured widow was ready to receive and press to her bosom her long absent, though not dead, husband. Just as they were about to break down the tomb, a gentleman happened to be passing, who surprised to see the churchyard filled with people, stepped up to know what was the matter. Having heard the story, he listened, and very distinctly heard the breathing, but instantly declared they were all mistaken, for it was the noise of young owls, and looking up to the eaves of a house just by, discovered the nest. A ladder was brought soon after, and four young owls taken, to the great joy of all present, but the enraptured widow and her daughters, who returned home in sorrow and despair, leaving the ashes of the dead undisturbed. The above is an absolute fact, and had not the discovery taken place, the tomb would have been opened; but the ignorant and superstitious would ever have imagined it was something supernatural which they had heard.

The Nottingham Journal
2 September 1786

Balloon Ascent in Yorkshire

Leeds, August 29

On Wednesday, at forty minutes after one o'clock, the gallant Lunardi fulfilled his engagement to the public by ascending with his Royal Balloon from Kettlewell's Orchard, behind the Minster, York, amid the acclaimations of several thousand spectators. The ascention was truly sublime, the balloon rose to a prodigious height, so as to be distinctly seen in every part of the town and took a N.E. direction. A very dark cloud for some minutes obscured the intrepid Aeronaut from the gazing multitude, who had, however, soon the pleasure of again observing his progress at a great distance, through the trackless atmosphere. Mr. Lunardi's dexterity in filling his balloon, which was done in little more than eighteen minutes, and every part of his conduct throughout the business, merited great praise and afforded the highest satisfaction to every beholder. Mr. Lunardi descended an hour after his ascent in a corn field, and observing the people flocking from every quarter towards him, by which he was apprehensive that the corn would be injured, he thereupon rose again and went out of sight.

At three o'clock he finally descended between two hills at a place called Grenock in the parish of Bishop Wilton, about 18 miles from York. A few shepherds came to his assistance after he was perfectly anchored and the number of his rustic visitors increasing, he discharged the inflammable air from the balloon, and with their assistance packed it up. Robert Denison, Esq., who had rode after him from his home at Kilnwick Percy, arrived in time to give proper directions for conveying the balloon safe to that place, and having accommodated Mr. Lunardi with his horse, took him home to dinner and afterwards most politely brought him in his own chaise and four to that city. Though it was night when they entered the town, the anxiety of the people for Mr. Lunardi's safety had been so great and the joy they felt on his appearance such that they took the horses from the carriage and drew him through the streets to his lodgings in triumph. Soon after Mr. Lunardi dressed, and paid his respects to the ladies and gentlemen in the Assembly Rooms, where he was received with the warmest expressions of welcome and applause. Mr. Lunardi when at a great elevation from the earth, experienced very inclement weather, had rain, hail and snow, and was also in the midst of electrical clouds.

The Nottingham Journal
2 September 1786

❋ *The first balloon ascent was by Pilâtre de Rozier in France in 1783. Vincent Lunardi, an attaché from the Neapolitan embassy, made the first balloon ascent from English soil, in 1784. He took*

off from Moorfields in London and landed in a village in
Hertfordshire. His visit to Yorkshire was in a series of provincial
ascents.

1787

Too Many Plums

On Friday last died at Bolton, in Lancashire, the Rev. Richard Godwin, of
Gateacre, near Liverpool. His Death is supposed to have been occasioned
by eating too large a Quantity of Plumbs the preceding Day after Dinner.

Drewry's Derby Mercury
Thursday, 16 August, to Thursday, 23 August, 1787

Cut off by Tide

Leeds, August 28
The following melancholy Accident happened during Saturday Evening,
the 11th. Instant. Mr. John Jackson, a respectable manufacturer, at
Silverdale, near Lancaster Sands, went for Amusement to gather Muscles
on a Place called the Stoneheap, upon the Sands, situate very near the
Lane, about which Heap the Channel runs. Being too eager in picking the
Muscles, he neglected to observe the Coming-in of the Tide, till he was
surrounded, when finding it impossible to get off, he set to work in
heaping up the Stones to save himself. He continued in this attempt for
about two Hours, when the Tide proving too strong for him, washed him
off in Sight of his near Relations and Neighbours, who had been
Spectators of his dismal Situation, most of the Time, without being able
to afford him any Assistance. His Body was found the next Morning not
far from the Place.

Drewry's Derby Mercury
Thursday, 30 August, to Thursday, 6 September, 1787

Curate conducted Own Wedding

An odd circumstance happened at Shepton-Mallet about a Fortnight since. Mr. F——, the Curate of that Place, published the Banns of Marriage of himself for three Sundays; the third Time and after the second Lesson he asked (aloud) if the Rector was present, or whether he had appointed a Deputy to marry him. On being answered in the Negative, he said he should perform the ceremony himself, which he did in the presence of the Congregation, and said the Rector must answer to the Bishop.

Drewry's Derby Mercury
Thursday, 6 September, to Thursday, 13 September, 1787

For Bite of a Mad Dog

A correspondent recommends the following Receipt for the bite of a mad Dog, which he always found successful, and which, for Humanity's sake, he wishes should be made public. Take 24 Grains of Cinebar, 24 Grains of fictitious Cinebar, and 10 Grains of Musk, reduce them into a very fine Powder, and give them as soon as possible, in a Tea-Cup full of any Kind of Spirits; if the Person has any symptoms of Madness, they are to take a second Dose immediately; and whether they are affected or not, the same must be repeated thirty Days after.

Drewry's Derby Mercury
Thursday, 20 September, to Thursday, 27 September, 1787

Tragedy at Harvest Home

A Melancholy Accident happened on Saturday Evening at the Celebrations of Harvest Home, at Stilton; as the Waggon was going thro' the Town with a Number of Men, Women and Children therein, a bystander was so inconsiderate and brutish as to throw a Brick Bat into the Waggon, which fractured the Skull of a Child, in a most Dreadful Manner. A Surgeon trepanned the Skull, but there is not the least Hopes of its surviving.

Drewry's Derby Mercury
Thursday, 20 September, to Thursday, 27 September, 1787

❀ *The wagon in this report carried the last load of harvest to the farmyard. At harvest home it was generally the custom for a pretty girl to have a seat of honour on the wagon; she was placed on the topmost sheaf.*

A Dreadful Accident

A few days ago the following melancholy accident happened at Hulton, near Kirby-Moor side. A woman having left her child (about half a year old) in the cradle, with a little boy to rock it till she came back; when, soon after she was gone, he left it alone and a pig belonging to the family went in, tore the child out of the cradle and ravenously devoured it.

The Maidstone Journal
9 October 1787

1788

Fox in Chimney

Wednesday last a Fox being observed to go into some hedge near the river, in the parish of Stour Provost, Mr. Galpine, of Marnhurst, went with a greyhound and two other dogs, roused him from his cover and coursed him about a mile to a neighbouring hamlet, when Reynard being hard pursued ran up the side of a house, and got into the chimney, but not finding good ground fell to the bottom, to the great confusion of a woman who sat by the fire. The fox was so much hurt by the fall that he died soon after.

The Bristol Gazette
24 January 1788

Villainy at Farm

Extract of a letter from Taunton, February 25
Since Monday last, many discoveries have been made here respecting the burglary, violent assault and other crimes lately committed at Sir William Yea's at Pyrland, in this neighbourhood; and such a scene of villainy begins to unfold itself as is scarcely to be paralleled. Six persons were principally concerned in the burglary there on the 8th. of last month (as mentioned in our paper), four of whom are taken, but the villains who entered the house with blacked faces are not of the number. It appears that the servant boy, who stood by and saw Sir William and his son so ill treated at that time, was in the plot and opened the door to let the others in; he is turned King's evidence and his testimony is corroborated by other witnesses of *good repute*. A substantial farmer, his wife and two brothers were concerned, it is said, in aiding and abetting the burglary,

and furnishing pistols and cords to bind the family. A certain *quondam* lady too, it is supposed, is not wholly ignorant of this business; and if all be true that is related of the many servants and dependants of this gentleman, it affords a most astonishing instance of depravity amongst them. Innumerable are the depredators and stealers of deer, sheep, wool and fowls that have already been discovered; five of these also are in prison, and several more are expected to be brought in thither tomorrow. Men, women and children have all been conspirators, and the whole country is in an uproar. We have strong evidence of 20 deer and as many sheep having been slaughtered and devoured in an old farm-house belonging to Sir William. The chambers of this house are a perfect Golgotha, and horse loads of deer skins have been sold at a time from hence. Three or four years' wool was stolen out of the lofts over his stables, packed up in the open court, and carried off without interruption during his absence. The deer were killed early in the morning if the Baronet was at home, or shot openly in the middle of the day if absent. The sheep were mostly eaten by his out-of-door workmen, and dependants, and five or six at a time have been driven away and sold by persons of this description. Five ewes and lambs returning home after they had been stolen and sold in the neighbourhood were stolen again a few nights afterwards, and effectually removed. These thieves used to play at cards on these nights of feasting, and the stake to be played for was always declared; perhaps three or four turkies, geese, or duck &c. and the loser was to go forth and steal them against the next entertainment, or *undergo a punishment*; of all these things we have strong proofs. C. W. Bempfylde, Esq., and the Mayor and Justices of Taunton, have been extremely vigilant in their endeavours to discover and secure this nefarious tribe and still perservere to the utmost in their laudable researches, in which they have every reason to hope for success.

The Salisbury Journal
quoted in The Bristol Gazette
6 March 1788

Gluttony

Perhaps the following instance of gluttony has scarcely been equalled. One Charles Tyte, of Stoke Abbott, in the county of Dorset, ate a few days since 133 eggs within an hour, together with a large piece of bacon and a quantity of bread and afterwards complained of a want of more eggs, and that he had not made a full supper.

The Bristol Gazette
13 March 1788

Getting rid of Smuggled Liquor

Lewes

Last Monday between two and three thousand gallons of spiritous liquors, which the Revenue Officers of this town and neighbourhood had seized within the last three or four years (and which it is thought, had it been sold, would have fetched upwards of six hundred pounds) were by them consigned to the Kennel, in a manner that produced a scene highly entertaining to the spectators; for the hour of action was no sooner arrived than there appeared a great concourse of people, composed of men, women and children, from five to fifty years of age, some of whom planted themselves at the entrance of the passage from whence the fountain of Aqua Vitæ was played off (and frequently, to increase the fun, high in the air) with uplifted pails and open mouths, to catch what they could of it in a pure state, before it reached the ground; while others less delicate in their pursuits, formed on one knee, a regular line on each side the gutter (which they had previously bayed up with slub) and with pots, pans, porringers and pipkins, fell eagerly to work in ladling up its contents, and happy were they who could obtain the most full buckets of this *rare puddle*; a little time, however, convinced us that what they saved had not been wholly committed to their *wooden* vessels. . . .

The novelty of this scene, added to the variety of comical figures, gesticulations and queer faces which it now exhibited, rendered it ludicrous almost beyond description, and such as would have furnished a most admirable subject for the pencil of Hogarth had he been living. But we were much concerned soon afterwards to find it get more serious, and at length to threaten fatal consequences, for the liquor was not much more than half consumed, when several were engaged in the *Broughtonian* science, and at the expense of black eyes, bloody noses and sore bones displayed the dexterity of *Humphreys* and *Mendoza*, while others were seen bruising themselves in another way, by tumbling head-long, and dead drunk on the pavement of the street. In short, the officers being now made sensible of the impropriety of persevering, wisely withheld their hand 'till the following morning, when in the presence of a few sober people, they destroyed the remainder of the liquor, and thereby prevented what in all probability would otherwise have happened, the loss of several lives.

Upwards of two thousand gallons of brandy, rum, and geneva were in like manner poured into the Kennel in the middle of the town of Horsham, which created as much drunkenness and confusion as there was at this place.

The Bristol Gazette
13 March 1788

⊕ *The 'Kennel' was a gutter at the side of the public highway. The*

'Broughtonian science' was boxing. John Broughton (1704–89) was England's champion for a number of years, and Humphreys and Mendoza were two other famous pugilists.

Whimsicall Bett*

A Whimsicall Bett, much the subject of conversation, has lately been made between the Duke of Bedford and Lord Barrymore. His Lordship bets the Duke a certain sum that he will produce a man who shall eat a live cat. The London papers have been hunting for precedents on this occasion. One of them relates that "for a wager of £50 a fellow who lived near the race-course of Kildare, in Ireland, devoured five fox cubs, and literally began eating each while alive. It is, however, to be observed that the devourer was a natural fool, having been born deaf, dumb and without a palate". Another story is told that "a fellow, a shepherd at Beverley, in Yorkshire, about eleven years ago, for a bet of five pounds, was produced, who was to devour a living cat. The one produced was a large black Tom Cat, which had not been fed for the purpose, but was chosen as being the largest in that neighbourhood. The day appointed was the Fair-Day at Beverley. The parties met. The man produced was a raw-boned fellow about forty. The cat was then given to him, on which he took hold of his four legs with one hand, and closing his mouth with the other, he killed him by biting his head to pieces immediately, and in less than a quarter of an hour devoured every part of the cat, tail, legs, claws, bones and everything. The man who laid the wager gave the fellow *Two Guineas* for doing it and the Shepherd appeared perfectly satisfied with the reward". After he had done it, he walked about the Fair the whole afternoon, and appeared neither sick nor sorry. He took no emetic—nor had this repast any effect upon him whatever.

The County Chronicle
18 March 1788

Seven Wives in Seven Years

A farmer is reported to be now living in some part of Norfolk, who having married and buried his wife in the year 1782, has had the very singular fortune to marry and bury one every year since. He is at the present time a widower . . . he declares seriously that he will never again enter the matrimonial state.

The Bristol Gazette
18 September 1788

Eagle captured on Skiddaw

Last week a gentleman fowling on a mountain called Skiddaw, in Cumberland, perceived a very large brown eagle drop from a precipice and attack a well-grown lamb of this season, which he seized in his talons, and was just going to mount, when the gentleman let fly and wounded him in the pinion of the left wing. He then approached the magnanimous bird, who held his prey, and with a kind of menacing look flared in his face for some time. The gentleman, willing to rescue the poor lamb, and equally unwilling to destroy so noble a creature, pulled a cord from his pocket, which he threw, with some danger, over the neck of the eagle, who finding himself noosed, quitted the lamb, and deemed to surrender. ... The gentleman led him gently to a burch tree round which he fastened the cord, and sat down watching, till some countrymen cutting peat on the mountain returned from work; two of them assisted in bringing the eagle to his house, where a place was prepared for his future residence. He is the largest of the kind ever remembered in Great Britain, being six feet three inches along the neck and back, from head to the end of the tail, four feet round the girth, and weighs sixty-two pounds, three quarters.

The Bristol Gazette
11 November 1788

Unfortunate Sweep

Last week, at Alburton, in Herefordshire, a chimney-sweeper, who, not satisfied with exercising the ordinary duties of his profession, thought it proper to shew his skill and resolution by standing on his head at the top of a chimney, when the bricks unfortunately giving way, put an end to his activity and his life.

The Bristol Gazette
27 November 1788

1789

'Extraordinary Operation of Nature'

There is at present a fine horse in the menage of the Earl of Pembroke, at Wilton-House, which, when worked, sweats exceedingly on one side, whilst on the other he is perfectly dry and cool, and this extraordinary operation of nature is so very exact, that it describes a palpably regular line, from the top of the nose, up the middle of the face, between the ears, and along the back of the tail.

The Salisbury Journal
23 November 1789

Penance in Public

Lewes, December 21
Last Sunday, one Woodridge, a carpenter, at Petworth, in this county, having married his late wife's sister, they both did penance together in the church at that place.

The Salisbury Journal
28 December 1789

VOLUNTEERS.

G. R. III.

God Save the King.

LET us, who are Englifhmen, protect and defend our good KING and COUNTRY againft the Attempts of all *Republicans* and *Levellers*, and againft the Defigns of our NATURAL ENEMIES, who intend in this Year to invade OLD ENGLAND, our happy Country, to murder our gracious KING as they have done *their own*; to make WHORES of our *Wives* and *Daughters*; to rob us of our Property, and teach us nothing but the *damn'd Art of murdering one another.*

ROYAL TARS
Of OLD ENGLAND,

If you love your COUNTRY, and your LIBERTY, now is the Time to fhew your Love.

R E P A I R,

All who have good Hearts, who love their KING, their COUNTRY, and RELIGION, who hate the FRENCH, and damn the POPE,

T O

Lieut. W. J. Stephens,

At his Rendezvous, SHOREHAM,

Where they will be allowed to Enter for any SHIP of WAR, AND THE FOLLOWING

BOUNTIES will be given by his MAJESTY.
in Addition to Two Months Advance.

To Able Seamen,	- - -	*Five Pounds.*
To Ordinary Seamen,	- - -	*Two Pounds Ten Shillings.*
To Landmen,	- - -	*Thirty Shillings.*

Conduct-Money paid to go by Land, and their Chefts and Bedding fent Carriage free. Thofe Men who have ferved as PETTY-OFFICERS, and thofe who are otherwife qualified, will be recommended accordingly.

L E W E S: PRINTED BY W. AND A. LEE.

1790-99

'LET US, WHO ARE ENGLISHMEN ...'
Recruiting poster published shortly after France declared war on Britain in February 1793.

1790

80 Years of Midwifery

Died a few days since at Horseley, in Derbyshire, a woman named Francis Barton, at the astonishing age of 107. She followed midwifery upwards of 80 years. It is said she remembered the Revolution in 1688, and that she danced at a merry-making on that glorious occasion.

The Newcastle Chronicle
23 January 1790

Hare amongst the Lawyers

A curious circumstance happened at Cockermouth, on Monday, while the Sessions were holding. A hare which had given her pursuers the slip near Papcastle (probably not conscious of the fact), fled with great terror and precipitation over Derwent Bridge, up the Street; and with wonderful agility, darting through a pane of glass in one of the windows of the Globe inn, presented herself upon the table, amongst a large heap of indictments, and other legal processes; the room being at that time occupied as an office by the Clerk of the Peace, and pretty much crowded with the Gentlemen of the law. As soon as the consternation, which took place amongst that learned body, had subsided, poor Puss was committed to the custody of the cook.

The Newcastle Chronicle
23 January 1790

❋ *Almost two hundred years after it provided temporary refuge for the hare, the Globe Inn still offers hospitality in Main Street, Cockermouth. It is now known as the Globe Hotel.*

Press-gang spoils Holiday

Monday last the meeting of the lads and lasses at the Ballast Mills, vulgarly yclept a Hopping, received a little alloy to its harmony by the introduction of a few unwelcome visitors in the shape of a press-gang, who, regardless of holiday cloathes, of the well-soaped pig, and the fair one's tears, contrived to select from the Company a few seasoned youths, to all appearance well calculated to assist in resenting the insult of the haughty Dons.

The Newcastle Chronicle
29 May 1790

❈ *The 'well-soaped pig', or pig with a greasy tail, was often the prize for he or she who could capture it in a competition at affairs of this sort.*

The reference to the 'haughty Dons' reminded readers that in its issue of 15 May 1790 the paper had reported the ratification of a treaty 'by the kings of Spain and Sardinia and the Empress of Russia, and the State of Venice, in order to resist by force the present policies of the British and Prussian cabinets'. Although a consequent conflict seemed likely, Britain did not go to war at this time.

Death among the Whortle-berries

A few days ago as a poor boy by the name of Newell, son of a besom-maker at Lockerly, Hants, was gathering whortle-berries in Lockerly Woods, he was bitten by an adder, in consequence of which his body swelled up very much, and he died in two days.

The Newcastle Chronicle
21 August 1790

❈ *Nowadays the whortleberry is more generally known as the bilberry, or blueberry.*

1791

The Pit Preacher

Lately died at the Coal-pits near Wednesbury in Staffordshire, Joseph Rawlins, commonly known by the appellation of the Pit Preacher, from the circumstance of his performing religious duties in the Methodissical manner, for a number of years past, among the colliers in that neighbourhood, and which he was first impelled to from ill-using Mr. J. Wesley, when preaching near that place in 1749. This singular pastor, though blind, worked on the week days as a collier and what is more extraordinary, distributed most of his earnings among his auditors, in cases of sickness &c.

> The Bristol Journal
> 11 June 1791

❀ *John Wesley, the founder of Methodism, had died in the previous March, at the great age of eighty-seven. The occasion when he was ill-used by the mob that included Joseph Rawlins was in the early years of his great preaching journeys, which were to cover a quarter of a million miles throughout Britain and Ireland. He referred to it in his Journal:*

October, 1749
On Tuesday, the 24th., about noon, we came to Dudley. At one I went to the Market-place, and proclaimed the name of the Lord, to an huge, unwieldy, noisy multitude, the greater part of whom seemed in nowise to know wherefore they were come together. I continued speaking about half an hour, and many grew serious and attentive, until some of Satan's servants pressed in, raging and blaspheming, and throwing whatever came to hand. I then retired to the house from which I came. The multitude poured after, and covered over with dirt many that were near me, but I had only a few specks. I preached in Wednesbury at four, to a nobler people, and was greatly comforted among them; so I was likewise in the morning. Wednesday the 25th. How does a praying congregation strengthen the Preacher!

Whimsical Curiosity

Some persons in the neighbourhood of Brigham, Yorkshire, found a toad on Good Friday, 1790, which, from a whimsical curiosity, they place in a pot with a slate upon the top of it, and buried it three feet deep in the earth, in a situation to prevent it receiving any moisture from the rains, &c., thereby to determine whether the wonderful relations respecting the subsistence of that reptile were true in any degree. The spot was marked, and it was resolved not to open it till the Good Friday, 1791. Accordingly a great number assembled on that day, and the pot, with its contents, was carefully dug out, when the toad was found not only living, but greatly improved in size. It was viewed for some time to observe whether it seemed affected by its exposure to the air, after so long a confinement; but no change was discovered; it was afterwards set at liberty.

The Maidstone Journal
28 June 1791

A Twenty-first Birthday

Lord Berwick's late *natal* day at Salop has been a *mortal* one to the animal creation. On this occasion (his Lordship having attained his majority) a rich profusion of solids and a powerful inundation of fluids were employed to enlarge the bellies and exhilarate the hearts of the multitude. Oxen roasted whole, and other unbasted delicacies were display'd— festive joy and harmony prevail'd—and the pulse of every man's heart beat high to the tune of Beef and Berwick forever.

The Chester Chronicle
4 November 1791

End of a Fiddler

A poor luckless fiddler, named Lucas, of this city (who had long been the Orpheus to the rural nymphs and swains at the adjacent wakes) came to a melancholy close a few days ago, at Willaston jubilee, where, ceasing awhile to ravish the ears of the Company, he put down his dulcet companion, the fiddle, to play upon a more substantial one—a good piece of beef, on which he was rarely *out of tune*; in this instance, however, an obstinate lump, which he was attempting to bolt, quarrelled with his *windpipe*, stopt *life's dance*—and in a few minutes the poor fiddler was laid out *B flat* upon the barn floor—another fiddler happening luckily to be at hand, the lads and lasses resumed the dance, and finished the harmony of the night.

The Chester Chronicle
18 November 1791

Wrecker's Fortune

A person lately died at Saltfleet, in Lincolnshire, who, on finding his end draw near, called his daughter to his bed-side, and taking a box out of his coat-pocket, which he had carried about with him upwards of twenty-five years, told her that it was all he had to bequeath, and that the real value of it was unknown to him, but advised her to offer it for sale after his death. This accordingly was done a few days since in London, when it was found that the box contained a set of jewels of immense value, which the deceased had betwixt twenty and thirty years ago gathered from a wreck on the coast; a circumstance never before his death divulged.

The Chester Chronicle
18 November 1791

1792

Bishop Blaize Festival

Godalming

On Monday last the workmen of Messrs. Holland & Co., Patentees of the Fleecy Hosiery Manufactory, carried on in this town, walked in procession. At the head of them, a man completely dressed in fleecy hosiery, followed by twelve boys in white, with caps, sashes and ruffles of fleece; next a shepherd and shepherdess with a lamb in a basket, Bishop Blaize and his chaplain dressed in canonicals on horseback, their horses led by boys in white. The woolcombers to the factory, dressed in fancy caps and sashes of wool, followed the Bishop; a band of musicians next, with flags emblematical of the manufactory, preceded one hundred and forty manufacturers dressed clean and neat, with cockades, sashes and ruffles, all made of fleece. In this manner they proceeded to the town of Guildford, where they were received with the ringing of bells at the three churches, amidst a vast concourse of people. Eleven pieces of small cannon were fired by order of Mr. Russell. Mayor of Guildford, in compliment of the procession. From Guildford they returned to the White Hart Inn in this town, where they were all regaled with a good dinner by the Patentees, and the day was spent in mirth and good harmony, to the satisfaction of all the party.

The County Chronicle
1 January 1792

⊛ *St Blasius or Blaize ('Bishop Blaize') was the woolcomber's patron saint. This was certainly among the very last of such celebrations in his honour in England, but they had been popular over many centuries.*

Cure for Dog-bite—in Church

The following receipt for the bite of a mad dog is hung up in Sunning-hill church, Berks.—Six ounces of rue picked from the stalk, and bruised; four ounces of garlick, bruised, four ounces of Venice Treacle, and four ounces scrapings of pewter. These are to be boiled in two quarts of strong ale over a slow fire, until reduced to one quart, the liquor then to be drained off, and kept close corked in a bottle. Nine spoonfuls to a man or woman fasting, for seven mornings successively, and six spoonfuls to a dog. Apply some of the ingredients warm, to the part bitten.

This receipt, our correspondent says, was taken from Gathorp church in Lincolnshire, where many persons have been bit by a mad dog. Those who used the medicine recovered; they who did not died mad.

The Derby Mercury
10 May 1792

A Long-lived Family

The history of longevity presents no instance of the kind equal to the following—There are now living in perfect health at Soulby, near Braugh under Stanmore, in Westmoreland, two brothers and a sister, Matthew, Robert and Anne Bousfield, whose united ages amount to three hundred and fifteen years. Robert, the youngest, 'tho one hundred and two, is gamekeeper to the Earl of Thanet and will engage to kill seven shots out of nine.

The Chester Chronicle
18 May 1792

1793

For King and Constitution

A correspondent informs us that on New-year's day the inhabitants of Ashbourne shewed their attachment to the King and Constitution, and their abhorence to the designs of republicans and levellers. Five sheep were roasted, and a great quantity of liquor given to the populace. The bells were rang and a procession made by the gentleman &c. with flags and a band of music, singing God Save The King, Rule Britannia &c. At the bonfire in the Market-place many patriotic toasts were drank and the effigy of the execrable author of the Rights of Man was first hanged and then burnt, as a punishment due to a person guilty of treason and seditious attempts.

The Derby Mercury
10 January 1793

❈ *This event took place just eleven days before the execution of Louis XVI and three weeks before the Revolutionary Government of France declared war against Britain. Similar affairs were organized in hundreds of towns and villages throughout the land, to assure George III that there was no possibility of a revolution in his realm.*

The 'execrable author' of The Rights of Man *was Tom Paine, the English Republican who had become a citizen of France. In earlier years (1774–87) he had lived in America, and strongly supported the colonists in the War of American Independence. He assisted their cause with his pen, and also served in the American army. He returned to America in 1802, and died there in 1809.*

The war with France continued until the Treaty of Amiens (1802) but was resumed in the following year. Peace finally came in 1815, with the defeat of Napoleon at Waterloo.

Little Mourning

On Wednesday, the 6th. instant, was buried at Cleve Prior, Worcestershire, Elizabeth, the wife of Thomas Melen, yeoman, and the next morning was married, in the parish church of Cleve Prior above mentioned, the aforesaid Thomas Melen to Margaret Brookes, relict of Francis Brookes, late of North Littleton, in the same county.

The Derby Mercury
28 February 1793

Frightened Animals leap over Cliff

A large flock of sheep and thirty or forty head of cattle that were grazing on the Downs near Purbeck, last week took fright at some uncommonly loud thunder, and ran to the cliffs, from whence they fell into the sea, at least 100 feet in height. They overtook a cart, the horses in which ran with them, and they fell together. A boy was on one of the horses, but got off just before they took the leap. Most of the sheep were picked up, but the animals were lost.

The Derby Mercury
7 March 1793

Landslide near Hereford

A very extraordinary and convulsive motion and sinking of a large spot of ground at Copley Wood, in the parish of Fanhope, near Hereford, has taken place within these few days. It was first remarked on Thursday se'nnight, by a man and a boy employed in hedging, who were alarmed by a noise which seemed to proceed from the wood, and immediately afterwards perceived some large stones in motion at a small distance from them; a part of the wood and wood ground was at the same time in apparent agitation, and slipped from its bed towards the low ground by the side of the river Wye. They were still more alarmed by the sudden motion of the ground whereon they stood, which opened in different places, and threw up small ridges of earth at short distances; and they had only time to make their escape before the hedge at which they were at work was nearly buried, the trees in and near it were thrust down and the road at the bottom of the wood was completely choaked up with earth, trees and stones to the height of 12 feet. The ground within the circuit of this motion has been ascertained to exceed four acres in extent and several very large apertures have been left, which have since continued to widen daily. What is very remarkable, a yew tree was removed to a distance of forty yards and now remains upright, without having suffered any apparent injury.

The Derby Mercury
18 April 1793

Women Pugilists

A pitched battle was lately fought at Elmstead, in the neighbourhood of Chelmsford, by two women; being stripped, without caps, and hair tied close, to it they set, and for forty-five minutes maintained a most desperate conflict. One of them, an adept in the science, beat her antagonist in a most shocking manner and would certainly have killed her, but for the interference of the spectators. To the vanquished heroine her husband was bottle-holder, and with a degree of barbarity that would have disgraced a savage, we are informed he instigated his fair rib to the fight.

The Cambridge Chronicle
27 July 1793

Sentenced to Pillory

William Roberts, of North Bovey, Exeter, for speaking treasonable and seditious words, is sentenced to be imprisoned in the common gaol for the term of one year, during which time he is to stand in the pillory of Moretonhampstead thrice; and at the expiration of his imprisonment to find security for his good behaviour for two years, himself in £50 and two sureties in £25 each.

The Cambridge Chronicle
3 August 1793

Two Diggers—10,000 Graves

Tuesday last died, at Shepton Mallet, a man known by the appelation of Digger Wright, whose predecessor and himself have been grave diggers in that parish upwards of 60 years, in which time it is computed that they have dug 10,000 graves.

The Bristol Journal
7 December 1793

1794

Quick Tea-drinking at St Ives

On Tuesday last the Mountebanks performed at St. Ives, when the quick art of tea drinking was proposed by Mr. Andrew as a method of drawing a company together for his benefit. He produced a pound of the best green tea for the first woman that could drink five cups boiling hot the quickest; this proposal set many mouths watering, as well as wishing for so great a prize; accordingly three women mounted the stage with Mr. Andrew, in order to perform that which they are well accustomed to, tea drinking. When the noble entertainment began it was amusing enough, but presently over, and the pound of tea clearly won by an old practitioner, who drank five cups boiling hot off the fire precisely in eight minutes, with as much unconcern and ease as possible, to the no little astonishment and good amusement of every spectator.

The Cambridge Chronicle
8 February 1794

Severe Weather

Great damage was done to the shipping on the different coasts of this Kingdom in the storm on Saturday se'nnight. Among the persons who perished on land that evening by the severity of the weather, the following have come to our knowledge: the wife of a mason at Potter Newton, near Leeds, a man, a woman and a boy, near Pickering: a woman at Loddington in Leicestershire; a pedlar, in a field near Kettering; a woman in crossing Salisbury Plain; and a poor man near Bath-Easton.

The Cambridge Chronicle
8 February 1794

A Funeral to Remember

A few days since was buried at Longford, near Newport, Shropshire, a widow Jones, of Newport, where the funeral was celebrated at the Talbot Inn, (agreeable to her request) at which upwards of forty persons dined upon 40 pounds of beef, 20 pounds of bacon, with fowls, puddings, &c., a very elegant and superb dinner. She tried on her shroud before she died; her coffin also she had made and tried, with many other strange and uncommon things.

The Cambridge Chronicle
8 March 1794

Woman aged 164

We learn from Abbey Laddercost, in Cumberland, that a woman called Jane Forester, who lives in that parish, is now in the 165th. year of her age. When Cromwell besieged the city of Carlisle, 1645, she can remember that a horse's head sold for 2s.6d. before the garrison surrendered. At the martyrdom of Charles I she was nineteen years of age. At Brampton, about six years ago, she made oath, before the commissioners in a Chancery suit, to have known an estate, the right of which was then disputed, to have been enjoyed by the ancestors of the present heir 101 years. She hath an only daughter living, aged 103. And, we are further informed, that there are six women now living in the same parish where she resides, the younger of whom is 99 years of age.

The Cambridge Chronicle
24 May 1794

1795

Christmas Cheer for Militia

On Christmas-day the ladies and gentleman of Hoddesdon and Broxbourne gave to the privates in the Derbyshire militia, who are quartered there, roast beef and plumb-pudding, and a pot of beer to each man, in consideration of their orderly behaviour in those towns, and at church.

The Cambridge Chronicle
3 January 1795

Dog hanged in Lincolnshire

At Hanworth Booths, a public-house, near Lincoln, a short time ago, a man dropped a five guinea Boston note, which disappeared in a moment, and strict search was made for it a long time without effect. At length a woman present recollected she saw a certain unlucky dog eat something white. This put an end to the life of the dog, for he was hanged up instantly, and his throat being opened the lost bill was found, in a very mangled state, but nevertheless cash was got for it at Boston.

The Birmingham Gazette
quoted in Staffordshire Advertiser
10 January 1795

Numbed by Cold—Saved by Dog

A reputable farmer at Bowbrink in Norfolk, on his return from Norwich last week, was so benumbed by the cold to be obliged to lie down and would have perished, but that his dog, as if sensible of his situation, got on his breast, and extending itself across him, preserved his lungs from the cold, which would otherwise have proved fatal. The dog, so situated for many hours, made a continual barking, and at length attracted attention.

The Cambridge Chronicle
2 February 1795

A Beautiful Ox

We are informed by a Gentleman in the Neighbourhood of Tenberly that he has lately sold, for One Hundred Guineas, an Ox of most uncommon Size and Beauty, and which was bred by the late Mr. Derrington of Devereaux Wootton, Herefordshire. His weight on the machine is one Ton, fourteen hundred and seven pounds—Height Nineteen Hands—Girth eleven Feet six Inches—Length from the Brow to the drop of the Tail Nine Feet, six Inches. Supposed to be the largest ever bred and is expected to come through Oxford, early in March, on the Road to London.

The Oxford Journal
28 February 1795

Horrible Spectacle near Beaconsfield

Tuesday morning last a most horrible Spectacle was discovered under a Hedge, about a hundred yards from the Road, in a field near Beaconsfield, Bucks, where the Body of a plain dressed man was found, that appeared to have lain dead for more than a Week, and whose dog remained along with the Corpse, and would scarce permit any Person to approach it, yet so famished by Hunger as to have eaten away all the upper Part of the poor man's Face, some of his Neck, and one of his shoulders. In this mangled State the body was removed to Beaconsfield Church, in order to be owned, and for taking an Inquest the same Day.

The Oxford Journal
21 March 1795

Mr Hastings's Acquittal

A correspondent from Chipping Norton informs us that on the Arrival of the News of Mr. Hastings acquittal, the Joy expressed by all Ranks was as diffusive as might be expected from the Generosity and Benevolence of his Character and the Regard due to so respectable a Family. The Gentlemen of Chipping Norton testified their Joy by giving an Entertainment in the principal Inn. The Bells throughout the adjacent Country rang unremittingly the whole Day and the Stow Band volunteers assembled at Dalesford House, where all Ranks of People were most hospitably entertained, while John and Arthur Jones, Esquires, of Chasleton, set the Example to the Gentlemen, &c. by throwing open their House and Cellar Doors; and in unison with every respectable Family within their vicinity, testified the high Esteem which is so justly borne to the present most worthy Possessor of Dalesford House.

The Oxford Journal
2 May 1795

⊛ *Warren Hastings had been Governor-General of India (1774–85). On his return to England he was impeached on charges of corruption. His acquittal in April 1795 followed a trial which had gone on for over eight years. The people of Chipping Norton had a special interest in the acquittal, for Hastings was by way of being a local resident. His home at Daylesford House was about five miles from their town.*

Rural Holyday

Extract of a Letter from Witney
On Wednesday last the inhabitants of this place were entertained with a rural Holyday. The Witney Band, consisting of performers on martial instruments of musick, having signified their intention of passing the day in Whitchwood Forest, it attracted a prodigous number of persons; no less than five thousand people were supposed to be assembled on the

occasion. The numerous parties spread upon the hills, others parading in the vallies, and not a few regaling under the shades of the venerable oaks formed a scene truly picturesque. Chearfulness dwelt on every countenance, all was good humour, the songs excellent, the musick delightful, and a more lively picture of rural felicity was never exhibited in the noble Forest of Whitchwood.

The Oxford Journal
24 October 1795

Exemplary Conduct

Oxford
On Monday next the Rutlandshire Fencible Cavalry, who have been quartered here during the summer, will march from here to Nantwich, in Cheshire. So strict has been their discipline, and so exemplary the conduct of this respectable corps that even the Publicans regret their departure.

The Oxford Journal
24 October 1795

1796

A Miserly Farmer

On Tuesday was found dead, in his bed, at Steeple Ashton, Wilts, George Kemp, who kept a small farm. He was a very penurious man, and would scarcely allow himself the necessaries of life; on examining the body two guineas were found in each hand, and two at each side of his mouth; indeed it is generally thought that he was choaked by this *precious bane*.

The York Herald
16 July 1796

The Musical Blacksmith—and Wife

The following is a copy of a manuscript hand-bill which was sticking up last week on the door of a blacksmith's shop in Staffordshire.

I T—— H—— dwellith within shows orses and meaks all the shows
gud as hin the koontrey. Teeches salmudy in parts for churches hevery
knight at height in ye hebbening Sundays and fair-times and other days
hecktept when notes is given for pitch pipes mead and sould by Mee
the Meaker Halo, prickt toones reddy mead for voose and likewise
antums for all hockashons Pickells and preserves sould by mee wife next
doar. Hand all these done by mee as affoorsed 16 of March and dom
1790 six Wissells and rattles for childer.

The Derby Mercury
21 July 1796

❀ *Another blacksmith—from Somerset—who had a number of*
sidelines and a wife who made a contribution to the family
business is noticed later on in this book (Coventry Mercury,
14 November 1814). He also believed in advertising his talents
by a shop-door list.

Maternal Affection*

In the month of September last year, the body of a young woman, dressed
in black silk, with a watch, a ring and a small sum of money was found
floating near Spithead by a lieutenant of the impress and conveyed to
Ryde in the isle of Wight. As no person owned it, a parish officer, who
was also an undertaker, took upon himself to inter it, for the property that
was attached to it, which was accordingly performed. One evening, about
a fortnight after the event, a poor man and woman were seen to come into
the village, and on applying to the undertaker for a view of the property
which belonged to the unfortunate drowned person, they declared it to
have been their daughter, who was overset in a boat as she was going to
Spithead to see her husband. They also wished to pay whatever expence
the undertaker had been at, and to receive the trinkets &c. which had so
lately been the property of one so dear to them, but this the undertaker
would by no means consent to. They repaired therefore to the churchyard,
where the woman, having prostrated herself on the grave of the deceased,
continued some time in silent meditation or prayer, then crying *Pillilew*!
after the manner of the Irish at funerals, she sorrowfully departed with
her husband.

The curiosity of the inhabitants of Ryde, excited by the first appearance
and behaviour of the Couple, was charged with wonder, when, returning
in less than three weeks, they accused the undertaker of having buried
their daughter without a shroud, saying she had appeared in a dream
complaining of the mercenary and sacrilegious undertaker and lamenting

the indignity, which would not let her spirit rest! The undertaker stoutly denied the charge—But the woman having secretly purchased a shroud (trying it on herself) at Upper Ryde, was watched by the seller, and followed about twelve o'clock at night into the church yard. After lying a short time on the grave, she began to remove the mould with her hands and, incredible as it may seem, by two o'clock had uncovered the coffin, which with much difficulty and the assistance of her husband, was lifted out of the grave. On opening it, the stench was almost intolerable, and stopped the operation for some time, but after having taken a pinch of snuff, she gently raised the head of the deceased, taking from the back of it, and the bottom of the coffin, not a shroud, but a dirty piece of flannel, with part of the hair sticking to it, and which the writer of this account saw lying on the hedge as lately as last month. Clothing the body with the shroud every thing was carefully replaced, and, on a second application, the undertaker, overwhelmed with shame, restored the property. The woman, whose fingers were actually worn to the bone with the operation, retired with her husband and has never been heard of since.

The Derby Mercury
28 July 1796

A Shocking Accident*

Last week as two men in the habit of travelling with a bear and three dancing dogs were on their way between Ormskirk and Wigan, they called at an inn at Newbro for refreshment; they secured the bear in a brew-house and gave him some bread to eat, but unfortunately left the door open. Soon after, a neighbour's wife passing by it, the animal having too much chain, rushed upon her, and tore her so much before she received assistance, that she expired about an hour afterwards. She was four months gone with child and has left a husband and four small children to regret her loss. The men are in custody.

The Reading Mercury
15 August 1796

Man mistaken for Mad Dog

The following singular accident lately happened near Hawkchurch, Dorset. In consequence of severai dogs having lately run away mad, the people were full of apprehensions of the mischief they might do, and a labouring man of the name of Bridle, being on his way home from an inn where he got himself intoxicated, fell down asleep by the side of the road, after it was dark, one of his neighbours happening to come by, heard him snore, and it struck him directly that it must be a mad dog growling. He immediately alarmed his neighbours, who armed with guns and pitchforks, came round the supposed dog, but fearful of advancing further for fear of being bit, one of them fired off his gun and the whole contents were lodged in the poor man's side and arm. But proper means having since been taken, the man is in a fair way of recovery.

The Derby Mercury
10 November 1796

Veteran Soldier

On Sunday week at the Scar, near Bromyard, Herefordshire, Jeremiah Atkins, aged 102 years. He was a soldier at the taking of the Havannah and Martinico and very near being scalped by the Indians, from whom he was rescued at the moment of the operation. He was likewise at the taking of Crown Point, in America, and at the Battle of Fontenoy, with the Duke of Cumberland, and fought against the Rebels in Scotland. He was also at the taking of Quebec, when General Wolfe was killed, and afterwards in the Battle of Tournay, in Flanders. This extraordinary man retained all his faculties, but that of hearing, to the period of his death.

The York Herald
17 December 1796

❀ *This much-travelled man, who had spent his last years in a quiet village after being in campaigns in Europe, North America and the West Indies, must have been one of the oldest soldiers ever known to the British Army on active service. The English conquest of Martinique was in 1762, when he would have been sixty-eight. Perhaps he had become an 'old soldier' in more ways than one.*

Soldiers Wanted

WANTED immediately, for the parishes of Burnham and Taplow, SEVERAL ABLE BODIED MEN to serve in his Majesty's Army or Navy during the War. A handsome bounty will be given, by applying to either of the Parish Officers on or before the 30th. instant.

The Reading Mercury
26 December 1796

1797

Healthy Tibshelf

In the small parish of Tibshelf in this county, which does not contain one hundred houses, there are now living betwixt 70 and 80 persons who are more than 60 years old, amongst whom there are 4 nearly 100 each, 18 betwixt 80 and 90—and 22 above 70; a circumstance which perhaps cannot be equall'd in this kingdom.

The Derby Mercury
12 January 1797

Pigeon saves Child in Convulsions

The following remarkable fact cannot be generally known. On Wednesday last the only child of Stephen Friar Gillham, Esq., of Sharfield, Brentwood, Essex, about a month old, was seized with convulsions, which were so violent that every moment was expected to be its last. As a last expedient, when every thing else failed, one of the servants provided a live pigeon, and plucking the feathers from the breast, applied that part to the pit of the child's stomach, who then lay apparently dead. At the expiration of ten minutes the pigeon became convulsed, and some symptoms of recovery were apparent in the child. The remedy was continued for near three quarters of an hour, at the end of which the child was completely recovered, but the pigeon was so violently convulsed that the servant could with difficulty hold it, and it died a few minutes after, in the utmost agony, having effectually extracted that affection from the child which proved its own destruction. The body of the bird was black all over.

The Derby Mercury
30 November 1797

Feast of Red Herrings

One very severe day last week two labourers who were at work on the road agreed to call at a public-house in Gleadless, near Sheffield, for a relish; and it was resolved between them that he whose jaws first failed should pay the shot for both. Red herrings were the food; of them the one devoured eighteen, the other twenty-two, with a proportionate quantity of oat bread, beside drinking as much ale as the fish might have swam in. After having cleared away heads and tails, bones, fins and everything, these animals, half men, half herrings, soberly returned to their work!

The County Chronicle
19 December 1797

Escape by Beer Cask

One day last week, a brewer's servant, who had been employed in carrying beer to Porchester prison, was committed to Winchester gaol, on a charge of having conveyed two French officers out of the prison in a large beer cask, by which means they escaped.

The Nottingham Journal
30 December 1797

1798

Pikes for the Peasantry

Pikes for arming the Peasantry in the event of invasion were last week deposited in the barracks at Weymouth, Dorchester, Bridport, Wareham and other places along the Southern coast.

The Nottingham Journal
17 March 1798

Watch-houses are Completed

The Beacon Masts and watch-houses are now compleated on the eastern coast by which the approach of an enemy's fleet can be announced from Yarmouth in five minutes.

The Nottingham Journal
14 April 1798

A Summons to Arms

In Hampshire every person from 15 to 60 years of age is summoned to arms, and the Mayor, Alderman and Burgesses of Portsmouth have unanimously offered their services in defence of his Majesty, his crown, his dignity and the integrity of the British Constitution against all enemies.

The Nottingham Journal
28 April 1798

Volunteers at Newmarket

A meeting was held at Newmarket on Sunday last, after Divine Service, for aiding government in case of invasion, pursuant to the regulations of Mr. Dundas's Defence Bill, when the inhabitants all came forward in a very laudable manner for that purpose, and most of the labourers offered their services to act as pioneers, or in any other capacity that may be deemed necessary.

The following stanza gives a lively description of the present military preparations:

On every heath, on every strand
New-raised battalions grace the land:
"To arms!" the hollow vallies sound
"To arms—to arms!" the hills rebound,
ECHO, well-pleased, repeats the voice around.

The Nottingham Journal
12 May 1798

Veteran with Javelin

At Newmarket, a hearty veteran, 94 years of age, attended the meeting for promoting Mr. Dundas's plan of defence, with a javelin on his shoulder, and signed his name without the use of spectacles.

The Nottingham Journal
19 May 1798

❁ *These measures against invasion were a few of many made necessary because of insurrection in Ireland and the threat of landings there by the French. In August 1798 an army of 900 Frenchmen actually landed in Mayo and fought a successful battle at Castlebar. They had to surrender to greatly superior forces in the following month.*

Too Many Nuts

Mortality having of late been more than ordinary prevalent among the soldiery at Silverhill, the bodies of several who died were in consequence opened, when it appeared, beyond a doubt, that their deaths were occasioned by eating too freely of nuts.

The Nottingham Journal
29 September 1798

A New Species of Cook*

There is at this time in the possession of Mr. Sample, of the Angel Inn, Felton, a hedgehog which performs the duty of a turnspit as well in every respect as the dog of that name, runs about the house as familiarly as any other domestic quadraped, displays a docility hitherto unknown in that class of animals and answers to the call of Tom.

The Derby Mercury
20 December 1798

❀ *The duties of a turnspit dog, as taken on by Tom the hedgehog, are referred to earlier in this book. (Report from the* Northampton Mercury, *30 July 1750.)*

1799

Lambs killed by Rats

Mr. Winton, a farmer from Sompting, Sussex, who on one night last week ordered his shepherd to place five lambs in a barn to shelter them from the severity of the weather, had the next morning the mortification to

find they had been all destroyed by rats, and that the hungry vermin, after killing the lambs, had torn out and feasted upon their entrails. Mr. Winton immediately sent for a rat catcher, who set his ferrets and dogs to work in the barn and by means thereof killed 90, which were for the most part of the larger Hanover kind.

The County Chronicle
14 May 1799

'For the Inspection of the Curious'

In consequence of an emetic given by Mr. Carrington, a surgeon, of Bakewell, Derbyshire, some time in the course of June last, to a young lady who went to Buxton for the benefit of her health, and who laboured under a very uncommon complaint, she parted with a live newt, three inches and a quarter long, which is preserved in spirits, and kept for the inspection of the curious at Mr. Carrington's shop, in Bakewell.

The County Chronicle
27 August 1799

Woman from the Seashore

On Thursday se'nnight a woman was brought to the Lunatic Hospital near Newcastle who has lived upwards of three years among the rocks on the sea-shore near Seaham. From whence, or in what manner she first came there is unknown, but she speaks in the Scottish dialect and talks of Loch Stewart and Aber Gordon in a rambling manner. She is about thirty-five years of age, inoffensive and cheerful, and during her residence among the rocks was fantastically dressed in the rags which chance or the wrecks threw in her way; she always kept a good fire of wood or coal, which the sea threw up, and it is supposed lived upon shell-fish &c. What is remarkable, a beard has grown upon the lower part of her chin, nearly an inch long, and bushy like the whiskers of a man.

The Portsmouth Telegraph
14 October 1799

1800-09

WHEN INVASION WAS IMMINENT
Cartoon drawn by James Gillray on 2 August 1803.

1800

Need for More Potatoes

The present unfortunate scarcity of grain demands the attention of every Member of the community, and as an encreased growth of potatoes is of the utmost importance this year, it is earnestly recommended to Noblemen and Gentlemen in all parts of the country, and all farmers and others who hold land, to promote the growth of that useful root to the utmost of their power.

Pieces of waste land, corners of fields, banks and young plantations of trees are very advantageous for potatoes, and if the proprietors would devote some acres to this purpose, they would show their patriotism in a most exemplary manner. In short it is the duty of every individual possessed of any portion of land to appropriate as much as he can possibly spare, for the use of his family, his neighbour and the public, and perhaps he cannot at the same time use his land so advantageously to himself as by the growth of this article.

Granting the use of waste land to labouring people to grow for themselves, giving the seed and lending them tools for planting is most earnestly recommended to all who have it in their power. If Parish Officers in the country would rent some land for the purpose and sell out the potatoes at a low price, it would tend very much to keep down the poor's rate.

The Times
22 February 1800

Raid on Potato Wagon

On Thursday a wagon-load of potatoes, purchased in Essex by a dealer near the City Road, was stopped on their way to town by a great number of men and women between Bocking and Romford, and notwithstanding the remonstrances of a great number of gentlemen who assembled on the occasion, they were all sold out in small quantities by the populace.

The Times
10 March 1800

Great Trouble at Farnham

On Thursday a very serious and alarming riot happened in the town of Farnham. A considerable number of Irish recruits for the 25th. and 27th. regiments being quartered there, they assembled in the evening at a fair held in the town, armed with large bludgeons, and upon a signal given by one of the party, they began an assault on several of the country people. Little resistance was at first made, and in a short time the Irish soldiers cleared the fair, knocking down every man, woman and child they could get at and using numbers of them with the greatest barbarity, so that they lay on the ground, notwithstanding the most spirited interference was made by their officers to prevent it. In a few minutes some of the townspeople joined those of the country and armed with hop-poles and clubs of all sorts returned to the fair, where they found the soldiers huzzaing, at having obtained a victory and destroyed the stalls &c. A most violent engagement ensued, and the Irish were in their turn compelled to fly, and some of them were most cruelly treated by the country people, who could not be restrained by the inhabitants of the town, but were proceeding to the utmost outrages, when fortunately the Farnham Volunteers, under Captain Hollest, arrived and prevented further mischief. The Riot Act was read, the wounded soldiers were protected to their quarters by the Volunteers and the mob was soon afterwards dispersed, a few being first taken into custody.

The great utility of Volunteer Corps was never more apparent than on this occasion, for had not the Farnham Volunteers instantly turned out, the whole town must have been in the greatest danger from a furious and provoked mob, and the Irish soldiers in quarters were every moment joining their comrades, who were becoming desperate.

The Coroner's Inquest sat on the bodies of the soldiers, and brought in their verdict— *justifiable homicide*.

The Times
3 June 1800

A June Harvest

About a fortnight ago, a person of Crossland Hedge, near Huddersfield, was enriched with the following increase of flock and family. At six o'clock in the morning, one of his cows was delivered of two calves, and at seven a heifer of one calf; at noon his sow brought eleven pigs, and before noon his wife presented him with twin heirs to all these blessings. Had the clouds rained calves and pigs and children on his head, he could hardly have picked them faster.

The Hull Packet
17 June 1800

The Matriarch

At a village near Shaftesbury, a respectable matron resides, aged 90, who is mother, grandmother, great and great great grandmother to upwards of three hundred children, whose ages, added to hers, mount to upwards of 5,600 years, and what is more remarkable, there are not more than twenty of her posterity reside at more than four miles distant from the house her own children were born in, the greater part of whom live in one manor, and milk upwards of 1,000 cows. Till within these few years she resided on the same farm where all her children were born (and one of her sons still occupies it) and made it a constant rule to dine all her sons and sons-in-law, daughters and daughters-in-law on Old Christmas Day; and the day after to have all the grandchildren, great grandchildren, &c.

The Hull Packet
2 December 1800

1801

Bullock in Public House

Cambridge

The following extraordinary incident took place at St. Ives on Monday, the 5th. instant. A bullock walked into the passage of the Royal Oak public-house in that town and the staircase door being open, it went upstairs into the dining room, and ran with such violence against the front window (which was a sash) as to drive the whole of the window-frame into the street, where the animal fell also (the height of more than 10 feet), but received no material injury, altho' so much terrified that it ran with great precipitancy down to the bridge and being stopped there, it leaped over the side, when it was carried down the current so rapidly, from a very high flood, that it has never since been heard of.

The Bury and Norwich Post
14 January 1801

Famous Run by Farmer Tiffin

Norwich
On Thursday se'nnight, Mr. Robert Tiffin, farmer, at Outwell, in this
county, undertook for a wager of £20 to run from the mile stone near
Outwell toll-gate, five miles on the road to Wisbech and back again in an
hour and a half, which he accomplished with ease in one hour and eleven
minutes.

The Bury and Norwich Post
18 March 1801

❀ *Farmer Tiffin was quite a runner, with an average speed of one
mile in 7·1 minutes. This compares very favourably with the
present United Kingdom (National) Record for men for the 'one-
hour' event—a distance of 12 miles and 1,268 yards in 60 minutes.
But this was established, in 1968, under competition arrangements
for a modern athletic event. Tiffin ran his race over bumpy pot-
holed roads of the early nineteenth century.*

Starling nests in Murderer's Body

About ten days ago a starling's nest, with young ones, was taken from out
of the breast of Watson, who hangs on the gibbet on Brodenham
common, near Swaffham, for the murder of his wife, which was
witnessed by hundreds of people as something very singular and
extraordinary.

The Lancaster Gazetteer
27 June 1801

Putrification in Thirty Minutes

Norwich
During the thunder storm on Wednesday se'nnight, a fat bullock
belonging to Mr. Barnes of Beeston, was struck dead by the lightning,
whilst drinking at a pond. No marks of violence were found on the
carcase, but in less than half an hour it was in a state of complete putridity.

The Bury and Norwich Post
15 July 1801

Eton's 'Aquatic Excursion'

The young Gentlemen of Eton, on leaving School for the Midsummer
vacation, took their annual aquatic excursion on Saturday to Surley-Hall,

where they were entertained with a sumptuous repast; after which Mrs. Townly Ward sent them ten bowls of syllabub. They drank the health of the Royal Family, and those of their patrons and preceptors. The company who assembled to see them was very numerous. They were seated in a curious Caravan, or Russian Waggon, presented to them by Lord Whitworth, which attracted the notice of every person present. The young Gentlemen exhibited great skill in the art of rowing, and were all attired in fancy dresses. In the evening some beautiful fireworks were let off, and the day concluded with festive mirth and innocent recreation.

The County Chronicle
4 August 1801

Fortune for Poor

A gentleman by the name of Robinson, who was born at Middleton in Suffolk, a short time since left £70,000 for the improvement and enlargement of a botanical garden. Some circumstances, however, rendering the request abortive, the executors made diligent enquiry for the lawful heirs and discovered them to be a poor man, of the name of Bedwell, residing at Clopton, near Woodbridge, and the wife of a labouring man with four children, at Middleton, between whom this large property is now divided. These persons are now placed in situations suitable to their fortunes. Their mother, it appears, was sister to the deceased.

The Lancaster Gazetteer
15 August 1801

1802

Old English Hospitality

The Earl of Moira is spending Christmas at Donnington, in the true style of old English hospitality. The poor of the village are fed every morning at his doors, while the unfortunate of the highest rank, whom anarchy and confusion drove from their country and estates, are entertained by him within.

The Weekly Dispatch
17 January 1802

Blind Henry

Last week Henry Harris, a blind man who goes by the name of *Blind Henry*, climbed up a poplar tree 60 feet high, which hangs over the river Stour, very near to Stourbridge, which he cropped in a workman-like manner, without any assistance. Two cart loads of the kidwood were afterwards taken out of the water.

The Weekly Dispatch
14 March 1802

❀ *It might be thought that 'kidwood' was 'young wood'. In fact it meant wood that could be made up into bundles and used for lighting fires. It was also known as 'kindling'.*

Sentenced to Death for stealing Lamb

Cambridge
At the sessions at Peterborough on Wednesday, Edward Harber, a lad about 12 years of age, was sentenced to suffer death for stealing and afterwards selling a lamb, the property of Henry Cole, Esq., of that city.

The Bury and Norwich Post
5 May 1802

Safeguarding the Navy

It will afford considerable public satisfaction to have it stated from authority that more than *eleven millions* of acorns have been planted this year in the royal forests and chaces, for the further increase of timber for the use of his Majesty's Navy.

The Weekly Dispatch
23 May 1802

Man killed by Stallion

On Wednesday se'nnight as a man was travelling in Cheshire with a vicious horse (a stallion) the animal seized him, and horrid to relate, tore his bowels out, so that he died almost instantaneously.

The Weekly Dispatch
22 August 1802

Bull-baiting at Lincoln

At Lincoln, on the 5th. of November, the annual festivities of the day began, as usual, by dragging a bull into the town, about eleven in the forenoon, amidst the shouts of all the vagabonds of the place. The animal being taken to Castle-hill, was tied to a stake and worried by dogs; when, after he had been some time tormented, he broke loose and rushed down the hill. It being market-day, the terrified country people made off in every direction, and several women, with their butter and geese, ran into St. Peter's church during the performance of divine service. The enraged animal attempted to cross the Witham, but failed; and after remaining in the water more than twenty minutes, he was dragged to the place of torture; here the victim exhibited a shocking spectacle, being extremely lacerated, and at four o'clock he fell down at the stake and instantly expired.

The Kentish Herald
18 November 1802

Tythes*

The following circumstance occured last autumn in Kent. A country squire, who, as it appears from his conduct, must be an enemy to the established clergy, sent notice to the Rector of his parish, who was in the habit of taking tythes in kind, to take up the tythe of *five* plumbs, which had been just picked off the tree. The parson saw that if he refused to comply with the notice, he was liable to be involved in a lawsuit; he submitted to the insult, and sent his servant to fetch *half* of one of the plumbs.

The Weekly Dispatch
19 December 1802

1803

Terrible Affair at Weymouth

A terrible affair happened on Saturday se'nnight at Weymouth. A press-gang from a frigate, lying at Portland Roads, consisting of the Captain and his Lieutenant, with the Lieutenant of Marines and 27 marines, and about as many sailors, came on shore at Portland Castle, and proceeded to the first village, called Chesselton. They impressed Henry Wiggot and Richard Way, without any interuption whatever; the people of the island took the alarm and fled to the village of Easin, which is situated about the centre of the island, where the people made a stand at the pond. The gang came up and the Captain took a man by the collar. The man pulled back, at which the Captain fired his pistol, at which signal the Lieutenant of Marines ordered his men to fire, which being done, three men fell dead, being all shot through the head, viz. Richard Flann, aged 42 years; A. Andrews, 47 years; and William Lano, 26 years, all married men, two of them quarry-men, and one a blacksmith. One man was shot through the thigh, and a young woman through the back; the ball is still in her body, and but little hopes are entertained of her recovery. Poor Lano, the blacksmith, was at his shop door, and there fell dead. An inquisition has been held, and a verdict given of Wilful Murder against the whole, leaving the law to discriminate the ringleaders.

The Leeds Mercury
16 April 1803

Horse Falls 60 Feet—and lives!

The following singular circumstance occurred on Tuesday se'nnight near Shields. A young horse, grazing in some fields in the neighbourhood of Cliffords Fort, being desirous of cropping the sweetest herbage, unluckily ventured so near the brow of the precipice which overlooks the sea, that down he fell! It is imagined that the descent is 60 feet perpendicular and that he was not dashed to pieces is a matter of surprise; the owner, who lives close by, joyfully led him away, perceiving no other alteration occasioned by the incident than that he moved his hind legs rather stiffly.

The Leeds Mercury
23 April 1803

Dog fostered Lamb

The following remarkable occurrence happened a short time since. A ewe belonging to Mr. Anthony Storey, of Crook, near Kendal, having died in yeaning, the lamb was saved and laid by the fire, where a cub bitch, who had all her welps drowned, was lying. She permitted the little animal to suck her teats, and actually fostered it till it came to its growth.

The Leeds Mercury
18 June 1803

Ready for Invasion

The parish of Beckenham in this county, consisting of about 250 inhabitants, held a meeting on Sunday evening, in a field near the village, for the purpose of tendering their services to Government. The meeting was attended by Lords Gwydir and Auckland. After Lord Gwydir had delivered a most impressive and eloquent speech, no less than 220 inhabitants of this small village entered their names, the greater part of whom are effective men.

The Sea Fencibles all along the coast enter with alacrity; a very considerable number have already enrolled themselves at Deal and Dover and other parts of the coast. 150 stout fellows are learning the use of the great guns at Archcliff Fort. Dover will be further strengthened in a day or two by several Companies of Infantry.

The Kentish Herald
28 July 1803

❋ *War with France had come to an end with the Peace of Amiens in March 1802, but it broke out again in little over a year, in May 1803. Napoleon, now First Consul of France, planned an early, full-scale invasion of England and assembled a camp of 100,000 men at Boulogne. They were to embark in a great armada of flat-bottomed boats.*

The 220 men of Beckenham and the 150 'stout fellows' at Archcliff Fort were part of a large army of 400,000 volunteers for the defence of Britain. As happened many years later, in 1940, class and party differences were forgotten; there was tremendous enthusiasm, and a great determination to defeat a ruthless dictator from over the Channel.

The danger of invasion was to continue, in growing intensity, until 1805, when it receded dramatically with Nelson's victory at Trafalgar.

Many of the preparations against invasion by the Home Guard of those two crucial years have a strange, almost eerie, resemblance to those taken in country districts in 1914 and again, to a still greater degree, to those in the earlier years of the Second World War.

Fine for breaking the Sabbath

Mr. Robert Hastings has been convicted before the Rev. S. Oldershaw of driving cattle through the parish of Starston, Norfolk, on Sunday the 24th. of July and paid the penalty of 20s.

The Ipswich Journal
13 August 1803

❀ *Mr Hastings's fine was imposed under one of several Sunday Observance Acts of the period 1625–1780. One of them specifically forbade the following of one's week-day job on Sunday, and another particularly prevented a carrier undertaking work on that day.*

Barley Wager

On Wednesday se'nnight Mr. Devereux, a gentleman farmer in the neighbourhood of Beccles, undertook for a considerable wager to cut 3 acres of barley, from sunrise to sunset, which he performed in 20 minutes under that time, to the great astonishment of all present.

The Ipswich Journal
20 August 1803

Invasion expected at any Moment

A Gentleman who has posted it hither coastways from Brighton reports our state of preparation and activity to be such on every assailable point of the whole as to set the slyest approach of the Corsican and his hordes in defiance. The enemy's camps on the opposite shore are clearly discernible from Dover, Sandgate, etc. and accounts have been received that at St. Omer's, about 25 miles from Calais, a camp of 50,000 men is posted, which is expected every moment will be ordered to proceed for embarkation.

The Kentish Herald
29 September 1803

The Beacons are establishing . . .

The Beacons are establishing at Canterbury, Shorn Cliff, Barham, Isle of Thanet, Shottenden, Hythe, Poslingdown, Westwell, Pluckley, Lynham-hill, Coxheath, Bexley-hill, Chatham Lines, Wrotham-hill, Tenterden,

Highgate and Hawkhurst and Goudhurst, which, beginning from Canterbury or Shorne Cliff, will be successively fired at the near approach or actual landing of the enemy on the coast of Kent, and on which signal everyone is to assemble at his known place of rendezvous, and there expect to receive orders from the General Officer under whose command the several Volunteer and other Corps may be placed, and to whose quarters, on the first alarm of such an event, the Commanding Officer of every corps is to despatch a mounted officer or non-commissioned officer to receive such orders as may be thought necessary. The fire Beacons are stakes of wood and other material with a pole passing through them, on the top of which is a small white flag to make their situation more visable. When the alarm is given in the day, means will be taken to make a great smoke accompany the fire.

The Kentish Herald
6 October 1803

Wagons for Women and Children

Waggons are ordered to be provided and kept in readiness in the principal towns along the coast, for the purpose of conveying into the interior of the county, the sick, the women and children, should the French succeed in effecting a landing. Those provided for the town of Dover were last Sunday collected on the Parade, for inspection by Mr. Pitt, as Lord Warden of the Cinque Ports.

The Kentish Herald
6 October 1803

A Dedicated Poacher

As a person said to be a notorious poacher on the manors of Worthen and Broction, in this county, was shooting at a covey of partridges, in the late fall of snow, the gun burst and took off two of the fingers of his left hand. On his return home he was met by a neighbour, who observed his hand bleeding pretty badly, and enquired what was the matter. The other replied "The gun has burst and blown off two of my fingers, but never mind that, mun, I ha got the birds".

The Salopian Journal
21 December 1803

Woman killed by Stag

A few days since, as a poor woman was going to Powderham Castle, Devon, to receive a portion of provisions daily allowed by Lord Courtenay to a number of poor people, a stag in the park furiously attacked and killed her on the spot. The animal was immediately shot.

The Salopian Journal
21 December 1803

1804

'Preston Fight' Treasure

On Saturday, 17th. ult., as George Whitaker, the inhabitant of a lone cottage about four miles from Blackburn, betwixt Whalley and Hibchester, whilst choosing a proper place for fixing a pole to hang up a pig he was going to kill, felt something hard betwixt the thatch and the wall, which he drew out, and was agreeably surprised to find it a purse inclosing five smaller ones containing some gold, and several crown and half-crown pieces of the reign of Charles the Second, James the Second, William and Mary, and Ann, and a Portugal moidare. It is supposed they have lain there ever since the year 1715, or Preston fight, as it is called, and deposited there by an old woman that inhabited the cottage, as it was afterwards occupied by one Anderton for sixty years, a man in rather low circumstances; the present occupier has lived therein eight years—he is wise enough not to mention the sum found, but by what information can be obtained it is thought to be pretty considerable.

The Leeds Mercury
21 January 1804

❀ *The 'fight' at Preston was between royalist forces and troops of the Old Pretender, James Edward Stuart. It took place on the outskirts of the town, and resulted in the surrender of 1,500 of the Jacobites. The coins were probably hidden in the mistaken belief that the rebels would be victorious, and advance further into Lancashire.*

A 'Lawless Court'

A very singular custom, connected with the Manor of Rochford, in Essex, is the holding of what is called a Lawless Court. Its origin is uncertain, but tradition represents it as arising from a conspiracy against the Lord of the Manor, projected during his absence, and overheard by him on his way home. As a punishment he ordered that all the tenants on his manor should ever afterwards assemble at a certain hour of the night, on the same spot where the conspirators met, and do homage for their lands. The court is held in the open air, on King's Hill, on the midnight of the first Wednesday after Michaelmas day; and all the business is transacted in whispers, the minutes being made with a coal, instead of pen and ink. The steward opens the court in as low a voice as possible; yet those tenants who neglect to answer are deeply fined and every absentee forfeit's double his rent in every hour's absence. The time of assembling is from twelve till cock-crow. The parties previously meet at the King's Head, in Rochford.

The Leeds Mercury
11 August 1804

❀ *The Lord of the Manor lived at Rochford Hall, thought to be the house in which Anne Boleyn was born. This custom lingered on until as recently as 1920. In the earlier years of this century Rochford Hall became a golf club.*

'The Walking Obelisk'

On Tuesday, J. Hawkesworth, many years gamekeeper to T. W. Coke, Esq., died at Holkham Hall, in the 70th. year of his age. He never associated with, or spoke to any person, unless he was first addressed. He was very penurious, had accumulated a considerable fortune, which he had hid from the fear of invasion, and his death was supposed to be occasioned by depriving himself of sufficient nourishment. Mr. Coke always furnished him with proper liveries, but his dress was of the most miserable kind, and he always wore an old painted hat, patched over with pieces of cloth. The liveries which he had by him at the time of his death and which had never been worn are supposed to be worth £100. He was known by the title of the Walking Obelisk.

The Leeds Mercury
25 August 1804

❀ *'The Walking Obelisk's' employer was the famous agriculturist*

'Coke of Norfolk', (1752–1842), who in 1837 became Earl of Leicester. He was also a great friend of America, and did much to bring the War of American Independence to an end.

Holkham Hall is a beautiful mansion full of many paintings and other treasures, about 35 miles from Norwich. It is open to the public.

Certain Cure for Adder-bite

Certain cure for the bite of an adder. Let the part affected be rubbed well with sweet oil, and a tablespoonful taken internally. This treatment has been known to restore persons in the last extremity.

The Leeds Mercury
8 September 1804

1805

St. Thomas's Day Benevolence

On St Thomas's Day last, and during the present winter, Lord and Lady Lowther's annual donation was distributed to the poor in the neighbouring villages of their delightful seat at Lowther, consisting of 124 lb. of excellent meat, upwards of 200 pairs of flannel blankets, and a great quantity of warm apparel. Besides all this, soup of an excellent quality is served out twice a week to a number of poor families in the vicinity.

The Lancaster Gazette
26 January 1805

✸ *St Thomas's Day (21 December) was the traditional occasion for dispensing charity. Benefaction boards in parish churches record many gifts of coal and money which were given out then. It was also known as 'Gooding Day', when the poor were given 'good things' for their Christmas dinners. But it was a sad day for farm beasts and poultry. This couplet reminded the farmers of the day on which they should make their last slaughters for the Christmas table:*

On St. Thomas the Divine
Kill all turkeys, geese and swine.

Invasion Alarm

On the night of Friday the 15th. ult. the inhabitants of Wensleydale were greatly alarmed by the burning of heath on Hamilton, which was mistaken for the beacon on the top of Roseberry; the alarm was immediately given to Colonel Straubenzee of the Wensleydale Volunteers, who ordered the drums to beat to arms and such was their alertness and activity that they were all under arms by four o'clock in the morning. The intelligence was communicated to Timothy Hutton, Esq. (the commander of the Masham volunteers in the absence of William Danby, Esq.) before nine o'clock, who instantly dispatched his servant to Masham, when men were sent to all the villages with orders for all the carts and waggons to be got in readiness, and although some of the men were five or six miles distant, they all assembled in the market-place by two o'clock, the waggons and carts loaded with baggage, blankets &c. and marched immediately in excellent spirits on their way to Malton, according to their orders. They arrived at Thirsk that evening, when, finding the cause of the alarm, they remained there that night, and returned to Masham the next morning, when they were met by the greatest part of the inhabitants to welcome their return. A few days after, they received a letter from General Newgill, complimenting them upon the great activity and intrepidity they shewed on the occasion; a certain proof that should the enemy attempt to invade our shore, the Wensleydale and Masham volunteers will not be the last in coming forward to give them a warm reception.

The Lancaster Gazette
6 April 1805

Boy killed by Toads

The following extraordinary and mournful event lately happened at a village in the neighbourhood of Alfreton, Derbyshire. Two brothers, sons of respectable parents there, having been amusing themselves by the side of a pool with catching and destroying toads, one of them, about twelve years of age, was as thoughtless and imprudent as to put a stick he had been using into his mouth; which having some of the venom of the toads adhering to it, infected his lip, which was sore, and produced so much swelling and inflammation as to occasion his death not many days later.

The Lancaster Gazette
20 April 1805

Poisoned by Duck Eggs

The following singular and fatal occurrence is said to have taken place. On the evening of Friday week, three drovers, a father and his two sons, called at the house of a farmer, not far from the village of Fifield, in Berkshire, for the purpose of taking some of his cattle to London. Here they partook of some refreshment, which chiefly consisted of duck eggs; very soon afterwards they were seized with a violent sickness, were put to bed and died before the next morning. The apothecary of the adjoining village, who was sent for, made enquiry as to the food they had eaten, and on finding they had eat duck eggs, he immediately gave directions that the pond to which the farmer's ducks resorted should be searched; this was done, and a toad of the enormous weight of seven pounds was found at the bottom of the pond. Some of the duck eggs that had not been used were examined, and black spots were observed inside the yolk, and some of the eggs were given to a dog, which caused his death in a very short while. The eggs must have been impregnated by the spawn of the toad.

The York Herald
7 June 1805

❂ *A fear of toad venom was very much a part of British folklore; the venom is often recorded as an important ingredient of a witch's brew. The Chronicles of the Abbey of St Albans related that the hated King John (1167–1216) met his death through a mixture of toad venom and ale offered to him by a monk at Swineshead Abbey in Lincolnshire. The monk put a toad in a cup, pricked it to release the venom and then added the ale.*

Cure for Rheumatism

A Mineral spring has been discovered in the small island of Hilbury, at the western extremity of Cheshire, possessing the powerful efficacy of curing the Rheumatism, &c. The property of the spring was accidently ascertained by a respectable Welsh farmer, who went to the island for the benefit of his health, and happening to wash his hands, much swollen from Rheumatic affection, in the waters found immediate relief.

The York Herald
15 June 1805

Death of Nelson

Lord Nelson, in his last will, expressed a desire that his body should be interred by the side of his reverend father at Burnham Thorpe, unless His

Majesty *should be graciously pleased to direct otherwise.* His Majesty, we understand, has ordered that his remains shall be buried in St. Paul's.

The York Herald
16 November 1805

✹ *The battle of Trafalgar, in which Nelson was killed, had taken place on 21 October 1805. Nelson was born at Burnham Thorpe, where his father was rector, in 1758. At the parish church there he is remembered in many ways. The lectern was made from oak from the* Victory, *and there is a copy of* The Times *that tells of his funeral at St Paul's. The village inn has a room in which Nelson is said to have given a dinner to parishioners of Burnham Thorpe to celebrate his appointment to command of the* Agamemnon *in 1793.*

Burnham Thorpe is deep in the Norfolk countryside, about thirty miles from Norwich.

Nelson's Protégé

A most curious circumstance, respecting the ever-to-be lamented Lord Nelson, happened on the 18th. inst. at Plymouth. As Colonel Tyrwhitt, Vice Warden of the Stanneries, Cornwall and Devon, was, with other gentlemen, looking through his telescope at the French prizes going up the harbour, he observed a fine little boy, of an open countenance, cheering with his playfellows, and heard him several times called Nelson. This raised (on being often repeated) a curiosity to know who the boy was. Colonel Tyrwhitt went to his father's cottage, who was a quarryman, and lived at Rusty Anchor, under the West Hoe. By this time the boy was returned, first appearing shy, but, on a little conversation, this wore off, and he said Lord Nelson was his god-father, but he was shot and killed the other day in a great battle. The Colonel then entered the hut, and found the father, who had lost a limb in the Minotaur, in the battle of the Nile, and his wife and four children, clean, though poorly dressed. Colonel Tyrwhitt then asked if the circumstance were true, of Lord Nelson's being god-father to this little boy, and was answered, yes. The mother then produced a certificate of his baptism, at the British Factory Chapel, Leghorn, July 1800, attested by the clergyman, Rev. Mr. Cummins—and signed

Emma Hamilton
William Hamilton
Nelson and Bronte.

The child was named Horatio Nelson—His mother was washer-woman on board the Minotaur, of 74 guns, Captain Louis. When the child was born, in the Bay of Leghorn, his Lordship and Sir Wm. and Lady Hamilton said they would stand sponsors. He had promised, when the boy grew up, to put him to sea, and give him a nautical education. But after the Peace of Amiens, these poor people, from ignorance, neglected (though desired by his Lordship when he sailed for England) to write him when they were settled. The Minotaur was paid off at Plymouth, and the father of the boy, with his small pension, has contrived to maintain his family ever since. After talking over the circumstance of the intended kindness of Lord Nelson to this poor little boy, if he had known their situation and place of abode, Colonel Tyrwhitt determined to follow up his Lordship's good wishes, took the boy as his protégé, and with his usual humanity, had him decently clothed and put to school, and means to give him a regular nautical education to fit him for the naval service of his country. A little purse, by way of subscription, for present purposes, has just been opened, under the patronage of Mrs. Admiral Sutton, which will, no doubt, be soon filled, out of respect to the memory of a hero, beloved, admired and almost adored; and whose memory will be cherished and entwined round the heart of every lover of British naval virtue and heroism.

The Lancaster Gazette
30 November 1805

1806

Smoking Sailor caused Wagon Fire

On Monday last, as the Hull waggon had got about five miles from Scarborough, it was perceived to be on fire, owing to an inconsiderate, imprudent sailor smoking a pipe in the waggon; the waggon and all the goods therein were damaged; and had it not been for great exertion, the horses would have been also burnt to death. With difficulty, a female passenger and child were got out a little scorched. Within these few years, similar accidents have happened; but it is hoped that drivers will, in future, be on their guard to prevent passengers from having pipes with them, lives and property being thereby endangered.

The York Herald
14 June 1806

Bull-fight in Berkshire

A Drover, at a village called Hurst, in the Vale of Berks, has been backed by a Sportsman, to combat with a ferocious bull, which has long been the terror of women and children in the neighbourhood. This singular exhibition will take place in the ensuing week for a considerable sum. The bull is backed by the owner. He who keeps within the field longest is to be declared the victor.

The Morning Chronicle
11 July 1806

Three Admirals from One Village

It is with satisfaction we learn that the County of Norfolk, in gratitude and affection to the memory of its dear, departed Nelson, has determined to place its column of commemoration at the native spot of the hero's birth, Burnham Thorpe. It is worthy of remark here, that, within a mile or two of Burnham Thorpe, stands the obscure village of Cockthorpe, a village of three houses, or rather of three hovels only, each of which produced, from humblest village life, its individual Admiral. The three Cockthorpe Admirals became Flag Officers of much renown; Sir Christopher Mimms, Sir John Narborough and Sir Cloudesley Shovel. . . .

The York Herald
13 September 1806

Fifth of November*

On Monday last, George Walkitt, farmer of Weaverthorpe, was convicted before Edward Topham, Esq., in the penalty of £5 for destroying hares on that day. We insert this as a caution, as some persons ignorantly conceive this to be a *day free from all law*.

The York Herald
15 November 1806

Bull Baiting*

The Bachelors of Windsor, having claimed their chartered right of the piece of ground called "Bachelor's Acre" in Windsor, will bait their game-bull again on Monday next, in Bachelor's Acre. They will give the following prizes to the owners of the dogs which bait; For the best dog, £3. 13s. 6d., to the second best, a silver collar value £3, to the third best £1. 1s. 0d, and to the fourth, a collar, value 15s. The bull, after baiting, will be killed, and distributed to the poor at Windsor.

The York Herald
22 November 1806

❀ *In 1974 a lady resident at Windsor successfully challenged a plan to build a multi-storey car park on Bachelor's Acre. When the case was heard before a High Court judge it was recalled that as well as bear-baiting and bull-baiting, Bachelor's Acre had been used for fairs and archery. There were archery butts there from 1651.*

Supposition of Murder*

On Sunday, the 20th. July last, Elizabeth Byram, a young woman, and servant to John Proctor, of Smeaton, butcher, had leave of absence from her mistress to see her friends, who reside at Protherton and Knottingley, a distance of five or six miles, and on her return home late the same evening, she was last seen on the cross roads from Pontefract to Campsall, and from Doncaster to Ferribridge, where she had informed some of her female acquaintances she expected to meet a young man, who paid his addresses to her, and who was seen on the same road late that same evening by other people; her disappearance from that time gave rise to a suspicion that he had murdered her and buried her in the plantation of F. L. Hodgson, Esq., at Stapleton, and he was accordingly apprehended and committed to Wakefield House of Correction by the Magistrate, before whom he underwent several strict examinations. But no circumstances sufficiently strong arising, he was restored to his liberty. The prejudices of the neighbourhood were still very great against him, and the inhabitants of the surrounding villages repeatedly examined and searched the extensive plantations and wastes to discover the remains of the unfortunate girl, but without effect.

The young man, whose existence was rendered miserable, was on the point of quitting his native village, to avoid the detestation of his neighbours, when last week a letter was received from London, by the girl's friends, informing them she is in a most deplorable state, and in St. Bartholomew's Hospital. It now appears, from her account, that a soldier who overtook her on the road enticed the frail one to accompany him, and after seducing her he left her to her fate; she at length reached the metropolis, and has been on the town, till disease drove her to her present asylum.

The neighbouring villagers are yet very unwilling to believe in the present existence of the girl and many affirm that they have seen her ghost in different places—and a celebrated *wiseman*, or *conjuror*, in the neighbourhood, who had been consulted, undertook to discover, by *his art*, the grave where the girl's remains were deposited, if his inquiries would gain the permission of the Magistrates!!

The York Herald
29 November 1806

1807

Prevention of Murder*

A few nights ago, as the driver of the Bedford stage-waggon was going along the road between Luton and the town of Bedford, at twelve o'clock at night, he perceived a light in a field adjoining the road, and his curiosity being excited, he unfastened his mastiff dog from under the waggon, and proceeded to the spot, where he found a man digging a hole in the ground. The waggoner accosted him familiarly, but the man angrily informed him he had nothing to do with him, or his business, and the former left him. He had not proceeded two hundred yards on the road, when he met a female with a box and a bundle under her arm, and he also interrogated her, and this without receiving any satisfactory answer. The curiosity of the waggoner was on its full stretch, when he saw the young woman cross to a foot-path which led to the man in the field, and he again untied his dog and followed her. She went to the man, and after a short conversation, he drew a pistol from his pocket and exclaimed "I've prepared your grave, and you must die". The waggoner, who had remained a few paces distant, rushed on the man, and the mastiff seized him, when the waggoner bound him, and conveyed him to safe custody, as well as the female, who wished to depart. The man has been committed for trial at Bedford. The woman, who is pregnant by the man, who is a rustic, was a bar-maid at Bedford, and she had met the man by appointment. She had left her situation, and had £70 in her pocket.

The Courier
2 April 1807

Chudleigh destroyed by Fire

The town of Chudleigh, in Devonshire, has been destroyed by fire! The dreadful conflagration began on Friday morning at ten o'clock. It is supposed that it commenced at a bake-house, and the greater number of buildings in the town, being thatched, the flames spread from house to house, from tenement to tenement, with astonishing rapidity. The terrified inhabitants had, ere night, the dismal prospect of every habitation enveloped in flames; they were left without shelter—almost without food and raiment; and on Saturday the whole scite of the town, with the exception of one or two detached buildings, was a heap of smoking ruins. The road was impassable, and the Mercury stage-coach made a circuit of two miles in consequence. As one alleviation of this dreadful visitation, we hear no lives were lost, and every exertion will doubtless be immediately made by the neighbouring Gentlemen to procure necessaries for the sufferers.

The Salisbury Journal
25 May 1807

Further News of Chudleigh Fire

The account given in our last of the calamitous event was too correct, as appears by the following narrative, published by the Committee to investigate the same:

On Friday morning, about eleven o'clock, this most fateful fire commenced. In less than one hour its ravages had spread over a considerable portion of the town. Unhappy for the inhabitants, every circumstance seemed to conspire their ruin. The buildings were principally covered with thatch, the fire engine was consumed a few minutes after the melancholy accident was discovered, but the very inadequate supply of water would have rendered any application of it of little avail. A strong wind blew the flames from one extremity to the other, carrying destruction to those dwellings which, from their remoteness, were considered safe and had become depositories of the most valuable effects. The consternation and confusion which ensued rendered it impossible to concert any measures, or combine any exertions that could arrest the fury of the flames. The wretched and terrified inhabitants endeavoured, indeed, to rescue from the fire some part of their property, but even this last hope was, in many instances, impracticable. What was saved at one moment, at the hazard of their lives, was burnt perhaps the next, in the place that was considered secure. The destruction became general; and the people, exhausted by great, but ineffectual exertions, abandoned themselves to the utmost despair. Of three hundred houses, of which the town was composed, above two hundred are now in ruins.

The Salisbury Journal
1 June 1807

London–Manchester in 20 Hours

In the year 1770 there was only one coach to London, and one to Liverpool, which went from or came into Manchester, and they set out only twice a week. There are now twenty-seven distinct coaches which run from Manchester, of which eighteen set out every day, and eight others three times a week, to their different places of destination. In the year 1754 a *flying coach* was advertised and it promised in the following words "However incredible it might appear it would actually arrive in London in four days and a half after leaving Manchester". The distance is one hundred and eighty-five miles and the journey is now performed by the mail-coaches in about thirty hours, and on some occasions it has been travelled in twenty hours.

The Weekly Dispatch
6 September 1807

The Great Fair at Howden

The great Fair for horses at Howden, in Yorkshire, is just over, where good horses of all descriptions, whether for harness, hunting or the road, sold at high prices. Good colts were scarce and sold well. Horses adapted for the cavalry and artillery service were in great demand, and the price for those of that description experienced a considerable advance. This, which is undisputably the largest fair for horses in the kingdom, commences annually on the 25th. of September, and continues till the 3rd. of October, being attended by all the principal dealers from London, Edinburgh, and from several of the great towns in the different counties of England. During every night of the time above-mentioned there are not less than 2,000 horses in the stables of the respective inn-keepers, or sent out to grass. The stables of the public-houses in the adjacent villages, to the extent of ten miles around Howden, are also completely full. So that it may be fairly estimated that not less than 4,000 horses are every day exposed to sale; and supposing that this number is renewed only four times during those ten days, which is a very moderate calculation, it follows that about 16,000 horses are disposed of at this fair, worth together not less than £200,000.

The Courier
9 November 1807

Hare ran on Stumps

Last Saturday, a hare was turned up before a brace of greyhounds, in Ringmer Chalk Pit, and so hardly pressed down a declivity of the hill, that to accelerate her escape, she leaped from it on the road below, and broke both her forelegs, after which the timid animal actually led her pursuers a considerable distance on her stumps, and until she was at length overtaken, and put out of her misery, in a field belonging to Mr. Farncomb, of Stoneham.

The Courier
20 November 1807

Peril in the Snow

An idea of the severity of the weather may be formed from the following circumstances which occured on Monday se'nnight.—As four drovers, on their return from the south, were passing over Shapfell, three of them were so overpowered by the cold, that they were unable to proceed further. In this emergency, the fourth took upon his shoulders one of his companions, who appeared more exhausted than the others, and conveyed him to the nearest public-house, at a distance of a mile and a half, though the poor man performed the journey without his shoes, having lost them in the snow. Having relieved himself of his burden, he instantly set out again in search of those he had left behind, whom he found somewhat recovered, they having, during his absence, killed a sheep which they found on the fell, and prevented the vital spark from being extinguished by wrapping its warm intestines around their benumbed feet and hands. On reaching the public-house, they observed their friend a lifeless corpse.

The Courier
2 December 1807

Life saved by Fiddle

A fidler returning home from a merry meeting, between Alston and Harwood, in Teesdale, in the stormy night of the 20th. ult., took shelter in a low out-house on Alston Moor, which was afterwards so overblown with the snow, that he could not get out, nor did any part of the house appear; and here he must have perished, had not some shepherds, who were seeking their sheep, discovered him by the sound of his fiddle under the snow; his playing on which unquestionably was the means of saving his life.

The Hull Packet
22 December 1807

1808

Receipt for the Cure of Sickness in Young Sheep

When the sheep is observed to be affected, let it be immediately brought into the house; then take a large table-spoonful of mustard, mix it with boiling water till it be of a proper consistence to be swallowed, and apply it as warm as the animal is able to bear it. Let the sheep stand twelve hours in the house after the mixture has been applied.

The Salisbury Journal
29 February 1808

Disgraced for cutting down Trees

On Saturday two young men were publicly whipped in the Market-place of this City. They brought this punlishment and disgrace to themselves by cutting and destroying young trees in the woods of the Earl of Radnor, of which they were convicted at the last Quarter Sessions, when the statute imperatively obliged the Bench to sentence them to three months imprisonment, to be three times publicly whipped and to give security for their good behaviour for two years. One of these young men has some property and good connections and had been before detected cutting a young pollard, and cautioned not to be guilty of the like again. They have two months imprisonment and two more whippings still to undergo. May their punishment deter others from evil.

The Salisbury Journal
7 March 1808

Sheep survives Three Weeks under Snow

Many well-authenticated cases of sheep living an astonishing length of time without food and buried under the snow are upon record, but the most remarkable instance of this sort, we believe, is that of a sheep belonging to Mr. John Turnill, of Dogsthorpe, near Peterborough, which, with seven others, was buried from Thursday night, the 11th. of February, till Friday, the 4th. of March, when it was found alive, and upon being extricated eagerly ate the rind of sticks, straw and whatever came in its way. The seven other sheep were dead.

The Northampton Mercury
19 March 1808

Attack on 'Witch' in Huntingdon

About half-past nine o'clock on Saturday night, the 7th. instant, the house of Wright Izzard, of Great Paxton, in the County of Huntingdon, was broken into, and Ann Izzard, his wife, was dragged out of bed by a man, at present unknown, who, with the assistance of two other men, with great violence, forced her into the yard without any clothes on; here a most barbarous assault was committed upon her person by three women, aided and abetted by several men; her head was injured by a pin or stick which fastened the door on the outside; she received a wound under her right eye; her right breast was very much bruised, while her arms and legs and other parts of her body were lacerated with pins, or some sharp-pointed instruments, till they were literally covered with blood. On the next evening an assault, very nearly similar, was again made upon her. The parties offending were brought before the bench of magistrates at

Huntingdon on Saturday se'nnight and were bound over to keep the peace and to appear at the ensuing assizes, to answer the charges which shall then be preferred against them. Ann Izzard is a very harmless, inoffensive woman, nearly sixty years of age, and is the mother of eight children. A few weeks ago some misguided people raised the cry of witchcraft against her; and at the moment the poor in general of the parishes of Great and Little Paxton, and some of the farmers also, really believe she is actually a witch.

The Northampton Mercury
28 May 1808

❀ *In their attack on poor Ann Izzard the people who ill-treated her were observing a practice followed by their ancestors over many centuries. It was believed that if a witch's blood was drawn her spells were weakened or ruined.*

Wonderful Escape from Destruction

The following wonderful escape from destruction occured at Atherstone, Warwickshire, on Saturday se'nnight. During the storm of wind on that day, the miller belonging to the windmill near that place, finding it out of his power to stop the sails of his mill, called in the assistance of a neighbouring millwright, who succeeded in stopping their progress, but afterwards, ascending the sails to fasten the cloth, he was by a sudden squall of wind carried round with them several times before assistance could be given to stop the rapidity of their motion, but which was at last effected, and the poor fellow descended without injury from his uncommon vehicle. The sails had once been stopped when he was on the upper sail, and consequently with his head downward.

The Northampton Mercury
22 October 1808

Large Meal in 38 Minutes

On Wednesday last, a corporal belonging to the Dunstable Volunteers undertook to eat twelve dozen raw herrings, two quartern loaves of bread and drink two gallons of ale in an hour, which he performed in 38 minutes, to the great astonishment of a number of spectators assembled at the White Hart Inn in that place.

The Northampton Mercury
19 November 1808

1809

Church Window blown down during Service

A great degree of consternation was excited in Sleaford church last Sunday. At the instant the officiating clergyman had pronounced the words in the prayer for the Clergy "Send down upon our Bishops and Curates, and all congregations committed to their charge", a sudden and violent gust of wind sent down the great church window. The crash was tremendous, and the alarm so great that few of the congregation waited the conclusion of the service.

The Observer
5 February 1809

Cure for Hoarseness

The chewing of transverse sections of horse radish, like lozenges, is a quick and infallible cure to hoarseness of the voice, and all catarrhal disorders.

The Observer
12 February 1809

Shepherd drowned in Mud

A shepherd to Mr. Fisher, of Cotham, Lincoln, was found drowned last week with a fat sheep, in one of the closes on the farm. The dog, it is supposed, drove the sheep in, and on the man endeavouring to get it out, the mud was so strong he could not extricate himself.

The Observer
11 June 1809

Drunken Labourer attacked by Rats

The dangerous consequences likely to result from sleeping in an out-house during a state of intoxication were singularly exemplified on Thursday last. A labourer in the employ of Mr. Laybourn, of Witney, near Oxford, having retired greatly inebriated, to recover from a debauch, was attacked by some rats. The liquor and sleep had so overpowered the unfortunate man that he was incapable either of repelling them, or calling for assistance. He continued in an agonising state for two hours, when his groans attracted the attention of a person passing the door, and who, on entering, found a number of rats of a large species assembled round the feet of the sufferer, seven of whose toes were entirely devoured by these ferocious animals.

The Observer
25 June 1809

The Corpulent Mr Lambert

Mr. D. Lambert, so celebrated for his corpulence, died, without any previous illness on Wednesday morning last, at Stamford, whither he had gone with intent to exhibit himself during the races. He was in his 40th. year, and upon being placed in the famous Caledonian balance, within a few days of his death, was found to weigh 52 stone, 11 lbs. (14 lbs. to the stone), which is 10 lbs. more than the celebrated Mr. Bright of Essex ever weighed. His coffin, which is 6 feet 4 inches long, 4 feet 4 inches wide, and 2 feet 4 inches deep, consists of 112 superficial feet of elm, is built upon two axle-trees and four clog-wheels; and upon these the remains of the poor man will be rolled into the grave, at St. Martin's. A regular descent will be made by cutting away the earth slopingly for some distance. The window and wall of the room in which he lies must be taken down, to allow the removal of his corpse.

The Observer
25 June 1809

❀ *Mr Lambert's claim to fame was because of his great weight, whereas Mr Rice of Sutton Bonington (see* Adams Weekly Courant *of 2 March 1773) was noted for his height (7 ft 4½ in). Daniel Lambert was 17½ inches shorter than Rice, but round the middle he measured 92 inches.*

Fox under the Bed

On Monday last the Cottesmore hounds unkennelled a fox at Tolthorpe Oaks, near Stamford, and after a chase of an hour and a quarter, ran into him at Ashton, in Northamptonshire. Reynard was so distressed that he took shelter in a cottage, passing through a room in which a woman was working, and secreted himself under the bed in an adjoining compartment. The hounds, however, came up in a few minutes, moved him from his hiding place and tore him to pieces. The Earl of Lonsdale immediately presented the poor woman with half-a-guinea, as a remuneration for the trepidation his noisy visitors had put her in.

The Hull Packet
12 December 1809

Fined One Guinea—for refusing to work

John Storey, James Hardy, and William Affleck, three servants in husbandry, to Mr. Oliphant, farmer, at Marlefield, in Kent, were lately fined by the Justices of the district, one guinea each, besides expences, for refusing to cut and bring home from their master's fields, green fodder for his cattle, which they conceived they were justified in refusing, after having done a yoke at plough, or a common day's work of 12 hours.

The Observer
12 November 1809

County Cricket—Fat Sheep Prize

A game of cricket was played on Tuesday se'nnight on Erridge Green, between the gentlemen of the counties of Kent and Sussex, for a fat sheep, to be roasted whole. On account of the shortness of the days, it was agreed that one innings should decide the game; which was accordingly commenced and well-contested, having terminated with three notches only in favour of the Sussex gentlemen.

The Observer
12 November 1809

1810-19

TEETH WERE DRAWN AT THE BLACKSMITH'S SHOP

1810

Fever Victims—5 Children from one Family

A greater mortality has seldom occurred in one family, and in so short a time, as in that of John Harrison, of Bingham, farmer; he having buried in little more than a month (and three of them in the short space of six days) five of his children, of the respective ages of three, nine, eleven, thirteen and eighteen years of age, by a malignant fever, which has been prevalent in that town for some time.

The Stamford News
13 July 1810

Fishermen find Bell from Ruined Church

On Friday last, as some fishermen were fishing about a mile and a half below Saltfleet, they caught in their net a bell-clapper of large dimensions, but in their endeavours to take it into their boat, it mouldered to pieces. It is supposed to have belonged to Saltfleet Church, which stood, it is thought, near the spot, but has been swallowed up by the sea some centuries past.

The Stamford News
20 July 1810

Landlady's Son climbed Moulton Church Steeple

A young man of the name of Thornton, son of the landlady of the White Horse public-house at Moulton sea's end, lately experienced a most providential escape from danger occasioned by an act of extreme temerity. He actually scaled the steeple of the parish church, which is not less than 170 feet high, by means of the crotchets, or small projections of stone attached to the exterior of the spire. Not content with having succeeded in gaining the stone which caps the summit, he aspired to substitute his cloth apron for the fane! Whilst climbing up the staff at the extremity of which the fane is fixed, it brake with his weight! His destruction appeared already to have taken place. But wonderful to tell, his body caught the stump of the staff, and he was thus arrested in his descent. While the horror-struck multitude expected him to be dashed a mangled corse at their feet, he reached the flat stone in safety, and shortly afterwards descended to the ground, by the same adventurous route which he traced in his ascent.

The Stamford News
31 August 1810

❀ *The 'fane'—nowadays we call it a 'vane'—was the church's weathercock.*

Died in Harvest Field, after denying Theft

On the 31st. ult., Eliza Hancock, while gleaning in a field in the parish of Box, near Bath, was accused of stealing wheat from the sheaves, which she denied, and wished she might be struck dead if she had; she was found dead in the field in about two hours after.

The Stamford News
21 September 1810

Harvesting at 95

A singular event occurred in the wheat field of Mr. Avan of Tenterden on Monday se'nnight, when Thomas Collins, of the advanced age of 95, reaped in company with his son, William, aged 72, and his daughter, Sarah, aged 66, and whose united ages amounted to 233. It is equally remarkable that the father is free from the infirmities peculiar to old age; and in order to commemorate the event, he has lately been presented with a scythe with an appropriate inscription thereon.

The Stamford News
21 September 1810

Many Pints of Yorkshire Stingo

Died at the Ewes farm-house, Yorkshire, Mr. Paul Parnell, farmer and malster, aged 76, who during his life time drank out of one silver pint cup, upwards of £2,000 of Yorkshire stingo!

The Shrewsbury Chronicle
16 November 1810

Ominous Visit by Golden Eagle

On Saturday, Mr. Bonsey, of St. Sebastians, observed a Golden Eagle, which, coming from the North, lighted in a field belonging to Mrs. Eason, of Nash, near Margate; but whilst he went home for a gun to arrest its further progress, the royal bird had plumed his lofty pinions and soared majestically away, amidst a tremendous storm of wind to the southward, which vainly endeavoured to impede it in its stately course. The migration of the Eagle is thought by the natives of Thanet to be ominous, and to portend some extraordinary convulsion in the social world, and a battle byeween the hostile armies is confidently expected by our ancient seers, to have taken place in Portugal on the day of this bird's appearance on the shores of Thanet.

The Stamford News
2 November 1810

❁ *At this time the British Army was heavily engaged in Spain and Portugal (Peninsular War 1809–14) under the command of Sir Arthur Wellesley, later to become Duke of Wellington.*

1811

Tooth-extraction

Mr. Cradock, of Langtoft, Lincolnshire, contrary to the advice of a surgeon, had a double tooth extracted by a blacksmith with a pair of pincers, which occasioned a broken jaw, and ultimately his death.

The Shrewsbury Chronicle
19 April 1811

Motherly Devotion

A few days ago, in the parish of Stanton, in this county, a gentleman observed a crow daringly pounce upon a fine leveret, but could not rise with it more than 6 or 8 feet from the ground. The captive's shrieks were heard by the parent, and pursued over two fields, jumping several times at the crow, till the prize was dropped, which puss immediately carried away in her mouth.

The Shrewsbury Chronicle
3 May 1811

14 Days' Imprisonment for playing Football

At Gloucester Sessions . . . an apprentice was convicted of profanation of the Sabbath, by playing at foot-ball on Sunday evening; sentenced to 14 days' imprisonment.

The Shrewsbury Chronicle
3 May 1811

Kiss from Footpad

A footpad stopped the carriage of Mr. Morris, surgeon, on Hounslow Heath, on Thursday se'nnight and robbed Mr. Morris of two five pound notes. Two ladies in the carriage tremulously held forth their money, begging him to take it, but he gallantly refused, saying he would have a kiss-a-piece from them instead. It was, he said, the first and should be the last, robbery he ever committed. He was a stout, well-looking man and he had the accent of an Irishman.

The Shrewsbury Chronicle
2 August 1811

Tragedy at Gleaning-time

On Wednesday a poor woman who was gleaning at Chiddingley, Sussex, imprudently placed an infant, two years of age, on the ground, who, being covered over with a cloak, fell asleep. Just after, a waggon loaded with corn approached the spot on its way to a wheat rick; the boy who drove it, either not perceiving the child, or supposing it to be the bare garment, suffered the vehicle to pursue its fatal course, when the wheels passed over the little innocent and killed it on the spot.

The Shrewsbury Chronicle
30 August 1811

Tithe Lambs*

It was laid down by the Chief Justice, at the Sussex assizes on this subject, that lambs are weanable when they can thrive on the same food that the dam subsists on, and that the farmer is bound to treat the parson's lamb in the same manner as he treats his own. This doctrine gives the parson the right to the tenth fatted lamb, and establishes a criterion upon the subject of tithe-lambs which can never be the subject of litigation, insomuch as the time of tithing is rendered certain, and the farmer has in his option to wean his lambs or not.

The Shrewsbury Chronicle
6 September 1811

Clever Sow

A gentleman passing through Burslem a few days since, had his attention arrested by the agitation of an oak tree, from whence the acorns fell in showers. On approaching it, he observed eleven young pigs faring on the fruit, whilst the mother-sow which had ascended the tree, clung with her fore legs to an upper branch, and shook the lower with her left *hind leg*.

The Shrewsbury Chronicle
25 October 1811

Instead of Horses

A man who holds a small farm near St. Alban's, and who is ever looked upon as a most eccentric being, made an entry into that place a few days since, mounted on a small car, actually *drawn by four large hogs*! He entered the town at a brisk trot, amid the acclaimations of hundreds. After making the tour of the market-place three or four times, he came into the Wool-Pack yard and had his swinish cattle unharnessed, and taken into a stable where they were regaled with beans and mash. They remained about two hours in the town, during which time he despatched his business at the market, when they were driven home.

This man has only had these animals under training six months. A gentleman offered him £50 for the concern as it stood but was indignantly refused.

The Shrewsbury Chronicle
1 November 1811

Hare Superstition

A poor man was convicted before the magistrates at Lewes, in the penalty of £5, for shooting a hare. On saying he was unable to pay the fine, he was asked if he had any household furniture, to which he replied he had *six* small children, and that to satisfy the *longings* of a pregnant wife and to prevent the deformity of the child, he had ventured to trespass by shooting the hare!

The Shrewsbury Chronicle
8 November 1811

✦ *Unlike the first excuse—his wife's longing for special food during pregnancy—the poacher's second one needs some explanation. The reference to deformity concerned a common belief to the effect that if a pregnant woman's path was crossed by a hare she would give birth to a child with a hare-lip.*

Cruel Exhibition

A cruel exhibition took place at Boston on Wednesday se'nnight. In the middle of the day, a live rat, which had been rubbed over with spirits of turpentine, was turned into the street, and a blacksmith's boy then set fire to the animal, which in that state ran about to the entertainment of the *humane* spectators, until being literally roasted alive, it died of the torture.

The Shrewsbury Chronicle
15 November 1811

1812

Imprisoned for Poor Work

William Hill, labourer, was committed by George Chetwynd, Esq., on Wednesday, the 25th. ult., to the house of correction for one month, he having been employed by Mr. Gilpin, of Wedge's mill, near Cannock, to thrash some barley and having left a quantity of grain in the straw, or in other words, not having thrashed it clean.

The Staffordshire Advertiser
4 April 1812

An Eccentric Parson

The Rev. Favell Hopkins, of Huntingdon, died lately at the age of 87. Though possessed of considerable funded property, he almost denied himself the common necessaries of life, and had more the appearance of a wretched mendicant than a respected clergyman. Walking one Sunday morning to do duty at a parish church in Cambridgeshire, he saw in a field a scarecrow, and going up to the figure took off its hat, examined it, and then his own, when finding the advantage to be in favour of the former, he fairly exchanged the one for the other.

The Observer
7 June 1812

End of a Pauper

A Coroner's inquisition was taken on Monday last, at Osbournby, near Falkingham, on the body of a man named Thomas Page, who had died under circumstances of peculiar horror. The deceased was a pauper, belonging to the parish of Silk Willoughby, but not chusing to stay in the workhouse, he was in the habit of strolling about from town to town, subsisting upon the provision which he begged. It was his custom to deposit what he procured in this way beyond the immediate cravings of nature, within his shirt, next to his body; and having a considerable store of meat and bread so placed, he, in the earlier part of last week, it is supposed, feeling unwell, laid himself down in a field, in the parish of Scredington, to sleep. The meat, from the heat of the weather, and of the man's body, soon becoming putrid, was struck by flies, and in a short time the maggots which occasioned, not only preyed upon the inanimate pieces of flesh, but began literally to consume the living substance. Favoured by the drowsiness and sloth of the wretched man, these loathsome vermin made such havoc in his body that when, on Thursday, he was found by some persons who were accidently passing in the field, he presented a sight shocking and disgusting in the extreme. White maggots, of an enormous size, were crawling in and upon his body, and the removal of the outer ones only served to shew hundreds of others, which had penetrated so deeply that it was clear the very vitals of the miserable man were invaded by them. Page was conveyed to Osbournby, and a surgeon was immediately procured, who dressed the parts affected, but the sufferer died a few hours afterwards, his case being beyond the reach of human skill. The Jury, on a full hearing of these extraordinary circumstances, returned a verdict to the effect that the deceased was "eaten to death by maggots".

The Observer
5 July 1812

Women in Search of Food

On Monday last several women assembled at Knottingley Lock for the purpose of intercepting a vessel supposed to have been laden with corn; but being disappointed in their object, they went the following morning to Knottingley, where they were joined by about 300 of their own sex, and proceeding to the shops demanded bread meal at 3s. per stone, which being complied with, they immediately sent the bellman to cry it as selling at that price. A number of women were in consequence induced to go from Brotherton to obtain flour at the above reduction.

The Observer
16 August 1812

❀ *During these later years of war the price of corn and meal obtained in the orthodox way was extremely high, Britain having long been cut off from normal sources of supply overseas. Militant women in many other parts of the country were to follow the example of their Knottingley sisters in the ensuing years of the earlier part of the nineteenth century.*

Search for Mermaid

Mr. J. Toupin, while on a sailing expedition last week, with a party of ladies and gentlemen, about a mile from Exmouth Bay, discovered in the water an animal resembling the description given of the Mermaid. One of the boatmen threw it some pieces of boiled fish, which it took and ate with apparent relish, and which induced it to remain for some time within a short distance. A medical gentleman offered a reward of £20 for taking this extraordinary animal; in consequence of which all the fishermen in the vicinity are busily preparing to ensnare it.

The Observer
30 August 1812

Farmer blows up Blacksmith's House

Yesterday se'nnight a Mr. Woodley, a farmer at Loynton, having purchased a quantity of gunpowder at Ashburton, took it in a bag to the shop of Mr. Chalk, a blacksmith, and while waiting for his horse, untied the mouth of the bag to put in a stone for the purpose of ballancing the weight; a spark of fire from the anvil communicating with the powder, it blew up the house and another adjoining. Chalk, his apprentice and three children were buried in the ruins, but were dug out without sustaining any material injury. Woodley had an arm broken. The shock was felt throughout the town.

The Observer
27 December 1812

From Rags to Riches

A person by the name of Baldock, who died lately at Canterbury, exhibited an instance of the accumulation of wealth from very small beginnings, in fact from nothing. He died at the age of little more than sixty, possessed of one million and one hundred thousand pounds. He was originally a poor boy employed to look after cows, and remarkable for dirtiness and slovenliness. He afterwards carried the hod as a bricklayer's labourer, and, at length, by dint of industry and parsimony, with some assistance, he amassed money enough to build the barracks at Canterbury, which he let to Government at the rate of 6d per week for each soldier, a practice which proved so profitable to him that in the course of a few years the whole building became his own, and continued to acquire wealth in various ways, till at the time of his death it amounted to the enormous sum stated above.

The Observer
27 December 1812

1813

Attack on Royal Gamekeepers

On Monday evening last between eight and nine o'clock, a most daring attack was made on two of his Majesty's gamekeepers, by five poachers, who were discovered in a plantation of Windsor Great Park, in the act of shooting the pheasant. These men were all armed with fire-arms and bludgeons, and some with long poles of a peculiar construction, with which they are accustomed to discharge the spring guns which are set in their way. By this unequal force the gamekeepers were overpowered, although they manfully fought with the pikes they usually carry when they expect a conflict, and inflicted many severe wounds on their opponents. One of the gamekeepers was so dreadfully beaten that his life is in the utmost danger from the severe blows he received on his head, with the butt-end of a gun, till it was shattered from the barrel, and the lock broken in pieces. One of the offenders is in custody, and a reward of £50 is offered for the apprehension of two others who have escaped.

Bell's Weekly Messenger
21 February 1813

The Cow and her Pigs*

Mr. Thomas Ade, a prosperous yeoman farmer of Milton, near Lewes, has a cow that having her calf taken from her about six weeks ago, seduced two very young pigs from a farrow of six, which, with the sow, were running in the same close, and has ever since suckled and nurtured them as her own, and is now so excessively fond of them that under a temporary separation, a few days since, she betrayed the strongest symptoms of uneasiness, bellowed incessantly and actually leaped a high hedge to recover her little grunting charges. The pigs are equally fond of the cow and on her milk they thrive rapidly.

Bell's Weekly Messenger
2 May 1813

Gigantic Gooseberry

A gooseberry was gathered in the garden of Thomas Tebbit, a gardener of Soham, at the beginning of August, which measured $4\frac{1}{2}$ inches in circumference.

The Cambridge Chronicle and Journal
27 August 1813

Boxing*

A boxing match of two hours duration, and in which 87 severe rounds took place, was fought in Bornham Meadows, a short distance from Gerrards'-cross, on Monday last, between Mr. Gabriel Jenner, a dealer in cattle, and a farmer, of the name of Gatton, for 10 guineas a side. It was a pitched battle, the stakes having been made a fortnight before. The dispute originated in an affair of jealousy, each courting a young widow in their neighbourhood. The combatants were complete novices in the art of boxing, never having even seen a fight. There were no easy falls, nor avoiding blows by judging distance. They met each other with native characteristic bravery, and used all the power nature had afforded them in hitting and throwing. In some rounds eight and ten crushing half-round blows were made, and in ten minutes after setting-to they were hideously beaten. Two and three minutes were sometimes spent between the rounds, from the inability of both to stand up, and in this state the combatants contended the last half-hour, but Jenner was unable to move, and Gatton won dearly.

Bell's Weekly Messenger
5 September 1813

Dog v. Goose*

Mr. John Little, at Nichol Forest, in this county, had a goose, which he kept, for the purpose of breeding, 33 years and which regularly brought up two broods of goslings each year. But a few days ago, a little dog, which like other *puppies*, was not too respectful to his seniors, wishing to play his pranks with one of her beloved goslings, was fiercely assailed by the ancient mother; but unfortunately, after a violent combat, the teeth of the canine brute proved too sharp for the beak and pinions of the hissing animal, which was stretched on the field of combat, leaving motherless a numerous progeny.

The Carlisle Journal
13 November 1813

1814

Eccentric Character deceased*

J. Mulford, Esq., whose death at Basinstoke, in the 94th. year of his age, was stated in our last paper, was a gentleman remarkable for several eccentricities. In his early days he associated for some time with the gipsy tribe. When his conduct assumed a more sober complexion, he resided in different places as a respectable gentleman, attracting notice by the peculiarity and even splendour of his dress. He afterwards professed an attention to the duties of a religious life, and built two chapels, with dwelling-houses for the ministers, at his own expence. Although he showed great generosity to others, his own expenditure in his kitchen, parlour, or wardrobe, was of the most frugal kind. His manner of life was somewhat in the hermit style. It need scarcely be said that he never entered into the matrimonial state. As to his family and its antiquity, Mr.

Mulford once said "My arms were three moles and three molehills, and my great ancestor was mole-catcher to William the Conqueror". About a year before his death Mr. Mulford found out that heads were never designed to fall beneath the tonsor's razor, and therefore his own chin was indulged with the venerable luxury of a long beard, which completed the costume of a patriarch. It was his wish for many years to leave the world suddenly, if it pleased God, that he might not occasion much trouble to any attendant. In this respect his wish was gratified. He died in his chair, in his parlour, across which he had walked several times, without pain, a few hours before his departure, having looked out of the window, and observed what a fine day it was for gossiping people to go about and say "Old Mulford is dead!" It is said that he left behind him £20,000, a considerable part of which is bequeathed to some poor relation, nor had he forgot the two chapels which he erected. While his death is gain to many, it will be a loss to many more, who will miss his frequent acts of benevolence, particularly the poor in his own neighbourhood.

The Hampshire Courier
31 January 1814

French Soldier killed at Lymington

Portsmouth
A serious affray took place at Lymington on Thursday night last. A party of sailors from the Swallow cutter then in port, proceeded to a house for the purpose of passing the evening with a few females; unfortunately the objects of their visit were found to be in the company of the same number of French soldiers. Indignant at being thus foiled in their pursuits and rendered more so by the idea that the cause was Frenchmen, the sailors proceeded to attempt dislodging their rivals, which being resisted, a most serious encounter took place, and we are sorry to add terminated in the death of one Frenchman, and two others very dangerously wounded. The seamen are in custody to answer for the offence. The resolution shown by them in the attack would have reflected great credit on our brave tars in a better cause.

The Hampshire Courier
31 January 1814

❀ *The soldiers were prisoners of war, for Napoleon was still Emperor of France, and continued to be so until he abdicated in April 1814. In the following year peace was restored by the Treaty of Paris. War broke out again when Napoleon escaped from Elba and returned to France in March 1815.*

Throwing at Cocks

All our readers, whose breasts are not utterly inaccessible to every just feeling of humanity towards the inferior creation, will rejoice to hear that the Magistrates of this County have determined to suppress the BASE AND BRUTAL CUSTOM of throwing at Game Cocks on Shrove Tuesday. We earnestly hope that the Magistrates of other Counties will follow so commendable an example by exerting their authority to prevent at once this cruel oppression of the brutish, and this shocking degradation of the human species.

The Warwick and Warwickshire Advertiser
19 February 1814

❀ *For this Shrove Tuesday 'game' the cock was tied to a stake and the competitors threw their missiles at it from a distance of twenty yards. 'Play' only ceased when the cock was killed. In some areas broomsticks were thrown at the bird. In Cornwall the victim was often a hen, rather than a cock. Hens which had not laid an egg by Shrove Tuesday were thrashed to death by flails, the contestants each aiming a blow at the bird in rotation. The man whose blow finally killed the hen received it as his prize.*

Supposed Murder*

A human skeleton has been dug up at Hursley, near this City, with a knife, the handle of which is mouldered to dust, sticking in its side. There are various conjectures respecting the circumstances, but nothing to lead to a discovery of the truth. An old person at Hursley says that nearly seventy years ago a young man, a butcher at that place, came to this City, and was known to have returned homeward from there, but was never after heard of; therefore it is generally believed he was murdered, and people are inclined to think that the skeleton now discovered is the remains of this unfortunate young man, who must have been buried by the murderers with the bloody knife sticking in his side.

The Hampshire Courier
21 February 1814

❀ *'This City' referred to in the above report was Winchester. Hursley is four miles from Winchester.*

Remarkable Circumstance*

Sunday week, the passengers from the Highflyer Coach observed a jack-ass worrying a sheep in a field at Dringhouses, near York. Had not the voracious animal been caught in the act, it would have been attributed to a dog.

The Carlisle Journal
2 April 1814

Wife sold at Hailsham Market

Hailsham Market last week presented a novelty which, though disgraceful to society, produced much merriment. A labouring man, of Westham, led his wife, a decently-dressed woman, into the market in a halter, and there exhibited her for sale, in which situation, however, he had not long placed her, before a tradesman of a neighbouring parish stepped up and bargained for her at five shillings! She was accordingly delivered, and her purchaser, after being offered seven shillings in advance for his bargain, took her off in triumph, amid the congratulations of a great number of spectators.

The Hampshire Courier
31 October 1814

A Comical Signboard*

Upon the door of a house occupied by a father and son, the former a blacksmith and publican, the latter a barber, near Bridgewater, in Somersetshire, is a board expressing as follows:

Burness and Son, blacksmith and barber's work done here, horse shoing and shaving; locks mended and hare curling, bleeding, teeth-drawing, and all other furriery work. All sorts of spiratus lickers according to the late comical treaty. Take notis my wife keeps skool, teaches reading and riting and all other langwitches; and has assistants if required to teach horitory, sowing an mathematics, and all other fashionable diversions.

The Coventry Mercury
14 November 1814

Herculean Feat

A few days since, as Mr. John Graham, a young man, shoemaker, resident in Walton, was at work, he espied a full-grown fox, deliberately walking up the road that leads through the above village; Graham immediately ran downstairs after Reynard, who instantly betaking himself to flight, was followed by this modern Hercules, and although encumbered with a pair of clogs, his apron, and other appendages, after a desperate race, for several minutes over hedges and ditches, during which he turned the animal several times, he succeeded in catching him and, seizing him by the neck, held him up to his astonished companions. In passing through the village, the fox leapt the wall of the churchyard, a height of six feet, without touching it, and was instantly followed by his athletic pursuer. Reynard was afterwards taken to Walton House, where he now remains.

The Carlisle Journal
3 December 1814

1815

Burial-place of Ancient Warriors

Last week, as some workmen were removing two large mounds of earth on Arreton Down, they discovered a number of human bones; on digging further they found a skeleton of a man complete, with an arrow through the back, and several others nearly whole. They are removed to the bone-house at Arreton Church, and may be seen there. Many people from Newport visited the Down, and the curious have preserved several articles, such as coins, a dagger and part of a pick axe. It is supposed to be the burying place of some ancient warriors, who fell in battle, perhaps on the very spot.

The Hampshire Courier
17 April 1815

❀ *Arreton is near Newport, Isle of Wight.*

May Day Celebrations

We have seldom witnessed a more pleasing scene among the rural revelry in this neighbourhood than that which took place at Cheriton, a village near here (Alresford), on the joyful anniversary of Maia† on Monday the 1st. inst. To heighten the effect and preserve a remembrance of the fascinating amusements which took place on the occasion, a May Pole was erected, about 70 feet high, and it had a very grand and pleasing appearance. After this was done, the youthful sons and daughters of the Goddess repaired to a commodious bower, erected near, with green boughs and tastefully ornamented with garlands and wreaths of flowers, where about 50 couples 'tripped the light fantastic toe' till night spread her sable vest over the hemisphere and warned them to depart. The next day (Tuesday) exhibited a re-assemblage of the gladdened villagers, the mirthful scene if possible far exceeded that of the preceding day, and the company were more numerous. Dancing was kept up with spirit to a late hour, and they separated with utmost unanimity and good humour, with the national air of "God Save the King". Many highly respected farmers were observed among the Assembly.

The Hampshire Courier
8 May 1815

† *The Romans sacrificed to Maia, the Mother of Mercury, on this day, whence the month derives its name.*

Death of Martha Gun

Died on Monday night, at Brighton, in the 89th. year of her age, after an illness of several months, that celebrated character, Martha Gun; her remains will be interred in the church-yard of that parish tomorrow afternoon; her numerous relations and bathing friends will follow them to the grave.

The Hampshire Courier
8 May 1815

❂ *Martha Gun—the name is more generally spelt as Gunn—was famed as a bathing-machine attendant, who 'ducked' many famous personages as they entered the water. These included George IV in his years as Prince Regent. Her weatherbeaten features are said to be remembered on Toby Jugs, which nowadays are collectors' pieces.*

Victory!

The inhabitants of Ashford manifested the pleasure they experienced on the receipt of the news of the surrender of Buonaparte, to Capt. Maitland, of the Bellerophone, by peals from the church bells, continued throughout the whole day, testifying a general joy at the very great acquisition to the general cause of Europe by the above event.

On Sunday last a very appropriate and patriotic sermon was delivered in Ashford Church by the Rev. J. Nance, D.D., from Jeremiah 49 chap. 11 verse,† after which a collection was made at the church door, which we have the pleasure to state amounted to the sum of £86. 9s. 6d., in aid of the fund for the relief of the families of our brave countrymen who suffered at the glorious battle of Waterloo.

The Kentish Gazette
28 July 1815

† *'Leave thy fatherless children, I will preserve them alive; and let thy widows trust in me.'*

❀ *The battle of Waterloo, in which Napoleon was finally defeated by the Allies, had taken place on 18 June 1815. The news was taken from the coast to London by messengers who travelled in coaches festooned with laurels.*

'Died by the Visitation of God'

Richard Richardson, who, as we stated in our last, was found dead on the downs, in the parish of Alceston, was supposed to have fallen a sacrifice to fatigue and want. He was in the habit of going every morning to the distance of four miles from home to work at 12s. per week. On the fatal day he got up at his usual hour and was about to start for his destination without taking any victuals with him, for all the food he possessed in the world consisted only of a three-penny loaf, and which he would fain have left for his family, as it was the only article of subsistence in the house, and he had no money or credit, and had been refused, as we understand, parochial support, when his wife, by repeated solicitations, induced him, though most reluctantly, to accept the loaf, with which he at length departed. On his return at night, it is supposed he sunk exhausted, as he was found lifeless on the downs, with the loaf, almost untouched, in his bag, intending no doubt to restore it to his half-starved wife and six children. The verdict returned was—Died by the visitation of God.

The Hampshire Courier
28 August 1815

Walter Scott at Waterloo

On Thursday last, Walter Scott, Esq., arrived at the hospitable mansion of J.B.S. Morritt, Esq., M.P., of Rokeby Park, Yorkshire, on his return from the plains of Waterloo. He has minutely inspected every part of that hallowed ground, preparatory to the publication of a Poem on the subject. He has brought off several of the trophies of the memorable 18th. of June, with which the plains are still plentifully strewed.

The Kentish Gazette
6 October 1815

❀ *Mr Scott is remembered today as Sir Walter Scott, author of the Waverley Novels, but he did not receive his baronetcy until 1820. His visit to France resulted in his poem 'The Field of Waterloo', published very soon after he got home. It was written as a means of raising money for the families of soldiers killed at Waterloo.*

Napoleon's Coach landed at Dover

Canterbury
The singular spectacle of Buonaparte's travelling carriage and horses taken at Charleroi, after the battle of Waterloo, yesterday forenoon attracted the attention of the inhabitants in its passing through this city from Dover, where it was landed on Sunday, out of the Chichester packet from Calais. It was drawn by four stallions and guided by the coachman, mounted on the near wheel horse, in the perfect French style. It conveyed the Prussian officer by whom it was captured, and a lady; and is, it is said, intended as a present to the Prince Regent.

The Kentish Gazette
24 October 1815

1816

Distresses in Staffordshire*

Sir,
    Your most obliging favour of the 8th. instant came safely to hand, enclosing £10 from a friend at Broxbourne. Should I acknowledge this in *The Times*?

I am sorry the Association does not go on better: why will they be so silly as to dispute, while our countrymen are starving? I rejoice to inform you, Sir, that while many are only *talking* about relieving the distresses of the county, other people are actually doing great and benevolent work: I received £50 by the post of today.

I yesterday called at *one hundred and twelve* cottages. I wish, Sir, you could have accompanied me. It was an affecting sight to me to witness so much misery. I could not, indeed, have borne it, had it not been for the prospect of affording my poor neighbours some relief—that relief, through your kindness, has been given. I found some families in a state of most consummate wretchedness; one especially, in a *hovel*, for *cottage* I cannot call it, in a most dreadful condition; the father was on a miserable bed with his thigh and arm broken; he belongs to no club, or benevolent society, has only a small pittance (half a crown a week) to sustain himself, his wife and three children. He said his poor limbs were getting better, but he was almost lost for want; he did not eat much he said, for fear the children should be starved. I crept back last night, after dusk, lest I should excite too much jealousy among the neighbours, and carried him two loaves and a little money; nor shall it be the last visit I will pay to that family. I could easily enlarge, but I spare you. I would fain, Sir, be a voice for the country, and send you testimonies of the most heartfelt gratitude.

Perhaps, if it be not too much trouble, you would get the Editor of *The Times* to acknowledge the following sum:—

TS, a little boy, who on hearing that a gentleman had sent £5 from London to buy mutton, promptly and voluntarily said then I will give £1 to buy potatoes. . .

Again, Sir, receive our best thanks. I am, dear Sir,
Respectfully and gratefully Yours,

> B. H. Draper
> Summer-hill, near Bilston,
> Staffordshire
> August 10, 1816.

The Times
13 August 1816

❀ *The poor in Britain were now in a state of acute distress. A great many of the thousands of soldiers demobilized at the end of the war had returned home, but there were no jobs for them. The agricultural interests had closed the ports against the importing of foreign corn under the Corn Law (1815) that prevented the landing of foreign corn until the price of home-grown corn was at the very high figure of 80 shillings per quarter. In the years that immediately followed conditions were made even worse by a succession of bad harvests.*

Singular Custom*

On Whitsunday, at St. Briavel's in Gloucestershire, several baskets full of bread and cheese, cut into small squares of about an inch each, are brought into the church, and immediately after divine service is ended, the churchwardens, or some other persons, take them into the galleries, where their contents are thrown amongst the congregation, who have a great scramble for them in the body of the church. This occasions as great a tumult and uproar as the amusements of a village wake, the inhabitants being always extremely anxious to attend worship on this day. The custom is holden for the purpose of preserving to the poor of St. Briavel's and Hervelsfield, the right of cutting and carrying away wood from 3,000 acres of coppice land, in Hudknolls and the Meendi, and for which every housekeeper is assessed 2d. to buy the bread and cheese which are given away.

The Times
7 October 1816

❀ *This custom has been observed at St Briavel's, in the Forest of Dean, since the twelfth century, when the Earl of Hereford was Lord High Constable of the forest. He had stopped the villagers from taking wood from the forest and only agreed to rescind the ban at the plea of his wife. As a mark of gratitude for the restoration of their privileges, each householder agreed to subscribe a penny every year for a distribution of bread and cheese to the poor on Whit Sunday after Mass.*

The scrambling in church continued for a further forty years after 1816. In 1857, however, it was thought that an outdoor ceremony would be more seemly; from then until recent years the recipients assembled in the churchyard and the bread and cheese was thrown down to them from the church tower.

The custom is still observed in these days of space flights. Nowadays, however, the distribution is made by the road outside the church, after Evensong on Whit Sunday. Surely this is one of the very oldest of customs of this kind in the country—covering an unbroken period of well over eight hundred years. It has always been the belief that, like hot-cross buns, bread and cheese from the St Briavel's distribution will never go mouldy. Local people carry it around as a charm against ill-fortune.

Terrible Journey for Smallpox Victim

On Saturday se'nnight an inquest was held at the House of Industry, Tewkesbury, on view of the body of Richard Godsall, a labourer, belonging to the parish of Powick, in the county of Worcester, who died there the previous evening, of that most dreadful malady, the confluent small pox. From the testimony of the widow of this poor, unfortunate and neglected man, it appeared that he was taken ill at Badgworth, where he had been in employ a considerable time, on the Wednesday se'nnight preceding; and that on the following Sunday application was made, on his behalf, to the parish officers, assembled in the churchyard, after divine service, from the behaviour of whom he was induced immediately to quit the place, and proceed on his way to his own home. From the advanced state of the disorder, however, he could only reach the neighbourhood of Churchdown that evening, where he and his wife lay in a desolate barn, without necessary sustenance, and without more clothes than his usual labouring dress. On the Monday he. with great difficulty reached the hamlet of Twigworth, in the parish of St. Mary de Lode, Glocester, where he could proceed no further, and applied to the overseer for relief, who put him into the hay-loft, where he lied all night among the hay and straw, without sheet or blanket, or covering of any kind save his own clothes. The disorder had now made such a rapid progress in his constitution that in the morning he exhibited a sad spectacle of human misery, totally blind, and so weak and emaciated that he was unable to stand. The overseer, notwithstanding, got him lifted into a cart and ordered him to be conveyed through several intervening parishes to Tewkesbury and there left. To save him from the jolting of the cart, his wife supported him in her arms the whole way, and when they arrived at Tewkesbury, the wretched state of the poor sufferer exceeded all description. He was immediately conveyed to the House of Industry, where the best medical aid and every solacing effort were promptly resorted to, but all was too late to save him, and he languished in increasing affliction until Friday morning. The Jury, after a minute investigation, returned a verdict "That the deceased being violently ill of the smallpox at Twigworth was removed from thence to Tewkesbury on the 29th. ult. and died of the said disease on the 1st. instant, and that his death was greatly accelerated and hastened by such removal".

The Cambridge Chronicle
15 November 1816

❖ *This unfortunate man was sent back to his home district under the* Poor Law *directive referred to in connection with the* Ipswich Journal *report of 18 February 1769.*

The parish officers at Badgworth were probably quite justified according to law *in sending him away from their village despite his serious condition. He was not one of their settled parishioners, and therefore must be considered the responsibility of the place to which they thought he really belonged.*

Unusual Friends

The circumstance of a hare, when a leveret, having taken refuge in the garden of a cottage at Sutton Cheney, in Leicestershire, in which it has ever since been domesticated, and is now grown grey in its security, calls to recollection a still more extraordinary fact. The present Margravine of Anspach, when Countess of Craven, had a young cub at Coombe -abbey which was reared in the kennel with Lord Craven's then crack pack of hounds. This sagacious animal was frequently taken out for her Ladyship's amusement, who was at that period partial to the sports of the field; reynard always left the kennel mounted behind the huntsman and, when turned out, afforded his canine friends an active chase, but when they came pretty near to his brush, he immediately turned round, and passing through the pack, leaped up again behind the huntsman and thus returned home. One day, however, whilst enjoying their customary amusement during the season, the poor fox was unfortunately run upon by a strange pack, who instantly killed the animal. The regret of her Ladyship and the whole of the hunt may more easily be imagined than described.

The Cambridge Chronicle
15 November 1816

Battle in Turnip Field

A banditti of turnip stealers, 40 in number, attacked and cruelly beat, on the 13th. inst., the four sons of Mr. Symes, a farmer of Yeovil, Somersetshire, who, with five others, were stationed to protect a turnip field from their depredations. The captain of the gang gave the word "Close your files, attack, attack", but although two of the farmer's party were so much beaten that their lives are in danger, they succeeded in repelling the plunderers and securing three of them, who were committed to Ilchester gaol for trial.

The Times
24 December 1816

1817

Wonderful Dream*

Thomas Page, a carpenter residing at Ewell, near Dover, having dreamed there was a large sum of money buried on the hill opposite River, above the lime-kiln which belongs to the Old Park and is the property of —— Every, Esq., Page applied for and obtained liberty to dig for the hidden property and set out on Monday last the 20th. January with several other persons under his direction; the spot being pointed out by Page, they commenced their labour, and after being at work a short time they found a scull and a canteen which were nearly decayed, when Page directed the people to dig a little more to the right and they would find a pot, which was done, and also another with a belt and breastplate; the two vessels have the appearance of large copper boilers, and are of very ancient make, they contained a quantity of old coins of gold, copper and other metals, some of them dated 117. This is supposed to be a miracle by the people residing in that neighbourhood, as Page could not have obtained any information from history, he being unable to read or write.

The Kentish Chronicle
28 January 1817

The account we gave on Tuesday last of Thomas Page, a carpenter at Ewell near Dover having found a quantity of old coins in consequence of his having dreamed that some treasure was hid on the hill opposite River, has induced a correspondent to furnish us with an account of the same man having had a similar dream nearly two years ago, when he searched at the same spot and found several silver ornaments, apparently Roman, and which it seems probably belonged to the belt of some warrior. We have seen these ornaments which are in fine preservation and they are inlaid with thin gold and some stones are set in one of them. The following memorandum was made by the Lady who now has the ornaments, at the time they came into her possession, which was shortly after they were found:

> Page, a journeyman carpenter, living at Ewell, near Dover, dreamed that if he dug up the ground at a certain place exactly pointed out in his dream, he should find great treasure, he accordingly in the morning proceeded to the spot, and with his knife only dug up these ornaments.

The place at which they were found is on the side of a hill, a little to the left of the turnpike road leading from Canterbury to Dover, about two miles from the latter place, and just by the corner of the road leading to Sandwich. It is reported that other persons in digging afterwards, in hopes of finding further treasures, discovered some human bones. April 1815.

The Kentish Chronicle
4 February 1817

Happy Pigs

On Monday last a party set out in a coach from Deal to spend the day in Waldershare Park, and instead of going to the Inn as most visitors do, they provided themselves with provisions, wines, spirits and porter, and when they alighted at the Park-gate, these refreshments were hid in a large amount of nettles, where it was supposed they would remain in safety. This, however, was not the case, for the party after taking a lounge in the Park found that some thieves, in the swinish shape, had arrived from the adjoining Farm-yard, and had devoured the whole of the eatables, and having broken the bottles, had drunk the liquors etc. and were ranging about in a state of intoxication; the looker in the Park was alarmed at the appearance of the animals and suspecting that they were seized with a complaint called the staggerbone, he immediately sent to Eythorne for a farrier, before whose arrival, however, the cause of their extraordinary appearance was discovered. The chagrin of the party at the loss of their refreshments may be more easily conceived than expressed.

The Kentish Chronicle
25 July 1817

Harvesting Woman causes Rick Fire

On Tuesday se'nnight the corn ricks of Mr. Neville of Whittington, near Lichfield, were set on fire, through an old harvesting woman smoking her pipe in the rick yard and thrusting it into the straw. Great damage would have ensued, except for the exertion of one Jervis, at great risk to himself. The loss sustained is calculated at £260.

The Nottingham Journal
4 October 1817

Attempt at Seduction*

A trial of a novel description of a countryman for attempting to seduce a servant-girl from the paths of virtue, took place at a public house at Upstreet a few days since, before an impartial jury of villagers there assembled: When after a most patient investigation of the case, the countryman was found guilty and sentenced to be hanged by the heels to the beam of the room for the space of twenty minutes, and to drink four pints of strong onion broth; two pints previous to, and the remaining two at the time of suspension. The delinquent on hearing the verdict endeavoured to make his escape and made great resistance at the sentence being carried out, but the honest rustics were not to be frustrated from showing their indignation at the heinousness of the crime, and immediately carried the same into execution, to the no small amusement and gratification of the Company present.

The Kentish Chronicle
9 December 1817

1818

Children sold by Auction

In a certain Borough town in the North of this county, the poor children who are bound as parish apprentices are actually put up for auction, and knocked down to the best bidder. At one of these sales lately, a fine hardy boy was bought for five pounds, while another less-favoured brought only five shillings. This mode is adopted to prevent the inconveniences that arise from distributing the children by lot, and to raise money by the sale.

The West Briton and Cornwall Advertiser
9 January 1818

Gamekeeper forced to spring Traps

On Wednesday, a gang of poachers, to the number of fifteen, knocked up the keeper of Mr. Lucas, of Filby, Norfolk, and seizing him insisted upon his accompanying them to the covers and springing the guns and traps before them. They were armed with guns and cutlasses. On the same night a gang of nine men also paid a visit to the woods of Cossey, and began to fire very near the house even before the family were in bed.

The County Chronicle
20 January 1818

❀ *Several barbaric man-traps and spring guns set to catch poachers can be seen nowadays in a public-house not far from Filby. It is the Gin Trap Inn at Ringstead, whose exhibits also include many animal traps as well as farm implements of earlier days. A great many of these antiques came from people living near by, who unearthed them from farm buildings and outhouses when the landlord told them of his plans to start his collection.*

Rider in the Sky

The following story has appeared in several papers:

Some months ago a very singular appearance presented itself in the sky to several persons at Hartfordbridge, near Basingstoke. About noon was distinctly seen by many persons, without any difference among them as to the form of the figures in the clouds, a man on horseback riding at full speed, pursued by an eagle, which soon darted upon his head, when he lost hold of the reins, fell backward, and eagle, horse and man were seen no more. The figures were apparently of the natural size.

The County Chronicle
10 February 1818

Honourable Badge of Distinction

The parish officers of Downham, near Ely, have come to a determination to furnish all such of their labourers as support themselves and families without parochial relief, with a good white hat. Upwards of 50 have already applied for and received this honourable badge of distinction, and seem highly proud of it, styling themselves "independent labourers".

The County Chronicle
17 February 1818

To keep away Foxes ...

Although but little known, it is pronounced a fact that a little tar, rubbed on the necks of young lambs, or geese, will prevent the depredations of foxes upon them, who have an unconquerable aversion to the smell of tar.

The County Chronicle
24 March 1818

Sermon for Dumb Animals

The late Thomas Ingram, Esq., of Ticknell, in Worcestershire, has left by his will £600, the interest of which is directed to be applied to the payment of a clergyman who shall annually preach, in Birmingham, a sermon to encourage and enforce humane treatment towards all dumb animals, particularly to horses.

The County Chronicle
21 July 1818

Dreadful Catastrophe*

On Saturday as three boys were playing in a field near Bennington, Herts, where some cows were feeding, one of them about 16 years of age, proposed to tie one of the others to a cow's tail, which, with the assistance of his remaining companion, he unfortunately accomplished, and, horrid to relate, the poor boy soon fell a victim to the barbarous whim of his associates, for the enraged animal dragged him up and down the field at full speed, plunging in all directions, and before he could be extricated from his perilous situation, life was totally extinct. His corpse was soon after taken home, and a coroner's inquest taken on view of the body on the Monday.

The County Chronicle
18 August 1818

1819

At Loggerheads?

In a village in Staffordshire, not a hundred miles from L—g—h, on examining the parish accounts the following curiosities appeared. One of the Overseers had made *sixty-three weeks* in the year; an item in the other Overseer's account was for a sum of money paid in aid of the *County Rats*; this caused a great deal of laughter, in which none joined more heartily than the Constable, who immediately afterwards produced an account which was a charge for holding a *conquest* over a man found dead.

The Leeds Mercury
6 February 1819

Man traps*

Lord Ilchester's gamekeeper was killed by a spring gun on the 6th. instant at Redlynch, Somerset, having trodden on the wire while setting it himself.

The York Chronicle
25 February 1819

Trial of Strength

An extraordinary trial of strength took place at Godalming, Surrey, on Tuesday morning, the 23rd. ult. A man named William Giles, aged 50, for a wager of 2s. only, undertook to carry a sack of flour, weighing 285 lbs., the distance of a mile without resting. This he actually accomplished, taking up his load at Eshing Mill, in the above parish, and carrying it up a steep hill, rendered slippery by the snow which had fallen just before, over a stile and a gate, and returning by the high road to the mill again. Giles effected his task with so much ease that he offered to repeat the wager within an hour after he had set down the load, but the spectators were so well satisfied with his prowess that no one could be found to accept the challenge.

The County Chronicle
9 March 1819

The Velocipede

The new machine, entitled a Velocipede, consisting of two wheels, one before the other, connected by a perch, on which the pedestrian rests the weight of his body, while with his feet he urges the machine forward, on the principle of skating, is already in very general use. The road from Ipswich to Whitton, says the Bury paper, "is travelled every evening by several pedestrian hobby-horses; no less than six are seen at a time, and the distance, which is three miles, is performed in 15 minutes. A military gentleman has made a bet to go to London by the side of the Coach.... It is said the present Velocipede will soon be superseded by one making by an ingenious person of Yarmouth, after the manner of the razor-grinding wheel—to be worked by a treadle for both feet. If it succeeds, it is expected it will move at the rapid rate of 12 miles an hour!"

The County Chronicle
23 March 1819

New Appointment to Haworth

We hear that the Rev. P. Bronte, curate of Thornton, has been nominated by the Vicar of Bradford, to the valuable Perpetual Curacy of Haworth, vacant by the death of the Rev. James Charnock; but that the inhabitants of the chapelry intend to resist the presentation, and have entered a caveat at York accordingly.

The York Chronicle
17 June 1819

❀ *As all the world knows, resistance to Mr Brontë's appointment to Haworth was not successful. He and his wife moved there in February 1820, with Charlotte (b.1816), Emily (b.1818) and Branwell (b.1817). Sister Anne was born in 1820; their mother died a year afterwards.*

  The value of Mr Brontë's appointment was £200 a year and the parsonage.

The King's Birthday—Celebrations at Bexhill

The King's birthday was celebrated this year at Bexhill (the male population of which place does not exceed 800, and it is supposed not to be equalled in England for its number of aged persons) on the Sussex coast, in an appropriate and pleasing manner. Considering the venerable age of our beloved Sovereign, 25 old men, inhabitants of that parish, whose united ages amounted to 2025, averaging 81 each, the age of the

King, dined together at the Bell Inn; and passed the day very cheerfully and happy. The dinner was set on table by 15 other old men, also of the above parish, whose united ages amounted to 71 each; and ten others whose ages amounted to 61 each, rang the bells on the occasion. The old men dined at one o'clock; and at half past two a public dinner was served up to the greater part of the respectable inhabitants to the number of 81, who were also the subscribers to the old men's dinner. The assembly room was decorated with several appropriate devices; and some of the old men, with the greater part of the loyal company, enjoyed themselves to a late hour.

The York Chronicle
24 June 1819

❁ *Bexhill was celebrating the 81st birthday of George III, who had reigned for almost sixty years. Although his subjects there enjoyed a happy day, the King himself was shut away at Windsor, insane, deaf and blind: for the last eight years his eldest son had been Prince Regent. These were the last birthday celebrations for George III—he was to die in January of the following year.*

Because of its climate, which gave it so many aged persons in 1819 Bexhill is to-day one of the most popular retirement towns on the South Coast. The population is now 35,000. And the 'Bell Inn' is still there, as the Bell Hotel.

Singular Voracity*

On Monday last, Thomas Tims, of Bletchington, Oxfordshire, for a trifling wager, undertook to devour a hedgehog, fried in bacon fat, for his breakfast, a rat, fried in candle fat, for his dinner, and a carrion crow, fried in train oil, for his supper, which the gormandizer accomplished to the gratification of his companions and to the disgust and astonishment of his more fastidious neighbours.

The County Chronicle
23 November 1819

1820-29

THE STATUTE FAIR
Here farm and domestic servants were engaged for the coming year.

1820

A Curious Occurrence

On Tuesday the 21st. ult. (St. Thomas's Day), as usual a stag was turned out from Blenheim Park, the property of the Duke of Marlborough. It directed its course towards Wickham, and from thence it took the high road and proceeded to Oxford; and then formed one of the most beautiful and picturesque sights that can be imagined. The stag and dogs, in close pursuit, followed by a great number of well-known and experienced sportsmen, proceeded up the High Street, as far as Brasenose College, when, to the no small astonishment of hundreds of spectators, the stag took refuge in the chapel, during divine service, where it was killed, sans ceremonie, by the eager dogs.

The County Chronicle
18 January 1820

John Clare

A Northamptonshire peasant, named John Clare, has lately published a volume of poems which evince considerable poetic talent. The Marquis of Exeter has granted him an annuity of £15 per annum, and other friends of rising genius have taken him by the hand, and by their bounty rendered him comfortable for life.

The County Chronicle
7 March 1820

❀ *The book referred to was John Clare's* Poems Descriptive of Rural Life and Scenery. *Clare was born at Helpstone, near Peterborough, in 1793, the son of a labourer. Although not in the first rank of English poets, he more than justified the confidence of the Marquess of Exeter and his other patrons, whose combined help brought him £45 a year. He was a true poet of the countryside.*

Gleaning*

The Magistrates for Beccles division, Suffolk, have officially published the following regulations respecting gleaning: No gleaning to be allowed before eight, nor after seven; no field to be entered until cleared; no preference to be given to the families of the reapers. The orders conclude by a request that the Clergy will notice them in their churches.

The County Chronicle
22 August 1820

❁ *In many parts of the country gleaning was not only 'noticed' in church, but was regulated by church bells. They rang at 8 a.m. to allow gleaners into the fields, and again at 7 p.m. to remind them it was time to finish for the day. The following are from opening and closing lines of a Suffolk poem about* 'Gleaning Time'.

Why, listen yow-be quiet, bo'!—the bell is tolling eight!
Why don't yow mind what you're about—? We're allers kind o'late! ...

Dear me! there goo the bell agin—'tis seven, I declare;
An' we don't 'pear to have got none:—the gleanin' now don't fare
To be worth nothin'; but I think—as far as I can tell—
We'll try a comb, some how, to scratch, if we be 'live an' well.

Loyal to the Queen

The King's Head, in Marlborough, Wilts, having undergone considerable alteration and improvement, the proprietors resolved to change the sign and to erect in its place a head of her Majesty the Queen. Accordingly on Tuesday last, the old sign was taken down and the favourite one erected. To celebrate the event, a numerous and respectable company of gentlemen dined together, a flag was displayed from the church, and the bells rang merrily the whole afternoon.

The County Chronicle
4 November 1820

❁ *The Queen referred to in this report was Caroline of Brunswick, wife of George IV, formerly the Prince Regent. After a long separation from her husband (in which she was alleged to have indulged in misconduct giving grounds for divorce), she had returned to England in the previous June. Shortly afterwards the Cabinet resolved to bring in a Bill of Pains and Penalties to deprive Her Majesty of her royal privileges and to dissolve the marriage. Marlborough was one of the very many towns and villages which sympathized with Caroline and supported her*

*against a royal husband whose own marital infidelities were
common knowledge.*

*The deeds of the Queen's Head at Marlborough (which never
reverted to its original name) show that the building was in
existence in 1701. It is scheduled as a building of Special
Architectural or Historic Interest.*

*The stories below (18 November 1820) are typical of many
rejoicings throughout the country when the Bill against the Queen
was carried in the Lords by only a very small majority and the
Cabinet consequently decided not to let it go back to the House of
Commons.* The County Chronicle *was not technically correct in
stating that the Bill had been 'thrown out'.*

*Queen Caroline died in the following year, after a humiliating scene
in which she was turned away from Westminster Abbey when she
attempted to attend her husband's Coronation.*

The Queen's Victory over her Enemies

Beaconsfield

At the moment I am writing this, all hearts are rejoicing at the news of
the Queen's victory over her enemies. There is not a house in this town, or
near it, but what is decorated from top to bottom with laurel, and every
body has left his employment to join in the General rejoicing. Sheep are
roasting, farmers and gentlemen are distributing strong ale, and
affording everything within their means to make the heart glad, and
there is no place in the district which has a steeple that has not the merry
sound of bells ringing. Indeed, there never was an occurrence within the
memory of the oldest inhabitant that tended to give such general
satisfaction, or caused such rejoicing.

Farringdon, Berks

When the mail brought the glorious intelligence that the Bill was thrown
out, many of the most respectable inhabitants ran towards the church,
and running up the belfry stairs, the bells instantly struck up a merry peal.
A white flag was hoisted on the tower, amidst the firing of guns and
sounds of martial music; at night the inhabitants paraded through the
town with white favours in their hats. The Rev. Mr. Cleobury ordered the
flag to be taken down, but the churchwardens refused to comply. All
business was at an end. Wednesday was fixed for an illumination, a ball
and a public dinner.

The County Chronicle
18 November 1820

1821

A Medical Wager

There is an idle notion that the flesh of the pigeon is peculiarly inflammatory food. A medical practitioner near Lewes (a Sussex paper tells us) to decide a bet on ten guineas to 7, which he made with a neighbouring worthy gentleman of the quorum, engaged to eat a pigeon a day for 30 successive days. The birds were provided and accordingly served up in regular succession for the 4 weeks and 2 days, and the bones of the last were as fairly picked as those of the first.

The Devizes and Wiltshire Gazette
28 June 1821

❀ *It is presumed that pigeon flesh was said to be inflammatory in the sense that it caused a swelling of the body through heat, and that the doctor did not suffer in this way. (It is, however, just possible that it was deemed 'inflammatory' because of a belief that it was an aphrodisiac.)*

Crow killed by Turkey

A curious circumstance happened on Wednesday at Turley. While a brood of young turkies were feeding in a field belonging to Mrs. Atwood, a crow pounced on one of them and was carrying it off, when the old turkey cock came to the assistance of the young bird, rescued it and killed the rapacious assailant. During the contest a magpie attempted to carry off the young turkey, but ineffectually.

The Devizes and Wiltshire Gazette
28 June 1821

Cure for Adder-bites

A young woman at Marchwood, near Southampton, getting over a stile accidently set her foot on an adder; the reptile coiled itself around her leg and inflicted several wounds with its venemous teeth; the sufferer was prodigiously swollen before medical assistance could be procured, but some of the country people killed a fowl and applied the warm inside to the affected part, which in some measure assauged the acute pain, and there are now hopes of her recovery.

The Devizes and Wiltshire Gazette
12 July 1821

1822

Emigration*

The final departure from Oswestry of three generations of one family took place on Monday, in the person of Mrs. Bickerton, widow, and her children and grandchildren. The heart-rending scene was witnessed by a vast concourse of their friends and fellow townsmen. The Chester Coach from that place was filled within and without by persons going to America.

The Hereford Journal
8 May 1822

❀ *Until it became independent in 1776, America had been the destination of thousands transported from Britain as convicts. Although the new country would not accept convicts, there was no such aversion to willing settlers.*

A Coming of Age

On Wednesday last, Sir Richard Acton, of Aldenham and Acton Round in this county, Baronet, eldest son and heir of Sir John Edward Acton, Bart., late Prime Minister to the King of the Two Sicilies, came of age, and the event was celebrated with every demonstration of joy and festivity at Bridgnorth, Wenlock and different parts of the Aldenham and Acton Round estates. At Morville Hall, by desire of the worthy Baronet, a very fine fat ox was roasted and distributed to the attending multitude, with several hogsheads of most excellent old beer, which was brewed for the occasion 21 years ago; during the distribution the assembly was treated with a dance on the green, whilst the church bells rung a merry peal, and a capital band played loyal tunes till the close of the day.

Upon every part of the estate all the tenants appeared to vie with each other in showing their respect; and we cannot help particularly noting the exertions of the Acton Round estate to celebrate the happy event. Several sheep were roasted and one of extraordinary size and fatness was placed whole on the middle of a very sumptuous table groaning under large pieces of roast beef, plum-puddings, &c. At this bountiful feast many hundreds were plentifully regaled with meat and drink of the best. Nothing could exceed the hilarity and mirth which abounded on this joyful event, and we hope the worthy Baronet will long live in health and every happiness to enjoy his fine estate.

The Salopian Journal
31 July 1822

Remarkable Horse

We mentioned on a former occasion, a remarkable horse, the property of the Company of Proprietors of the Mersey and Irwell Navigation; that they had remitted him from his labours, and sent him to graze away the remainder of his days. On Wednesday se'nnight this faithful servant died, and at an age which has seldom been recorded of a horse: he was on his sixty-second year.

The Salopian Journal
11 December 1822

❀ *This horse, 'Old Billy', had been in the service of the Mersey and Irwell Navigation Company since the age of two. After a working life of 57 years, towing barges, he had been retired to a farm in 1819. It would seem that to date no horse has lived to a greater age. You may see 'Old Billy's' skull in the Manchester Museum. His stuffed head is preserved at Bedford Museum.*

Fight Extraordinary*

A short time since, Thos. Dawson, labourer, of Garford, Berks, aged 91, had a quarrel with another labourer, of the same village, aged 85, which they agreed to settle à la Belcher, in a neighbouring close. The battle was contested, each party displayed the most determined spirit, and victory for a time was doubtful. At length the fight terminated in favour of Dawson, who was not a little pleased at having beaten a man younger than himself. On the following day (although apparently not much injured) he was too unwell to go to work, and gradually grew worse until the seventh day after the fight, when he expired. Dawson had been a labourer on the farm now occupied by Mr. Hamman, of Garford for nearly 70 years, and was never known to be absent from his work on a single day until after the fight.

The Salopian Journal
11 December 1822

Poetical Thieves

A robbery of 20 coombs of wheat was effected last week at Sibton. Mr. White, the proprietor, a few days after received the sacks, with a note containing the following lines:

> We have got your wheat
> And you can't find it;
> 'Twas a famous wind
> That help'd to grind it.

The Ipswich Journal
28 December 1822

1823

Shields from Battle of Shrewsbury

Two ancient shields, which no doubt were worn in the celebrated Battle of Shrewsbury, and were ploughed up at Battlefield, are now in the possession of Sir Andrew Corbet, Bart., of Acton Reynold Hall. The one is a specimen of those worn by the horse-soldier, and the other of those worn by the foot-soldier.

The Salopian Journal
8 January 1823

❀ *Battlefield is two miles from Shrewsbury. The battle from which it gets its name was fought in 1403, when the army of Henry IV defeated rebels led by 'Hotspur', son of the Earl of Northumberland.*

Very Bold Robins

On Wednesday week some men employed in felling timber in Newbigging-Wood, near Carlise, sat down to dinner and were immediately surrounded by a number of red-breasts, which, without ceremony, lighted on their knees and fed from their hands, and as one man was putting a piece of bread into his mouth, a robin, still more impudent than his fellows, flew at it with great avidity, perched on the man's chin and (being permitted to remain) actually picked the food from his mouth.

The Weekly Register
9 February 1823

Sagacious Raven

Mr. John Wallenger, at the Black Bull Inn, at Long Stanton, in Cambridgeshire, is in possession of a very sagacious raven, which frequently goes out hunting along with a dog that was brought up with him. On their arrival at a cover, the dog enters, and drives the timid hares and scampering rabbits from the thicket, while his crafty companion judiciously posts himself on the outside [of] the maze, and courageously seizes every one that comes his way, when the dog immediately hastens to his assistance, and by their united efforts nothing escapes. On various occasions, however, the raven has proved of more use than the ferret; and on a late occasion actually entered a barn with several dogs and enjoyed the sport of rat hunting. The dog is of the wire terrier race, and in the possession of Mr. J. Coy of Chesterton.

The Weekly Register
9 March 1823

Death in Chimney

Last week as a chimney sweep's boy, who was sweeping the chimney of Mr. John Collinson of Crowle, in Lincolnshire, had ascended up the chamber chimney and while in the act of sweeping had caused some soot to fall down another flue in the parlour, in which there was a fire; the soot caused it to blaze, and melancholy to relate, the poor boy was burnt to death in the chimney. Mr. C. did not know that the chimney had any communication.

The Yorkshire Gazette
10 May 1823

Cock attacks Child

Monday se'nnight, at the Fighting Cocks Inn, at Winfarthing, a large cock of the true fighting breed, attacked a beautiful child about a year and a half old, belonging to the family of the landlord, and wounded him in several places in the head and face, and if timely assistance had not been at hand, there is little doubt he would have repeated his attacks till he had deprived him of sight, if not of his life. The cock was killed immediately.

The Weekly Register
8 June 1823

Rook Pie*

At Maidstone Assizes last week a rookery cause was heard before Mr. Baron Graham and a Special Jury. The action was brought against a farmer for shooting rooks, and he justified his conduct on the ground that the rooks entered his field and did considerable mischief. Mr. Walford, for the defendant, said that if the notion was correct that these birds did no harm to the farmer's fields, why were crow-boys employed? Another question was, by what medium were they to estimate the damages? How were they to ascertain the value for the rooks? It had been said that the young rooks had been sent to the poulterers in London. It was true, he believed, that the unwary cockney sometimes ate rook in his pie while he fancied he was eating a pigeon. It was the first time in his life he had ever heard of a rook pie! Mr. Baron Graham, in summing up, said it was the first time he had ever heard of the sale of young rooks to make pies. Those palates could not be very delicate, he thought, that could eat a rook-pie; it was only a strong stomach, he fancied, that would be disposed to encounter such a repast. The good folk in the West of England will be amused by reading this; a strong stomach to encounter a rook-pie? If Mr. Baron Graham should ever happen to pass through Dorchester when young perchers are beginning to caw, we would engage to provide him with a rook-pie equal, if not superior, to any powdered pigeon reared in the kingdom of Cockaigne.

The Weymouth Gazette
quoted in The Weekly Register
24 August 1823

A Crafty Sportsman

A sportsman in the vicinity of Bath, whose son (not being qualified) was seen sporting on a neighbouring manor, fearing an information against him for this offence against the game laws, cunningly anticipated the movements of the enemy, by appearing on Friday to lay an information against his own son, for illegimately carrying a gun for the destruction of game. By this novel measure, he saves 50s., as the informer is entitled to half the penalty, which is five pounds.

The Leicester Journal
quoted in The Yorkshire Gazette
11 October 1823

Annual Payments put in Tomb

At the village of Thornford, near Sherborne, Dorset, an ancient custom exists among the tenants of putting five shillings in a hole in a certain tomb in the church yard, which prevents the Lord of the Manor taking tithes of hay during the year. This must be invariably done on St. Thomas' Day before twelve o'clock; the tenant of the manor farm then takes the money.

The Durham County Advertiser
29 November 1823

❀ *This custom disappeared when the Lord of the Manor brought a successful lawsuit which gave him the tithes in spite of the old tradition. Visitors to Thornford churchyard will find that the tomb has a scooped-out hole in the stonework, and the tenants used to put their money into this. It used to be covered by a hinged metal grating.*

1824

Priority Order

The following is the exact copy of a letter from the farming servant of a London Baronet: "Sir Thos the number of ship 300-66(366) all well horsses pigs and cows all well Sir Thos my por wife is no mor Tuesday nite haf pas seven o'clock."

The Times
20 January 1824

Foiling the Body-snatchers

Some bodies having been stolen from the church-yard of a remote parish in Northumberland, the owner of the estate, to prevent such depradation in future, has directed the graves to be made rather shorter than the coffin, and to be excavated at the bottom, so as to admit the head under the solid ground. It is then impossible to raise it by the feet and the ground must be cut away above the head—a work of more time than could always be commanded by the operation. In addition, a mixture of percussion powder and gunpowder, placed on a wire in the inside of the coffin, to explode on its being opened, has been resorted to. This will retain its explosive power for a month, in which time the corpse will be generally unfit for dissection.

The Carlisle Journal
quoted in The Times
17 February 1824

❀ *Body-snatchers, or 'Resurrectionists' as they were more generally known, plied their gruesome trade until 1832, when dissection of bodies at schools of anatomy was legalized. Until then hospital lecturers were offered bodies at nine guineas each, subject to their first paying a retainer of fifty guineas for the exclusive services of the band of body-snatchers involved.*

Manchester Mail in Accident

An accident befell the Manchester mail at four o'clock yesterday morning as it was entering St. Albans. A donkey which had been left astray on the road, got between the leaders, and one of the wheel-horses fell. The coachman and two outside passengers were thrown from their seats and much injured. The former had the presence of mind to retain the reins, which prevented further mischief. The passengers made a subscription to requite the coachman for his meritorious conduct. This should operate as a warning to deter persons from leaving animals astray in the public thoroughfares.

The Times
27 February 1824

Cure by the Kick of a Horse

An extraordinary instance of the sudden recovery of speech occurred at Forest-row, near Brighton, the other day. A man named Newman, who is horsekeeper to Mr. Hoare, of Lewes, had been dumb for twenty-seven years. About three weeks ago he received a kick from a horse which he was combing down, and was laid up in consequence for a week. Upon leaving his room he was seized with a severe attack of nerves and became delirious. He continued in that condition for some days, and upon recovering his senses he returned immediately to his old occupation, but did not remain long at it when he was again desperately afflicted. The third attack, it seems, was the charm. He appeared in the yard where he had been accustomed to answer all enquiries as to his health with a turn of the head, and when his master said "Well, Dick, how are you?" "A great deal better, thank you Master" was the reply, to the astonishment of Mr. Hoare, who actually staggered at the miracle. The poor man, we understand, continues in good health.

The Times
13 April 1824

Amputation of the Leg of a Cow*

Last week, near Exeter, a cow belonging to Mr. John Edwards, broke the lower part of the fore-leg, a compound fracture. Amputation was supposed by the vetinary surgeon to be the only thing to save the animal, and as she was a valuable milch cow, the farmer requested it to be done. The operation was performed, and a most ingenious wooden leg constructed, by which the animal will be able to walk tolerably well.

The Medical Adviser
quoted in The Leeds Mercury
18 September 1824

1825

Large Gangs of Poachers in Gloucestershire

Several most daring attacks have been made this season by unprecedentedly large gangs of poachers, on the property of Colonel Kingscote, in Gloucestershire. The audacity over one on Monday se'nnight exceeded all attacks. Above 40 men with white handkerchiefs round their hats, marching in files, drew up on seeing the keepers and their assistants (about ten in number) and a desperate battle ensued. But though the keepers made a spirited resistance, they were overcome by numbers, and unable to see any of the depredators, who, after the conflict, formed by word of command and marched off. They had with them, also, a horse and a dark lanthorn. At a preceding visit of 20 of the above gang, a number of them surrounded the house of the head-keeper and kept him prisoner, while the others shot in the preserve behind the house.

The York Herald
1 January 1825

Farmer killed by Cricket-ball

A few days since, at a match of Cricket at Lord Dacre's park, Mr. James Males, a respectable farmer, at Kimpton, received a blow from the ball upon his nose, which continued to bleed, with very little intermission, until Friday, when he died from the excessive loss of blood. His funeral was attended by all the members of the club, with whom he was playing when he received the fatal blow.

The Hertfordshire Mercury
6 August 1825

Road-makers find Gold Coins

On Wednesday, as some labourers were making a road at Shrivenham, Berks, they discovered, about four feet beneath the surface, 38 pieces of Gold Coin, of the reigns of Charles I and Charles II, and one of the reign of Mary. Those of the Charleses were nearly of the diameter of a crown, and the thickness of a sixpence, but that of Mary of the superficies of an eighteen-penny token, and of the thickness of the rest. The value of the gold is about £50. Mr. Dawson, we understand, claimed the pieces for Viscount Barrington, who is lord of the manor.

The Hertfordshire Mercury
6 August 1825

Pinching Match*

At the Bell Inn, at Widford, in this county, a delightful amusement has sprung up, quite novel, and which may vie with any of the present day entertainments of "the Fancy". It is that of a set-to between two persons which can bear the most pinching, and continue to pinch his opponent for the longest time; observing that if during the engagement any party betray any angry feeling, or swear, the party so offending to forfeit whatever wager depends upon the issue. A set-to of this sort occurred on

Tuesday last at the above place, between a Knight of the Thimble of small stature and puny appearance, and a stout athletic husbandman. They held on pinching each other, *with great pleasure*, for upwards of an hour, chiefly upon the fleshy parts of the arm, when at length the arms of the stout man fell powerless to his side, and he was obliged to give in from exhaustion and pain. The gallant Knight immediately offered to combat with any man in England for the championship of pinching.

The Hertfordshire Mercury
20 August 1825

❀ *The building in which these pinching contests took place has been in existence for well over 400 years. It has been an inn, under 'the name and signe of ye Bell' since 1730. Its most famous customer, Charles Lamb (1775–1834), the essayist, lived near by and mentioned the inn in his 'Confessions of a Drunkard'. It is recalled that after an evening's jollification there he would often plunge his head into a horse trough by the front door, to get rid of a hangover before walking home.*

Lamb is remembered at 'The Bell' to-day by his portrait and by a picture of the inn as he knew it. He would certainly have known of the pinching contests, and it is quite possible he took part in them.

The Statute Fair

At Aylesbury . . . in the Statute fair, the common wages for ploughmen and carters were from eight to ten pounds a-year, with board and lodging, and for inferior servants in the husbandry line from six to eight. The wages of a good dairymaid may be stated at ten pounds a -year and those of other female servants in a farm house about six, or, in other words, according to qualifications. At this time, the weekly wages of husbandry labourers in the neighbourhood of Aylesbury are about ten shillings a week, with beer at hay time and corn harvest.

The County Chronicle
4 October 1825

❀ *The Statute Fair was an event at which servants were engaged for the coming year. They would stand together in the street in line, with their boxes containing their clothing and other scanty possessions piled near by. The men particularly would stand with straws in their mouths to show they were disengaged. Some of them carried a tool, or other indication of the job in which they were skilled. A carter, for example, would carry his whip. The usual amusements of a fair would follow the serious business of hiring, and the day would end with a great deal of dancing and drinking.*

1826

Raffling Day at Peterborough

Peterborough

Crowland Shrove Tuesday fair, or "raffling day" as it is generally called, it being the custom to cast dice for sweetmeats in lieu of purchasing them, was attended by most of the blithe and bonny lasses of the neighbourhood; and some of the beau-monde of Postland were not the least conspicuous. In the evening there were groups of dancers at the different public-houses, particularly at the Crown, where all was fun and revelry; several country dances were managed with adroitness and elegance too.

The Huntingdon, Bedford and Peterbro Gazette
11 February 1826

Eccentric Will

At Stevenage in this county, in the year 1724, a person named Henry Trigg, made an eccentric will, the basis of which was the necessity enjoined upon his executor, under the forfeiture of the property left, provided such executor did not comply with the condition of placing his body "to the West end of the hovel, to be decently laid there, upon the purlins, for the purpose". The condition of the will was complied with, and the coffin has ever since been an object of curiosity to those travelling through Stevenage. A few days since, some fellows, who had been drinking at the public-house behind which the hovel is situated, determined upon breaking open the coffin, which they did; they discovered the entire skeleton and extracted several teeth, which were in excellent preservation, notwithstanding upwards of a century had elapsed since it was deposited there.

The Hertfordshire Mercury
1 April 1826

❀ *The coffin was deposited in the roof of the hovel, among the rafters. A 'purlin' is a horizontal beam.*

1827

Imprisonment a Luxury

John Johnson, a labourer, was on Wednesday committed to Peterborough, for 3 months, to atone for the offence of being taken, by one of the Marquis of Exeter's gamekeepers, with a hare in his basket. The keeper had previously traced footsteps in the snow which led to a snare, and upon watching, saw Johnson go to it on his way home, but take nothing, for the best of reasons, there was nothing to take. He, however, followed him, and found he had a hare in his possession. The culprit, if such he can be called under all the circumstances, is a hardworking labourer with a wife and two children. He walked every morning from Ketton to Southorp, and back every evening—a journey of sixteen miles: in the interim he performed a day's work: and at the end of the week he received as a reward for his labour the pittance of eight shillings. No wonder that he picked up a hare to eke out such an existence. Upon being committed he said that but for the feelings he had for his wife and children, imprisonment would be to him a luxury.

The Stamford News
quoted in The Leicester Chronicle
3 February 1827

A Quick Proposal—and Acceptance

Died at Parsonby, parish of Plumbland, on the 19th. ult., Elizabeth Smith, late of Wigston, aged 86. Her husband died about four years ago at the age of 96. Their marriage was rather a singular one. He was a tailor by trade and about the age of 46 he went into a harvest field in the above parish were a number of women were sheeving and proposed himself for a husband to any one who would accept of him, giving them a quarter of an hour to consider of it. His late wife immediately looked up and said "I'll have thee". "Very well, my lass, then to-morrow morn is our wedding morn". In this respect he was as good as his word, for the very next morning they were wed.

The Leicester Chronicle
10 February 1827

Izaak Walton's Bounty

This week has been dispensed to the poor of the Borough of Stafford, the bounty of the celebrated and ingenious "Izaak Walton", who was a native of the place, and who bequeathed a portion of the "rents and profits of a farme" to the purchase of coals "for some poor people", to be delivered in January or February. "I say *then*" runs the words of the humane testator "because I take that time to be the hardest and most pinching times with poor people". The farm in question is now of considerable value, bringing in we believe about £80 a year, and after deducting a moiety of the profits directed to be applied to the apprenticing of two boys and in a gift to a maid-servant, or some honest poor man's daughter, a sufficient sum has this year remained for the purchase of a small allowance of coal to almost every poor family, which has this week been distributed. The instrument was dated "August the 9th. 1683" and the testator was in his ninetyeth year.

> The Stafford Advertiser
> quoted in The Leicester Chronicle of
> 10 February 1827

❀ *The wishes of the famous angler were observed through the years, and continued to be carried out in a modified form until quite recently. Then operating on an annual income of £40, 'Izaak Walton's Charity' gave a sum of £5 annually for a maidservant, or poor man's daughter, under the terms of the original bequest, and provided coal for the poor to the value of the remaining £35.*

Death of a Poacher

On Friday last a coroner's inquest was held at the Cardigan Arms, at Corby, Northamptonshire, on the body of a poacher named John Bailey, who had died in consequence of being wounded by the gamekeepers of the Earl of Winchelsea on the previous Tuesday night, in Rockingham Forest. On that night, in consequence of some information given, eleven of the keepers repaired to the Forest, and found a body of about twenty

poachers engaged in netting rabbits. Notwithstanding mild remonstrances were at first used by the principal keeper, the poachers drew
themselves up in array, their leader gave the signal to attack, and a
desperate conflict was begun, but the keepers being well armed, the
poachers were compelled to retreat, leaving behind them many dozens
of rabbits, and a very large quantity of netting. During the conflict, one of
the poachers was dreadfully cut with a spear in the belly; but although his
bowels in consequence protruded, he contrived to walk to his home, a
distance of two miles, where he died on Thursday. Mr. Billson, surgeon of
Weldon, being called before the coroner and jury, deposed that he was
sent for on the night of Wednesday to attend the deceased, that he found
he had received a wound three inches in length on the left side of the body,
and that the bowels were issuing from it: he dressed the wound and
advised that Mr. Clarke, the parish surgeon, should be sent for. Mr.
Clarke, surgeon of Weldon, deposed that he saw the deceased the next
morning, that he staid with him till he died, and that he took down a
deposition of the deceased as to the manner in which he came by his
death. A person named Nixon, of Corby, deposed that he saw the
deceased on Wednesday night; he was lying with his bowels in his hand,
and said "Nixon, I am a dead man; John Miller is the man who stabbed
me". The deposition taken by the surgeon also stated that Miller had
inflicted the wound; a verdict of manslaughter was therefore returned
against him, and he was committed to Northampton, where the Grand
Jury at the Assizes this week threw out the bill, and he was discharged.
Miller is Lord Winchelsea's forest keeper and was the defendant in the
great cause some time ago, "Meadows v. Miller", on the subject of the
rights of common on Rockingham Forest.

The Leicester Chronicle
10 March 1827

New Use for Gibbet

The gibbet which has been standing 40 years near Stoke Church, was
lately blown down. It has since been brought on shore by some young men
who found it floating down the river, and having attracted some gazers,
the idea of making snuff boxes of the solid remains was broached by one
of them. The thought quickly flew, and not a portion sufficiently
substantial, but soon found its way to the carvers and turners, and the
putrid dust that so long hung on it, will no doubt give an excellent zest to
the titilating dust it is now doomed to carry.

The Exeter Weekly Times
20 October 1827

1828

Horned Visitor at Midnight

A few days since an extraordinary circumstance happened at the village of Fimpsall, near Wakefield. The report that a poor woman residing there had "a small matter beforehand" induced a neighbouring butcher to disguise himself with a buck's head and horns and to visit his ancient crony through the chimney. With dreadful bellowings he announced woe and punishment to come, if £100 were not produced before the fatal hour of twelve the following night. The threatened dame waited next morning upon her bankers at Wakefield to obtain the money; and in the urgency of her fears, she stated the cause of her withdrawing *so serious* a sum out of their hands. These gentlemen sent a couple of stout fellows to see fair play on the occasion. At the midnight hour, vivid flashes of lightning were seen in the chimney, and the horrid bellowings repeated. In five minutes, Horne, the hunter, was taken into custody and is now exercising in the House of Correction.

The Exeter Weekly Times
23 February 1828

❖ *Herne was a demon hunter said to haunt Windsor Great Park. Herne's Oak is referred to in* The Merry Wives of Windsor, *and the eerie huntsman figures prominently in Harrison Ainsworth's* Windsor Castle.

Throwing Lent-shards

John Incledon of Heanton Ponchardon, preferred a complaint against ten young men, who, according to the deposition of the complainant, beset his house on the night of the 18th. ult., with broken pottery, stones and other missiles, with which they broke in his door, and did him other damage. It appeared that the ancient practice of throwing lent-shards continues to be practised in the parish of Heanton, much to the annoyance of the inhabitants. Three were acquitted, no evidence appearing that they actually threw shards, though they were seen in the mob; the other seven were fined 6s. each

The Exeter Weekly Times
15 March 1828

✸ *This custom was also known as 'Lent Crocking'. At that season parties of boys would tour their villages and knock up the householders, when the leader would ask for food for himself and his companions. In many areas the leader would make his plea by reciting these two verses, all his friends joining in the chorus:*

> A-shrovin, a-shroving,
> I be come a-shrovin
> A piece of bread, a piece of cheese,
> A bit of your fat bacon,
> Or a dish of dough-nuts,
> All of your own makin!
>
> A-shrovin, a-shrovin,
> I be come a-shrovin,
> Nice meat in a pie,
> My mouth is very dry!
> I wish a wuz zoo well-a-wet
> I'de zing the louder for a nut!
>
> Chorus- A -shrovin, a-shrovin
> We be come a-shrovin!

✸ *If the food was forthcoming the party went away well pleased, but if the householder refused to open his door it was bombarded with broken cups, saucers, plates and dishes–'shards' and crockery resulting from kitchen breakages since the previous Lent.*

Mr Incledon evidently gave a firm refusal to the request for good cheer, or decided to ignore it.

Dreadful Results of Smuggling*

There have been committed to Horsham gaol within the last few weeks no less than 13 men, charged with being concerned in the affray between the coast blockade and a formidable gang of smugglers, in which a quarter-master of the service, of the name of Collins, and an old smuggler of the name of Timothy Smithurst, were killed in a lane leading from the village of Bexhill to Sidley-green, six miles to the westward of Hastings. A coroner's inquest, which was held on the body of Collins, returned a verdict of "Wilful murder against some person or persons unknown" and in a day or two after, a girl, who had been some time known as of loose character, gave information to the district commander of the coast blockade, lieutenant Green, which led to the apprehension of a young man named Charles Hills, alias Louckhurst, a resident of Bexhill, and other persons. They were confined in one of the Martello towers for some days, and then taken before F. F. North, Esq., one of the magistrates of the hundred of Hastings, on several successive days. At length Hills made a voluntary offer to become an approver, and his evidence was accepted; the consequence of which was, that six men were at once sent to Horsham for trial for the murder and a great number of warrants (we believe upwards of sixty) were issued against other individuals. Lieutenant Green and his men were out scouring the country night after night for weeks, in search of the accused persons, and many houses were broken into by main force, in some of which were found the objects of their search, in others they were unsuccessful. The villages round Hastings, for a circuit of twenty miles, were continually in a state of terror and alarm which it is impossible to describe. These were principally Bexhill, Sidley, Hooe, Westfield, Pett and Peasemarch. At Peasemarch they apprehended two brothers named Whiteman, who were stated by Hills to be two of the leaders in the affair. The men, as they were apprehended by the officers and identified before Mr. North by Hills, were committed to Horsham. Another man, named Buffard, a native of Pett, on being taken into custody, became an evidence for the crown, and pointed out the residence of persons said to be implicated, who lived in his own neighbourhood, and were not so well known by Hills. The distress occasioned round a considerable extent of country by this unfortunate occurrence is almost beyond conception. A great number of men, beside those actually in custody, have absconded, leaving no other resource to their families, but the workhouse; and in one parish alone, Bexhill, no less than 25 families have been thrown upon the parochial funds, which were before very heavily burdened. Consequences of a still more melancholy nature have been produced in some of the families, resulting from this unhappy conflict. In one instance a young woman, who had lain-in but a few hours, experienced so dreadful a shock on seeing her husband, one of the accused, dragged from the house, that she died in a state of madness the following day. In another case a wife similarly situated was delirious for several days, and only narrowly escaped the jaws of death.

The Exeter Weekly Times
5 April 1828

Ominous Dream*

A few days since, the remains of an adult human body was dug up in an orchard at Kingston-Deverell; from many circumstances it is suspected that a murderer had placed it there. It is singular that the discovery was made in consequence of a dream in which the Uncle of the person who found it had been warned that money was buried in the spot where the body was found, and which is marked by a bush grown over it.

The Exeter Weekly Times
12 April 1828

Divination

Some of the sapient inhabitants of Bukfastleigh, both male and female, had a few weeks since, a rare peep into futurity, and which no doubt in *future*, will prevent their being so easily duped. Report had spread the fame of a Gypsey just arrived in the neighbourhood, and her levees were nightly crowded with

Fair ones sighing out their love,
And doubting love-sick swains
Who sought the future to foresee,
To ease their present pains

How far she succeeded in this is a question we cannot answer, but she certainly contrived to ease them of their cash. Silver was required to cross her palm before the oracle could utter a word, and Gold not infrequently gave fluency to her wondrous tale. She told them all their past loves and jealoucies—of all their feuds and secret enemies; scepticism was therefore set at nought, for what better argument of being able to tell the future than such minute details of the past. Envy, however, has a keen eye, and rests not while fame sounds a trump. One lynx-eyed varlet pry'd so closely into the oracles physog. as to discover a cut in the nose which he had seen in other quarters. He blowed the roast; and they soon proceeded to roast the sybil; not as they would in olden time, at the stake for a witch, but merely by plucking her of her borrowed disguise, when she proved to be a girl of the village, about 18, who worked in one of the factories; and who heard, with no doubt much self satisfaction, the stories related of herself; and daily gleaned fresh food for her evening visitors.

Exeter Weekly Times
17 May 1828

1829

Treasure in Thatch

An inquisition has been taken before Mr. Charsley, coroner, at Wooburn, in Bucks, concerning a certain treasure which has lately been found in the thatch of a cottage of Northern Woods. In the month of May last, a Mr. Harris, the lessee of such cottage, employed some thatchers to unroof the cottage, which was in a decayed state, and to newly thatch it, and when the men so engaged had nearly completed the work, they suddenly left it and soon convinced the neighbourhood that they had had some extraordinary change of fortune, and one of the men, in particular, newly equipped himself, became the purchaser of pigs and a good watch, and exhibited quantities of old guineas in many different public-houses, gave a public feast, and became, in fact, quite the independent man, and not requiring or performing any more labour. He appeared to have been proud to acknowledge his new state, and admitted that although a young man, he had found sufficient money to maintain him for the rest of his life without labour. It was clear, therefore, that such individual had had "a lucky find". Although there was no evidence before the coroner of the ownership or identity of the property, yet conjectures were formed as to who were the depositers of the hidden treasure, as the guineas bore the stamp of the Sovereigns, King James II, Queen Anne and George II, and it was known to old persons living at the retired spot that, above 60 years ago, an old man of penurious habits had resided in the cottage, who had been accustomed to hide his money in apple-trees, and it is thought that if the finder of the money were to produce some writings which he appears to have suppressed, the owner of the coin would be identified. Amongst the old thatch which has been taken from the roof and conveyed to Mr. Harris's, there were found several old guineas, and also an old empty canvas purse, with a hole in the corner of it, and it is supposed it must have contained 1000 guineas. However, after a long investigation, during which the coroner had to examine parties who most reluctantly told the truth, and several of whom were guilty of most gross prevarications, not to say perjury, and who were most unwilling to appear before him, a verdict was returned by the patient and respectable Jury, "That William Higgins, the son of the thatcher who had been so employed, had found 700 guineas, and upwards, of ancient gold coin, hidden under the old thatch of the said cottage, which he concealed from the knowledge of the coroner, or those authorised to receive information thereof on behalf of our Sovereign Lord the King". He has absconded and no part of the treasure has been recovered. The constable was bound over to prosecute.

The Oxford Journal
27 June 1829

Wrestling in Cornwall

TRURO
Grand Wrestling Match
Will take place on Monday and
Tuesday, the 27th. and 28th. inst., when
the Following Prizes
will be awarded, viz.

To the Best Man	—	TWENTY SOVEREIGNS
Second-best ditto	—	TEN SOVEREIGNS
Third-best ditto	—	FIVE SOVEREIGNS
Fourth-best ditto	—	TWO SOVEREIGNS
Fifth-best ditto	—	A GOLD-LACED HAT
		A SILVER-LACED HAT
		A PLAIN SILK HAT

The Wrestling will commence each day precisely at Ten o'clock; and as the prizes undoubtedly exceed any that have been offered in this county, it is confidently anticipated that the Games will be attended by the very best of men in this and probably the adjoining county. Competent, respectable and impartial Umpires will be chosen from different districts and every man, come from whence he may, will have fair play shown him.

The Falmouth Packet
18 July 1829

Ship without Crew

On Tuesday, the 4th. instant, the body of a sailor was washed on shore at Lower St. Columb Porth; he had on a red frock and duck trowsers, with braces to them. The inhabitants of that place suppose it to be one of the crew of the vessel which lately came into Penzance without any person on board.

The Falmouth Packet
15 August 1829

❀ *This story was as mysterious to the people of Cornwall as was the epic of the* Mary Celeste *to a far greater number of people in 1872. The* Mary Celeste, *a brig of 282 tons, was found about 600 miles off Gibraltar without any of its crew, or any indication of what had happened to them.*

'The Old Sow'

A woman named Charlotte Phinmore, the wife of a labourer resident in a place called Blackstone, has suckled a pig to her breast in order to rear it. She continued the practice in the presence of several witnesses and appeared to take as much care of it as if it had been a child. She was finally induced to desist by the interposition of several respectable persons. The neighbours have given the pig, which is about two weeks old, the name of *Charlotte*, while its *nurse* is known by the cognomen of the old sow. The pig and her infant have both been seen on her lap at the same time.

The Plymouth Herald
quoted in The Falmouth Packet
20 August 1829

Lost on Dartmoor

In the early part of July last, when the weather was in its most inclement state, two boys, named Beer, the sons of a labouring man at South Zeal, one aged 13 and the other only six, were sent with a donkey to a part of Dartmoor to gather heath. After they had executed the mission, one of those tempests, which so frequently sweep over that desolate plain, took place, and no doubt hastened their return. It seems that the elder had sent his brother to collect a bundle of heath, which had been bound up for the purpose a short distance from them; he continued his way slowly home, accounted for his brother's not overtaking him by the supposition that he had passed him unobserved, and had reached home before him. When, however, he got to his father's cottage, he found that nothing had been seen of him, and it was evident that the poor little boy had lost himself upon the plains. Upwards of one hundred persons immediately started in search, but no trace of him was discovered. About three weeks since, when it was generally supposed that the little fellow had been washed away by the floods, a shepherd passing across the moor not more than a quarter of a mile from the spot where the child was first missed, discovered a leather cap, and upon searching further, the girth that had been used to tie the heath, and the thigh bone apparently of a child about six years of age. There were no other remains, but the wetness of the season and the immense number of foxes and birds of prey abounding on these desolate and almost interminable moors render it too certain that the child had been torn piecemeal by them, and that his clothes, which must have become rotten, were dragged away with the human flesh attached to them. It is of the opinion of those that went in search of him that neither the poor child, or any human being lost upon Dartmoor, and scantily clothed as he was, could have lived through a night so dreadfully tempestuous.

The Falmouth Packet
14 November 1829

Cider for the Trees

Exeter, November 12

It is a very common remark in this county at this moment, so abundant is the crop of apples, that there are "some for the boys to steal". This refers to a singular custom performed yearly on the eve of the Epiphany, when the farmer, his family and labourers go to the orchard, and encircling the oldest or the largest apple tree, with lights in their hands, and pitcher, or bowl of toast and cider, repeat the following lines:

> Here's to the old apple tree,
> Bud and blow,
> And bear apples enow,
> Hats-full, caps-full, three bushel bags-full
> And some for the boys to steal.

A libation of the cider is sometimes poured at the foot of the tree, amidst loud cheers and discharges of fire-arms, and many farmers are so superstitious as to believe that if they neglect this custom, the trees will bear no apples. The evening is spent in rural games and much merriment within doors.

The Falmouth Packet
14 November 1829

'A Diabolical Letter'

An inflammatory and diabolical letter has been sent to Mr. Kingham, the overseer of North Marston, Bucks, threatening to murder him for stopping money from the poor, adding that sooner than starve they will be up to their knees in blood and burn him in his house, if they cannot do for him in other ways. Mr. Kingham has offered £10 reward to discover the writer.

The Oxford Journal
19 December 1829

1830-39

WHEN SOUTHERN ENGLAND WAS ABLAZE
Rick-burning in Kent during the Agrarian Rebellion.

1830

The 'Sir Loin Table'

There is now at Friday-Hill House, in the parish of Chingford, Essex, the oak table upon which King Charles knighted the loin of beef. The house is now the property of——Heathcote, Esq. It is a large building, containing more than 30 rooms, in a dilapidated state, but is now undergoing considerable repair. Report has it that it was originally a hunting seat of Queen Elizabeth. The table, thick and of a clumsy appearance, is made of English oak, which, from the effect of time, is a little decayed.

The County Chronicle
12 January 1830

❀ *Another story has it that 'Sir Loin' was knighted by James I, father of Charles I, at Hoghton Towers in Lancashire. The 17-ft oaken table used for the ceremony at Hoghton Towers was much in the news in 1969, when it became the subject of a High Court Order.*

Hoghton Towers, five miles from Preston, is open to the public during many week-ends throughout the year.

Men pull Wagons to support Families

Coventry
On the evening of Friday se'nnight a waggon load of barley, drawn by 22 agricultural labourers, arrived in this City from Daventry, and was taken to the Thistle public-house, West Orchard. As these poor men have no employment, they adopted this plan to obtain a trifle towards supporting themselves and families. On Saturday morning they proceeded to Bedworth for a load of coals, and returned with them in the same manner to Daventry.

The Coventry Mercury
14 February 1830

❀ *On the Friday these men would have drawn the wagon a distance of approximately 23 miles. With only a night's rest in between, on the Saturday they would have pulled it over a journey of about 10 miles.*

Gipsy Funeral*

Highworth, Wilts, June 8

The mortal remains of an aged female belonging to this singular people were on Thursday last consigned to the dust in Highworth church-yard, attended by a great concourse of spectators, whom the interesting novelty of the spectacle had invited to the spot. The interment was conducted with the greatest decorum, the interest of the scene being heightened instead of *damped* by the incessant rain, which fell in torrents on the venerable, uncovered locks of the husband, who acted as chief mourner on the occasion, and who, with his numerous offspring (forming the procession) "the pitiless storm assailed in vain", but who appeared fully impressed with the sad solemnity of the last duty they were about to perform for one who had been a wife and a mother for nearly three score years and ten. When living she was a perfect *Meg Merriles* in appearance, and it is even said she was the identical person Walter Scott had in view when he wrote that inimitable character in Guy Mannering; be that as it may, for considerably more than half a century has she exercised her *oracular* powers in propounding the "good or bad fortune" of all the fair-going damsels for many miles round. . . . Perhaps it should have been said before that the "old lady" made her mortal exit in a lane near Highworth; and inclosed with the body in the coffin were *a knife and fork, with a plate*; and five tapers (not wax, we presume) were kept constantly burning on the lid of the coffin till the removal for interment; after which the whole of the defunct's wardrobe was committed to the flames, and her dog and donkey butchered "in order that they might follow their mistress"—a regular and superstitious custom amongst this people, and which was borrowed perhaps from some of the barbarous "tribes" in the East, where, on the demise of a person of distinction, his whole household are *obliged* to bid adieu to this world also, so that they might be in readiness to attend their lord and master in the next.

The Oxford Journal
12 June 1830

A Vigorous Appetite*

An elderly woman was tried at Hereford Assizes the other day for stealing a ram. According to her own account to the constable, she went to Mr. Tibbatt's field, in the parish of Avenbury, and having driven all the sheep to a gap in the hedge, as they were getting through she caught hold of the ram. The ram pushed her down, but she held him for a considerable time, though she was down. At last, being tired, she was obliged to let go, and the ram was escaping, when she caught him by the leg, and threw him, and drew her knife across his throat. After the ram was dead, she looked round to see if any one was about, and not seeing any one, she skinned it, and cut the meat into joints, and hid them. The prisoner, when called on for her defence, said "My Lord, I was perishing from hunger. When I caught the ram I was almost ready to eat the wool off his skin". She was found guilty, but recommended to mercy. The hunger of the old lady appears to have strengthened her arm as well as her appetite.

The Coventry Mercury
29 August 1830

❀ *1830 was the year of the 'Agrarian Rebellion', when the farm-workers of England, mainly those of the Southern Counties, rose in revolt against their low wages, hunger and living conditions generally. Serious rioting was the product of festering grievances over many years, including widespread unemployment since the end of the Napoleonic War and the high price of bread and other essentials. The immediate cause of the uprising was the introduction of threshing machines, which took away winter work from men who had beaten out the grain with the flail, in the way that their forebears had threshed it over many centuries.*

The riots started in June, in Kent. Until November they were mainly confined to Kent, Surrey and Sussex, but in that month there was a formidable increase after the poor harvest of 1830. In December there were uprisings in practically all the Southern Counties.

The following reports, from the Coventry Mercury *for the first week of December, tell of rioting, rick-burning and machine-breaking. There were a great many similar happenings in many other parts of rural England at the same time:*

Southern England Ablaze

Middlesex
Last night the property of Mr. J. Higgs, farmer, of Preston, near Harrow on the Hill, was consumed. The fire broke out about six o'clock in the evening, when three ricks were discovered to be in flames at the same moment. They were entirely consumed; and two ricks of hay were considerably damaged. The arrival of the engines prevented the house and other buildings from being consumed. No doubt can be entertained that this was the work of peasantry in the neighbourhood. By far the greater number evinced the most praiseworthy anxiety to assist in extinguishing the flames, and their exertions were exceedingly useful; but

the conduct of several was altogether the reverse. About twenty fellows indulged themselves in making fun of the matter: and at the one time, when the engines were obliged to stop for want of water, on being solicited to assist they sneeringly refused, exclaiming that they hoped to see a good many more such bonfires. The expressions used by óne fellow, as well as his general demeanour, were such as to induce the gentlemen present to take him into custody. He will be examined before the magistrates this day. Nearly all the farmers throughout that district received the "Swing" letters on Saturday. At Hendon, Hampstead, Kingsbury, and Edgeware, there is scarcely an individual whose property is exposed, but who has been threatened. We understand that Mr. Higgs, in consequence of the low prices obtained for agricultural produce, was compelled on Saturday last to reduce the wages of his labourers 2s. per week, and to that step the occurrence is principally attributed.

We are sorry to add that Gloucester and Hereford have not been free from the diabolical deeds of the incendiaries. At Bourton-on-the-Hill, Gloucestershire, on Saturday night, a hay-stack belonging to the Rev. Dr. Warnefield was set on fire, but happily the damage done was not to a serious extent.

On Friday evening last, a party of labourers and others, from the neighbourhood of Tetbury, Gloucestershire, assembled together to the number of about eighty, broke some threshing machines, and extorted money from some of the farmers in the neighbourhood of that town. The real mischief occasioned by this lawless and misguided mob was comparatively trifling, but the fear and dismay which the reports of their proceedings occasioned, may be easily conceived. In the evening of that day, between twenty and thirty of the most active of these marauders had proceeded as far as Tiltup's Inn, which is situated on the Bath Road and within a short distance of Nailsworth; here they had ordered a good supper, which, however, they did not partake of. Colonel Kingscote, a most active magistrate, on intimation being given him of the riot, instantly dispatched a messenger to Dursley and Wootton for the military, who are stationed in those towns; on their arrival they hastened to the Inn above mentioned, and succeeded in capturing every one of the rioters, who were waiting for the supper to be brought in: they were immediately marched off to the House of Correction; the next day, the greater part were committed to Gloucester county gaol, the rest have since been sent to the same prison. As a proper precautionary measure, every respectable inhabitant of the borough of Tewkesbury has been sworn into the office of special constable.

A gentleman who arrived in Bath on Saturday, from Hungerford, describes the lawless conduct of the people as most alarming. They went to the Magistrates assembled at the Town-hall, Hungerford, on Tuesday, and demanded five guineas, which were given them. They then went and compelled every farmer to give them two guineas, and destroyed every threshing machine in the neighbourhood, and demolished the furniture of a tanner. Similar depredations were committed at Ramsbury, where the depredators amounted to 400 in number, carrying a tricoloured flag. They visited Littlecott, the seat of Gen. Popham, and demanded that he would raise the labourer's wages to 12s. per week, and reduce his rents, to enable the farmers to do the same. They then ordered something to eat and to drink, and after regaling themselves, went thence to Chippen Lodge, the seat of Mr. Pearce, M.P. for Devizes, and made similar demands. The same day they visited the farmers around, and where resisted, forcibly broke into their cellars, and the same evening billeted themselves as a regiment of soldiers on the inhabitants of the village. The coaches were attacked during the day, and, as Mr. Coddrington was addressing them on the illegality of their conduct, a hammer was thrown at him, which wounded him severely on the head.

At Woodborough, Wilts, 28 men were taken prisoners at a public-house, where they were making merry with money they had extorted by intimidation from persons in the neighbourhood.

Hampshire

No fewer than 200 persons are now in Winchester Gaol, charged with various outrages. The peasantry, who at first employed themselves only in the destruction of machinery, and limited their demands to the increase of wages, have since degenerated into predatory bands, traversing the country, and levying by force money and provisions from the gentry. All round Winchester these bands have spread themselves. *Several inhabitants of Winchester and other towns, and persons in full employment at high wages, as mechanics*, have been apprehended and lodged in prison as ringleaders of the most flagrant outrages. Women and boys take their share in these outrages, which are concluded by a division and expenditure of the spoil at public-houses and beer-shops, which last prove convenient places of meeting and rendezvous. Some have been heard to declare that they will not work while they can earn so much by mobbing. The man who struck Mr. Baring with a sledge hammer is in custody. The Magistrates, aided by the military, are constantly on the alert. At Selbourne, the mob went to the house of the Vicar, who, being intimidated, signed a paper to the effect that he would be content with £300 a year. They also compelled some farmers to sign an agreement that they would have no more hired guardians of the poor.

Huntingdon

On Wednesday evening a party of from 40 to 50 men assembled in the village of Sawtry, and proceeded to demolish two thrashing machines. On the following evening a more formidable party, from the villages of Upton, Alconbury, &c. uniting with the above, commenced their work of destruction on other machines in the neighbourhood; and, amongst the rest, destroyed a very valuable one on the farm of Mr. Sturton, at Alconbury-hill; another at Mr. Dann's, at Stukeley Lodge; and another at Mr. Wright's, at Monk's Wood House. The party at this time was between two and three hundred strong. Having finished their work here, they proceeded to Buckworth, where they arrived between two and three o'clock in the morning, their numbers having a little diminished by the way, and immediately sawed and broke to pieces two thrashing-machines used on the farms of Mr. Gray, and Mr. Bowker. On Saturday morning a party of about fifty commenced operations in the neighbourhood of Stilton, and the Rev. Mr. Gordon, having placed himself at the head of several gentlemen, farmers and others, resolved to oppose them, and after a severe skirmish, in which one of the rioters had his arm broken, succeeded in capturing eighteen of the ringleaders, who were immediately sent under a safe escort to Huntingdon gaol. Meanwhile a number of special constables were sworn in at Huntingdon, and started for the villages where offences had been committed. In the course of the night twenty-five of the gang were sent in safe custody to the county prison, together with three poachers, making a total capture of fifty in one day. The instigators of these disturbances, and the first to act in them, were men *earning from 12s. to 15s. per week and in constant employ.*

The Coventry Mercury
5 December 1830

❀ *The report from Middlesex refers to letters from 'Swing'. These were warning notes said to have come from the leader of the uprising, who was known as Captain Swing. They were received by hundreds of farmers at this time.*

In asking for wages of 12s. weekly the rioters who called on General Popham at Littlecott were demanding what in several counties would have been an increase of 33⅓%, for the current wage was generally about 9s.

At Selborne in Hampshire, where the vicar agreed an annual stipend of £300, the rioters also burned down the workhouse. The curate there for very many years was the famous Gilbert White, the naturalist, whose Natural History of Selborne *was first published in 1789. But White did not live to see these riotous happenings in his beloved Selborne: he had died nearly forty years previously.*

Banbury, December 2

In the country around, the demolition of machines continues, but in every case I believe the work is being accomplished in the open fields—to which indeed the farmers have many of them conveyed their machines, leaving the labourers to destroy them at their pleasure, and out of reach of danger to other property. In some places agricultural wages have risen to 10s. a week, in the hope of deterring the men from illegal conduct. In others the labourers demand more, and have refused to work in consequence of its not being pledged them.

The Coventry Mercury
5 December 1830

☘ *The farmers of Oxfordshire were not alone in handing over the threshing machines to the labourers for destruction. Many others endeavoured to pacify the rebels in this way. In Norfolk farmers were urged by the magistrates 'to discontinue the use of Thrashing machines and to take them to pieces'. They issued notices with this advice on them.*

Machine burnt to Ashes

A few days since, Mrs. Nicholls, of the Sun-Rising, Edge-hill, ordered her threshing machines to be taken into one of her fields and covered with stubble. On this being made known in the neighbourhood, a lawless set of fellows assembled, and by setting fire to the stubble, burnt the machines to ashes.

The Coventry Mercury
12 December 1830

Over Thirty Stacks fired at Coton

Cambridge

A fire broke out soon after six o'clock yesterday evening on the premises of Mr. Angler, a large farmer at Coton, three miles west of this place, and in the course of a few hours the farm buildings and thirty-two stacks of corn and hay, principally belonging to Mr. Angler, were burnt down. The engines from this town were in attendance, as were a large concourse of inhabitants and students, who actively exerted themselves to subdue the fire. We lament to add that a number of countrymen stood by, and would render no assistance.

The Coventry Mercury
12 December 1830

Diabolical Spirit in Cumberland

In Cumberland, we regret to say, the spirit exhibited is most diabolical.
On Tuesday night, two fires took place in opposite directions near
Carlisle. A large mob assembled from Carlisle and not only refused to give
assistance, but did everything they could to prevent the fire being
extinguished, by throwing the buckets into the flames, cutting the pipes,
&c., exclaiming "This will teach them to make corn laws. . . . This will
enlighten the borough-mongers" &c.

The Coventry Mercury
12 December 1830

1831

A Letter to Captain Swing

We copy the following from *The Taunton Courier*:

To Swing

If the following short, but most melancholy narrative can be of any use
in deterring your peasantry from similar excesses and guarding them
from similar misfortunes, the Editor will be doing good by making it
public:

I am curate of a small parish in Hampshire, and hearing that there was
a great gathering of people in the immediate neighbourhood, I arose early
in the morning to use my influence with my parishioners to keep out of
the mischief. The first thing I saw was seven persons, all married men,
with bludgeons in their hands, repairing to the general assemblage of
labourers. I begged, intreated and implored them to remain where they
were; I brought out their wives and children to assist me, but it was all in
vain; they treated me with respect, but were determined, and I lost sight
of them; in forty-eight hours from that period, this was their condition.
John Symonds (wife and four children) skull fractured in five places, quite
insensible and life in imminent danger—Francis Dorking, a widower
(five children) committed to Devizes jail, for machine breaking, will be
tried for his life—William Farmer, left cheek cut down to the bone with a
yeoman's sword—three cuts in the arm, so bad that his arm was taken off
that night—John Freeling, absconded with three warrants out against

him for capital offences, and seven children and wife chargeable to the parish.—Abraham Tucker, trampled upon by cavalry, cannot possibly recover, was just married. Daniel Jones and John Vigor, two excellent young men, became intoxicated, plundered houses—are committed to take their trial, and will, in all probability, perish upon the gallows, leaving nine children to deplore the madness and folly of that fatal day. It falls to my unhappy lot to visit daily these miserable mothers and deserted children, and if the boldest peasant who had taken up his bludgeon against the magistrates and the law could see it, I believe his heart would die within him, and he would return in humbleness of spirit to the plough. It is a fearful thing to be cursed by the poor, but day and night these unhappy people call down the curses of heaven upon *Swing*.

The Sussex Advertiser
3 January 1831

Harrowing Scenes at Winchester Gaol

Winchester
The scenes of distress in and about the gaol are most terrible. The number of men who are to be torn from their homes and connexions is so great that there is scarcely a hamlet in the county into which anguish and tribulation have not entered. Wives, sisters, mothers, children beset the gates daily, and the governor of the gaol says that the scenes which he is obliged to witness at the time of locking up the prison are truly heart-breaking.

The Falmouth Packet
15 January 1831

The Trials at Reading

Berks.
The trials of the rioters at Reading concluded on Tuesday, when the awful sentence of death was passed upon three of the prisoners, viz. William Oakley, W. Winterbourne and Alfred Darling (the last-named having been convicted of robbery and other crimes and the two others of destroying machinery); twenty-three capitally convicted of robberies, destroying machinery &c. had sentences of death recorded against them, and will be transported for life; nineteen were sentenced to transportation for fourteen years; and the remainder to seven years transportation, or various periods of imprisonment.

The Falmouth Packet
15 January 1831

❀ *In Southern England, in all about two thousand men were put on trial after the labourers' uprising, many of them only a week or two after the flames of the burning rickyards of that unhappy December had died down. Two of the prisoners at Winchester were executed on 15 January 1831, the day on which the* Falmouth Packet *reports were published.*

Curious Fact*

Mr. Charles Parker, of Arundel, brought home three very young rabbits, which for the sake of warmth were placed before the fire. The house cat had kittened the same day, and on discovering the young rabbits showed great affection for them; on the following morning all the kittens but one were destroyed, and the rabbits placed under the care of the cat, who has ever since shewed the greatest solicitude for their welfare, and they are now thriving under the kind offices of their feline foster-mother.

The Sussex Advertiser
4 April 1831

1832

Off to the Canadas

A plan of emigration on a limited scale has recently been attempted in the parish of Lenham. Our worthy High Sheriff, George Douglas, Esq., of Chilston, lent £1,000 to the authorities of that parish, which sum was employed in fitting out a certain number of labourers and shipping them for the Canadas. After the emigrants have reached the place of their destination, a small sum of money, varying according to the number of children, is given. The sum advanced to the parish will, of course, be repaid by instalments. Many farmers in Headcorn, Ulcomb, and in other parts of the Weald, are selling off their agricultural implements and other property, to embark for the new world. The reasons for quitting their father-land are the low price of agricultural produce, the pressure of the rates, and the utter impossibility of bettering their conditions by the most persevering industry.

The Maidstone Gazette
quoted in The Lichfield Mercury
6 April 1832

⊛ *Two years after the loan to the village of Lenham by the High Sheriff, parish authorities were able to borrow money from the Governments in order to help emigrants. They could do so under the Poor Law Amendment Act of 1834. But the arrangement was restricted to money to speed the departure of paupers who would otherwise have continued to be a charge on local funds.*

156 Emigrants from Frome

One hundred and fifty-six persons left Frome on Sunday evening last, on their way to Bristol, to embark for Canada. The greater proportion of these emigrants leave the country in consequence of the entreaties of their friends who have gone before them and prospered.

The Lichfield Mercury
6 April 1832

The Reform Bill is passed

The welcome intelligence that the Reform Bill had been read a third time in the House of Lords, and passed by a large majority, reached this city shortly before ten o'clock on Tuesday morning. It was communicated by an express from that active and obliging newspaper, *The Sun*. The public joy was speedily manifested, and so great was the curiosity to become acquainted with the particulars that, notwithstanding the display of the intelligence in the office window and the circulation of notes to as many of our friends as time permitted, we were overwhelmed with enquiries, and some hours of our time were occupied in the gratifying task of answering interrogatories on the subject. At least thirty or forty times we were called upon to give to audiences of occasionally eight or ten persons, a short account of the proceedings.

Congratulations were universal; and even passengers by the coaches, hearing that particulars of the intelligence were to be obtained at our office, came to it, at the risk of losing their places, and joined in the general expression of delight. . . . The bells of the cathedral and the other churches rang merrily and continuously throughout the day, and it is intended to celebrate the joyous event of the Royal Assent being given to the Bill by numerous public dinners. Many names, we hear, have been put down for this purpose.

The Lichfield Mercury
8 June 1832

Reform Celebrations at Leek

Leek
Since the joyous intelligence of the third reading of the bill first arrived in this place, the town has presented an enlivened and animated appearance. The bells for several days continued to peal forth the merry sounds of gladness—banners with appropriate and striking devices were everywhere hoisted, and the inhabitants await with impatience the announcement of the appointed day of general exultation that they may contribute their mite to the common cause, and, however humble, attest the sincerity of their satisfaction—and the happy termination of the arduous and important struggle.

The Staffordshire Gazette
13 June 1832

❀ *The Reform Bill of 1832 enfranchised nearly a quarter of a million people in England and Wales who had not previously enjoyed the right to vote, and it ensured a much fairer distribution of parliamentary seats through the elimination of 'Rotten Boroughs'. The third reading was on 4 June, and the Royal Assent followed three days later.*

Alarm at Eton*

A very sudden and fatal attack of cholera, which has taken place at Chalvery, a hamlet of Upton, near Eaton, has excited so much alarm in the neighbourhood that circulars have been sent to the parents of students at Eton College, communicating the occurrence of the disease—and of course giving the option of removing them previous to the vacation, which commences on Monday, the 30th. inst. Five poor persons, all males, have been attacked, and all have died, although they received every attention from the parish authorities, and from a medical gentleman well acquainted with the disease in India. The eldest was fifty-five year of age, and the youngest eight; one of them died in six hours from the first attack of the disease, and another lasted nineteen hours. All the cases occurred on Sunday and Monday and as no new case has since appeared, and every precaution has been taken of covering the bodies with lime and committing them to an extra deep grave the same day, lime-washing the houses and fumigating or dressing the clothes, &c., we hope, although the attack was violent and fatal, it is now over.

The Wolverhampton Chronicle
25 July 1832

1833

Wild Boar Hunting in Buckinghamshire*

A short time since, a wild boar, the property of Charles Shaw, Esq., of Hedgerley Park, escaped from his stye, and a number of persons were employed till Saturday last to find his haunt. On that day he was found in a thick cover in Dropmore Park, and was immediately pursued by men and dogs, but he appeared to put them all at defiance, killing one bull dog and very much injuring another. In fact some of the gallant sportsmen were compelled to climb the trees for safety. The boar was not taken after all, his pursuers losing him in the strong covers near East Burnham, where he is supposed to be at present.

The Windsor and Eton Express
14 February 1833

Extraordinary Produce*

A standard pear tree, by no means a large one, in the garden of the Rev. T. O. Bartlett, rector of Swanich, has this year borne the astonishing number of two thousand, one hundred and twenty one pears, weighing altogether but a few pounds short of half a ton. The fruit is of the species called The Iron, or baking pear; and the same tree, a few years since, produced a pear which weighed two pounds, two ounces and a half.

The Dorset County Chronicle
31 October 1833

Guy Fawkes Day in Hampshire

Fordingbridge
In order to prevent a further repetition of the disgraceful and dangerous proceedings which have taken place for several years past on the evening

of the 5th. of November, about 40 of the inhabitants were on Monday sworn in as special constables and by their vigilance the lighting of bonfires and letting off fireworks in the streets on Tuesday evening was entirely suppressed.

The Dorset County Chronicle
14 November 1833

November 5th in Taunton

The 5th. of November was as usual in this town celebrated by a variety of squibs, crackers and fire balls let off in the centre of the town, to the annoyance of all peaceable inhabitants and the danger of their property. It is to be wished that the scene of action were transferred to some neighbouring field, where they could not endanger the safety of travellers, but this has several times been endeavoured to be effected by the constables, and as often failed. Last Tuesday, Jarvis, the constable, in an attempt to put a stop to the proceedings of the crowd, was attacked, his coat was pulled off his back and he was much bruised. The most effectual stop to the fireworks, however, was occasioned by the circulation of a hand bill, to the effect that a German by the name of Van Heiglar would give a display of fireworks in a field about a mile from the town. The greater part of the people immediately rushed thither, but of course they found no fireworks, and they found too late they had been hoaxed. This prevented the display in the town being as good as usual.

The Dorset County Chronicle
14 November 1833

King Charles's Face

A short time ago was discovered at Wentworth Castle, in Yorkshire, an oak box, containing a plaister cast, taken from the face of King Charles the First after his execution. The features bear an extraordinary resemblance to the portraits painted of him by Vandyke, and exhibit a calm serenity of expression very different from what a violent death would lead us to suspect. The box which has been in the possession of the descendants of Thomas, Earl of Strafford, ever since the execution of the Monarch, had been thrown amongst some empty packing cases in an outer office where it lay concealed and forgotten.

The Leicester Journal
27 December 1833

1834

Extraordinary Baking Pear

An extraordinary common baking pear, weighing 17½ oz. and measuring 13½ inches in circumference was gathered on New Year's Day in the garden of Mr. Clarke, of Brixham. It will be presented for exhibition at the next Devon and Exeter Horticultural Show.

Dorset County Chronicle
16 January 1834

Prizes for High Moral Character

Cornwall

At the annual parish meeting at St. Austell on Tuesday last, much satisfaction was expressed at the exhibition of the overseer's and waywardens' accounts, and at the general management of the parish affairs, by the select vestry during the year. Compared with the former and preceding years, there was a diminution of expenditure. . . . It was not the least gratifying part of the proceedings to witness the distribution of the prizes offered by the vestry to those individuals who have maintained the highest reputation as to moral character. Ten pounds were appropriated for that purpose several months previously, and the resolutions of the vestry duly advertised. This sum was thus awarded:

First Prize   £4 to Richard Williams, in the Higher Quarter, or Upland part of the parish, with eight children, average earnings of the family 9s.6d. per week—never aided by the parish.

Second Prize   £3 to Henry Cock, Mulvra, Lower Quarter, nine children under 20, average earnings of the family during the year 15s. a week—no parochial aid recently. Assisted some years since during sickness.

Third and Fourth Prize   £2 and £1, divided equally between Launcelot Hore, John Hore and John Henwood of the High Quarter, each with six young children, maintained on ordinary labouring wages, without parish help.

The successful candidates were decorated with ribbands, and were addressed in an admirable and impressive speech by the worthy vicar, the distributor of the rewards. A like sum of ten pounds was voted by the meeting for a similar purpose next year.

The Dorset County Chronicle
3 April 1834

Hen survives Five-week Burial

A hen belonging to Mr. Nuttall, of West Monkton, on the 18th. ult. was discovered under a mass of straw, which had been accidently thrown upon her as far back as the 12th. of February. It was exceedingly weak and had entirely changed colour from its long confinement. It is now quite recovered.

The Dorset County Chronicle
3 April 1834

Trades Unions*

The misguided men who were convicted at our late Assizes of administering unlawful Oaths in their secret meetings as Trades Unionists were removed on Thursday morning from the County Jail, to be placed on board the *York* hulk in Gosport Harbour, preparatory to being banished from their native country in pursuance of the sentence passed upon them of Seven Years' Transportation beyond the seas.
James Loveless, who it appeared by the evidence against him, took a prominent part in the secret transactions of the society, and John Loveless, his brother, were itinerant preachers, and in the possession of the former the following lines were found:

> God is our guide; from field, from wave,
> From plough, from anvil, and from loom,
> We come our Country's rights to save,
> And speak a tyrant faction's doom.
>   We raise the watchword 'Liberty'!
>   We will, we will, we will be free!
>
> God is our guide, no swords we draw,
> We kindle not war's battle fires
> By reason, union, justice, law,
> We claim the birthright of our sires.
>   We raise the watchword 'Liberty'!
>   We will, we will, we will be free!

Dorset County Chronicle
3 April 1834

❀ *The Loveless brothers and their fellow-prisoners were the famous
'Martyrs', agricultural labourers from the Dorset village of
Tolpuddle. Although they were convicted of administering
unlawful oaths, the real purpose of the charge was the
Government's determination, by way of a savage sentence, to
discourage farmworkers from forming trade-unions, although these
had been lawful since 1824. The Tolpuddle men, who had formed
a Friendly Society of Agricultural Labourers, were arrested on
24 February, 1834, had to walk the six miles to Dorchester and were
there sentenced towards the end of the following month. They
were all transported to Australia, but because of a great outcry
initiated by the trade-unions all six men were given a free pardon
in 1836. George Loveless, their leader (mistakenly referred to as
'James' in the* Dorset Chronicle) *came home in 1837, and his
brother James (not 'John') returned in the following March, as did
Thomas Standfield and his son, John, and also James Brine. James
Hammett did not see Tolpuddle again until 1839.*

*The 'Tolpuddle Martyrs' are remembered in their home village
in several ways. Six memorial cottages and a hall were built there
in 1934 by the Trades Union Congress. Each cottage bears the
name of one of the men, and provides a home for a retired
agricultural worker. The hall contains many fascinating records and
mementoes of the six men. There is a memorial seat by a tree
under which they held their meetings, and a tablet marks a house
in which Thomas Standfield lived. James Hammett's grave is in
the churchyard; he was the only one who stayed in Tolpuddle after
the return from Australia. Five of the men were Methodist lay
preachers. There is a memorial arch in front of the Methodist
chapel.*

Superstition*

The vapours of superstition have not yet been dissipated in the light of
education. An elderly dame, last week, ran breathlessly towards a
gentleman riding near Taunton on a white horse, eagerly asking him for a
remedy for her child, who had the hooping cough. The silly creature was
referred to a medical gentleman as the proper person for such an appeal,
but the old woman insisted on it that he would not do, no prescription
being of the least use unless given by the first person she met on a white
horse.

The Dorset County Chronicle
3 April 1834

Curious Circumstance*

On Sunday, April 13, as the clerk of Collingbourne Kingston Church was looking out the lessons for the day, he perceived something under the Bible in the reading-desk and, in a hollow place, found a robin's nest containing two eggs. The bird, not having been distracted, laid six eggs, which were hatched on the 4th. instant. They are now to be seen and have been viewed by the churchwardens and many respectable persons. It is singular that the cock bird, which worked hard to procure food for its mate, should have even brought it in its bill and fed its partner during the hour of divine service, which is performed twice each Sabbath day.

The Dorset County Chronicle
15 May 1834

❀ *Robins continued to make use of church lecterns in this way. At the church of the Holy Trinity at Blythburgh, Suffolk, a robin is embroidered on the lectern cover and the churchwardens' staves are tipped by a robin in bronze. They commemorate the hatching out of two robin's eggs in the fifteenth-century lectern in the 1880s, and that a robin nested there again about fifty years later, in 1931. Another strange nesting place for a robin is the subject of a subsequent story, from the* Cumberland Pacquet *of 13 June 1843. Yet another report showing that the robin has little fear of man is given earlier in this book, from* The Weekly Register *for 9 February 1823.*

300 Labourers demand Higher Wages

Between two and three hundred labourers assembled in the parish of Stansted Mountfitchet on the 22d. inst. and proceeding to the different farmhouses compelled all engaged about the premises to leave their work and join in a combination, the avowed purpose of which was to demand a higher rate of wages. Men who were at plough were taken away by the mob, and in one instance a man who was unloading corn was taken off the wagon and by force compelled to join them. Two of the ring-leaders, named George Willis and George Sapseed, have been apprehended and were on Saturday committed to Springfield Convict Gaol for trial.

The Chelmsford Chronicle
3 October 1834

Inflammatory Songs*

Two men were on the 29th, ult. apprehended in Sculcoats, singing and vending a ludicrous and inflammatory burlesque upon the New Poor Law Bill. On the following day their stock-in-trade was burnt by order of the Magistrates, and they were discharged on promising never to do the like again—*Hull Advertiser* (Two vagabonds were vending the same inflammatory papers in this county during last week. We trust the authorities will look to them—Ed.)

The Chelmsford Chronicle
7 November 1834

❀ *The subject of these songs would have been the Poor Law Amendment Act of 1834, which was brought in to combat a poor rate amounting to more than seven million pounds annually. The significance of this figure is the fact that it was about three and a half times as much as was needed fifty years previously, although the population was still less than double that of the 1780s. (For details of the measure, see subsequent extract from* Falmouth Packet *of 24 September 1836.)*

This very high expenditure was largely due to the Speenhamland System, which derived from a meeting of Justices of the Peace at the village of Speen, in the district of Speenhamland in Berkshire in 1795, and was subsequently adopted for the greater part of the rest of the country. Through the Speenhamland System, the justices agreed on the amount which a labourer needed to maintain his family with the essentials of life, in terms of food, clothing and shelter, the amount rising with an increase in family and fluctuating according to the price of bread. If the labourer's wages failed to meet that figure the deficit was met through the rates.

Chace Extraordinary*

A spirited chace commenced last week at Heckington, by the Constable of that place and several men charged to assist him, to take two poachers named Medlar and Burgess. One being in bed, made his escape out of the window, with nothing on but his shirt, and showed real game, taking hedges, ditches, roads and ploughed fields, without shoe or stocking, and was closely pursued through seven parishes for the whole day: night coming on, and the hunters running by sight, not by scent, lost him, and were compelled to give him credit for resolution and activity. The other, Burgess, took shelter under a large brewing tub; one of the pursuers suspected that to be the case, and got upon it and held him down, while the others came up and secured him.

The Chelmsford Chronicle
26 December 1834

1835

Christmas Pie*

We are informed that Mrs. Kirk, of the Old Ship Inn, Rotherham, has, with her accustomed liberality, provided for her friends, and especially for her Sheffield friends, a Christmas pie which, when taken to the oven, weighed upwards of seventeen stone; it consists of one rump of beef, two legs of veal, two legs of pork, three hares, three couple of rabits, three geese, two brace of pheasants, four brace of partridges, two turkeys, two couple of fowls, with 7½ stone of best flour. We have no doubt that the good landlady of the Ship will be honoured with lots of visitors, not only to look at, but partake of that extraordinary pie during Christmas.

The Doncaster Gazette
quoted in The Devonshire Chronicle
17 January 1835

Grim Reminders of Civil War

Some labourers who were employed digging stones on Epsom Downs on the 19th. instant, discovered 14 skeletons that had evidently been interred a great deal of time, and apparently in haste, as the graves were only from one and a half foot to two foot deep, and appeared as if dug where the bodies fell, as they were found lying in all directions. Some few of the graves contained two bodies, as the whole only occupied a few rods of ground, situated on the brow of the hill by the road-side leading from Epsom to Reigate. The remains were carefully collected and interred in Epsom Church-yard, and the stone diggers were desired not to disturb any more soil near the spot, as it was probable many more would have been found. The following is abridged from Clarendon's History of the Rebellion and for want of better information may account for the above discovery:

In May 1648 a meeting of the Royalists was held on Epsom Downs under the pretence of a horse-race, and 600 horses were collected and marched to Reigate. Sir Michael Levesey sent Major Audeley from Hounslow with three troop of horse to prevent the meeting and take possession of Lord Monson's castle at Reigate, but they were too late and the Royalists arrived in Reigate before them. Audeley rested on Red Hill, and the Royalists left Reigate and marched to Dorking; the next morning they returned to Reigate, but finding it occupied by the Parliament forces they marched for Kingston. Two hours afterwards the Parliament forces, consisting of five troops of horses and three of foot, marched from Red Hill in pursuit of them, and made such speed that the horse overtook the Royalists *before they reached Ewell, where a sharp skirmish took place.* The Royalists continued to retreat before the Parliament forces until they reached Kingston, which they entered in good order, and the Parliament forces were repulsed at the entrance of the town.

The Surrey Standard
28 February 1835

Execution*

James Passfield, who was convicted at the last Essex Assizes of setting fire to the stack-yard of Mr. Isaac Davie, of Toppesfield, suffered the last sentence of the law in front of the Convict Gaol, at Springfield, near Chelmsford, on Friday last. Previous to being led forth to the scaffold, he made a full confession of his guilt and died penitent. He was only 23 years of age.

The Leicester Journal
3 April 1835

Burial after Thirty Years

A few days ago the remains of a farmer were interred at Stevenage, in Hertfordshire, who died many years ago; and bequeathed his estate, worth £400 a year, to his two brothers, and if they should die, to his nephew, to be enjoyed by them for thirty years, at the expiration of which he expected to return to life, when his estate was to return to him. He provided for his re-appearance by ordering his coffin to be fixed on a beam in his barn, locked and the key inclosed, that he might let himself out. He was allowed four days grace beyond the time limited, and not presenting himself was then honoured with Christian burial.

The Leicester Journal
24 April 1835

✿ *It might seem that the farmer buried at Stevenage was influenced by the curious instructions left by his fellow-townsman, Henry Trigg (see extract from the* Hertfordshire Mercury *of 1 April 1826).*

Riots in Kent*

At the first sitting of the Kent Special Sessions, which was holden on Wednesday, at St. Augustines, near Canterbury, the grand jury found a true bill against eighteen persons, most of whom were labourers, for having been concerned in the riots at Sittingbourne and Doddington, which took place on the introduction of the new Poor Law Bill in that district a few weeks ago. In the course of the day several other true bills were found by the grand jury against persons implicated in the same riots; the indictment contained five different counts, and charged the prisoners with riotously assembling to obstruct the execution of an Act of Parliament. Mr. Bodkin appeared for the prosecution and Mr. Wells for the defence. Several witnesses were called for the prosecution, who stated that on the 4th. of May last, the poor of the parish of Doddington had expressed great dissatisfaction at receiving relief half in kind and half in money, according to the provisions of the new Poor Law Bill, and that a mob of several hundred persons had assembled round the workhouse, making use of the most violent language against the magistrates. Some of them went around with bludgeons and laid violent hands on Dr. Poore and Gen. Gosselin, and had also ill-treated such of the paupers as were willing to accept relief in the manner offered by the magistrates and enacted by the legislature. Mr. Wells was briefly heard in the defence. He thought, he said, that great allowance would be made for excitement amongst persons not having had the benefit of education, and in a case where a great change in the political economy, and that change affecting such persons, had taken place. Mr. Wells then adverted to the difference between Lord Brougham and one of the Poor Law Commissioners, as to the Poor Law Bill's authorising the separation of man and wife, and the feeling of many of the working men in Court was about to display itself in condemnation of such a separation, but it was immediately repressed. Several of the prisoners received good characters from some of the parochial authorities of Doddington and four other persons. The chairman briefly summed up, recapitulating the evidence, and the jury, after a few minutes' consultation, returned a verdict of guilty against all the prisoners, but recommended them to mercy.

The Surrey Standard
6 June 1835

Good Marriage by Mail-cart Man

We insert the following as we received it from our Salisbury correspondent—

Mr. Thomas Gill, son of Mr. Gill, of the French Horn Inn, Sarum, was married on the 28th. of June at St. Edmund's Church, Salisbury, by the Rev. Dr. Hawes, to a Miss Angell, late of Newfoundland, by which marriage he will shortly come into the possession of a number of estates and money, amounting in value to £1,000,000, left by a Mr. Angell, who died some 60 years since. The Chrois estate, near Lambeth, forms part of the landed property, and to possess which he must bear the name and arms of the Angell family. He is at present the mail-cart man on the line of the road from Warminster to Sarum.

The Devizes Gazette
quoted in The Times
25 July 1835

Wonderful Manifestation at Chewton Mendip

Wonders will never cease and miracles are not yet out of fashion, especially at Chewton Mendip, where (it is gravely affirmed by the *Bath Herald* "on authority") 30 or 40 of the good people, all wearing heads on their shoulders, have been favoured with a wonderful manifestation. Thus the story runs:

On Sunday evening se'nnight, between six and seven o'clock, there was seen at Chewton Mendip, a most extraordinary and unaccountable phenomenon in the heavens. It was the appearance of a regiment of horse, with swords drawn, every trooper being distinctly visible, and the whole performing their evolutions as in the field of battle, both horses and soldiers appearing perfectly black. The sight lasted a considerable time, and was witnessed, with no small degree of consternation and dismay, by not less than 30 or 40 individuals, one of whom, named Tyte, gamekeeper to Anthony Blagrave, Esq., of Harptree-court, instantly descended the hill from Chewton, under considerable agitation of feelings. A woman also of the village was so terrified by the spectacle, that she has not recovered from the fright at the present moment, and is really seriously indisposed. There are many recorded examples of similar sights, from Josephus down to the year 1745, when previous to the great rebellion, celestial phenomena of the same character were said to have been seen by wondering multititudes of all classes of people.

The Times
8 October 1835

❀ *A report of a similar 'phenomenon'—much later than 1745—is given earlier in this book, from the County Chronicle of 10 February 1818. Many present readers will recall that soldiers of the First World War told of 'Angels of Mons' who appeared in the sky at a time of very bitter fighting—a belief buttressed (or engendered) by Machen's famous short story.*

Extraordinary Discovery*

A few days since, as a labourer in the employ of Mr. Fawcett was digging in a field adjoining one belonging to Mr. Holmes, of Dunstable, for the purpose of putting in a post at a depth of about 6 feet, he found something which resisted the force of the spade and pick axe. Mr. Fawcett proceeded to the spot, and on clearing away the ground, found four complete stone steps of considerable breadth and width, with the base of a column or pillar at each end, and then in the same condition as they had evidently been when used as the means of access to the building to which they had belonged. This led to a further search, when the entire foundation and some of the walls of a church were most distinctly traced; in addition was also found a large quantity of stained glass, and some very curious paving, which is conceived to be the flooring of an altar-piece. On inspection a coffin was found, the wood of which had completely assimilated itself with the surrounding earth. The former leaden coffin remained quite entire, although evidently injured by time. The leaden coffin, on being opened, was found to contain the perfect skeleton of a human frame, the flesh of which had totally wasted, and had left all the bones as they had been placed at the time of interment. Tuesday afternoon the parochial authorities determined in consequence of the immense number of persons who had flocked to see the coffin and its contents, to have it re-interred in the church-yard of the present church, which was done. Some time since, Mr. Fawcett, while digging in the same field, found a quantity of stone under the surface sufficient to build a stable; and some time subsequently to a fire, which occurred at the Saracen's Head, a quantity of old and rare coins and other curiosities were found, some of which are in the possession of the landlord. From the fact of Dunstable having been destroyed by a fire in the reign of John, no doubt exists that the things found form part of the ruins of the old town.

The Times
15 December 1835

1836

A Strange Yule Custom

Had not the following anecdote been told to us on the authority of a
gentleman of high respectability, we should have found some difficulty in
believing that so strange a superstition still had influence over the minds
of the inhabitants of the West Riding. On the night of Christmas-day, our
informant was returning to Leeds in a gig, from a town a few miles off,
and wished to light a cigar. He stopped at a cottage by the way-side and
begged to be allowed a light. "No" was the reply "thou'lt get no light here
to-night". Somewhat surprised at this surly reply, he drove on for a mile
or two, and arriving at a toll-gate, again preferred his request. "No Sir"
said the gate-keeper "I shall let no light go out of my house to-night". As
there was no mending the matter, our friend again proceeded to another
toll-bar, and a third time requested a light. He was very civilly told that he
should have had a light with pleasure, had it not been Christmas-night,
but that, on that night, to allow a light to be taken out of the house *would
ensure bad luck throughout the next year*. This silly superstition was
cause which led to the refusals which so astonished the traveller.

The Times
quoted in
The York Chronicle
14 January 1836

An Unusual Family

Mr. Samuel Oldfield, grazier, of Cleatop, near Settle, has successfully tried
a novel method of bringing up four lambs, whose mothers are dead; three
of them may now be seen sucking a cow, which regularly comes to the
little creatures of that purpose at their feeding time! The other lamb he is
rearing by another ewe. What makes the circumstance more remarkable
is that one of the lambs, being very small, perches on a stool to enable it to
reach its adopted mother.

The York Chronicle
4 May 1836

Tragedy at Brough Rock

A shocking accident occurred last week at the Brough Rock near the Lizard. A young man attempted the scarcely human task of climbing to the summit of this rock, which is 250 feet high (there being only one instance on record of the feat having been previously performed) and succeeded. After lowering down some sea birds' eggs, he fell over the tremendous precipice, and was of course dashed to pieces. The cause of his falling is not known and never will be. The Rock is detached from the main land, and the ascent to the summit is extremely perilous—as in several places to be passed in the ascent, the projections overhang.

The Cornubian
30 June 1836

Longevity*

There is now living in and near Liskeard, three old men, called Bowden, Tremain and Oliver, whose united ages amount to 301 years. Bowden, the eldest of the three, is 104 years of age, and attends his church regularly.

The Cornubian
14 July 1836

New Poor Law Act

A meeting was held at the Town-hall, Liskeard, on Monday last, when Mr. Gilbert, the Assistant Poor Law Commissioner, attended to explain the mode of administering the new poor laws. Several influential gentlemen of the neighbourhood were present. The chair was taken by John Buller, Esq., of Morval. Mr. Gilbert observed it was important when any great change took place in the administration of the laws that such change should be well understood. In this instance the consent of the community was not necessary, the power of joining any number of parishes being vested in the commissioners. The object of the Poor Law Amendment Act was to economise the parochial funds and to create a proper executive to carry the law into effect. The board of guardians would consist of the nobility and magistrates of the district, and of one or more of the most respectable inhabitants of each parish, elected by the owners and occupiers of property in each parish; to the board would be entrusted the management of the funds and the affairs of the union. The paupers were divided into two classes—those who received out-door relief, and others who were sent to the workhouse: of the former were the aged and infirm, the workhouse being employed as a test for the idle and disorderly. There was no law which made it compulsory on all paupers indiscriminately to go into the workhouse. In reply to questions proposed by Mr. Lyne and the Rev. T. Grylls, Mr. Gilbert stated it was imperative on the board of guardians to classify the inmates of the union workhouse, and that consequently husband and wife, parent and child were separated from each other. Application for relief is made to the relieving officer, who lays the same before the board of guardians at their weekly meeting. Each parish would pay for the maintenance of its own paupers in the workhouse, the incidental expenses of the union, borne by the several parishes, would be regulated by the average expenditure of each parish during the last three years. The union will include 27 parishes; and its operations are likely to commence early in the ensuing year. Thanks were accorded to Mr. Gilbert and the meeting broke up.

The Falmouth Packet
24 September 1836

❀ *There were parish workhouses in Britain long before the Poor Law Amendment Act, but under this new measure one large workhouse for a 'Union' of parishes became compulsory. Earlier measures had specifically laid down, however, that able-bodied men must be found some sort of job outside the workhouse. As Mr Gilbert made clear, the new Act required that such men must definitely go to the workhouse. Outdoor relief, which had risen to a very high annual figure, was most certainly barred to them. Mr Gilbert, incidentally, was a very busy man who visited many parts of the country to explain the Act. In March of the previous year, for example, the* Surrey Standard *reported a visit to Buckingham, where he had ordered the formation of about thirty parishes into a Union.*

A Curious Loaf*

A correspondent writes: There is a loaf of bread in the possession of Mr. Soars of Thurlestone, Derbyshire, upwards of 400 years old. It is a funeral loaf, bearing the date of 1436, and was discovered upwards of two years ago, in a chest with some old writings belonging to a family estate. The writer has been acquainted with the said loaf upwards of 50 years and called the attention of the public to the *old bread* some years ago. Since then it has become a Lion and has suffered by the handlings and pilferings of the curious. Mrs. Soars has placed it on a handsome glass salver and beehive cover, which adds greatly to its presentation and appearance. As

Mrs. S. is noted for the excellence of her dairy, she can truly (and often does) reply to interrogations "How are you getting on?". "Well, pretty well, we have an old loaf *uncut* in the house, and some decent cheese."

The Nottingham Mercury
quoted in The Harrogate Advertiser
26 September 1836

1837

A Great Walker and Teetotaller

Petworth
A short time since the Earl of Egremont had the portrait of Mr. Thomas Holt, one of his oldest tenants taken by Mr. Phillips, jun. and it has since been engraved and dedicated to the Temperance Society. Mr. Holt is a wonderful man. He has been in the habit generally every year of walking from his house to London, a distance of about fifty miles, and returning on foot the next day but one. In October last, although then in the 85th. year of his age, he performed his accustomed journey, and in the usual time, thirteen hours. Mr. Holt is a remarkably striking instance of the inestimable advantages of temperance. In his 85th. year we see him capable of walking at the rate of nearly four miles an hour for thirteen consecutive hours!! This gentleman knows not the use of either wine, spirits, or fermented liquor of any kind. His only beverage through life has been milk, tea and water. He remembers not to have suffered from illness these forty years past, except latterly when he had an attack of the prevailing epidemic. Mr. Holt proposes, if he should be blessed with continued health, to perform his usual journey to the metropolis this year, nor does he in the least doubt his ability to accomplish it as usual. In the year 1807, on the occasion of a contested election, Mr. Holt walked from Petworth to Lewes, a distance of thirty five miles and a half; having given his vote to the Hon. Charles Wyndham, and partaken of some bread and cheese and a draught of water, he returned home the same day, having performed a journey of no less than seventy-one miles with perfect ease to himself.

The Sussex Agricultural Express
18 February 1837

❀ *The 'prevailing epidemic'? Influenza.*

Death in Dairy Jar

Billingshurst
An inquest was held on the 24th. instant, at the house of Mr. T. Baker, of Cobbethall farm, in this parish, on the body of Edwin Baker, a little boy, the son of Mr. T. Baker, a little more than two years old. It appeared from the evidence that on Tuesday morning last the deceased was with his mother in the wash-house, who was attending to her dairy affairs, and had been scalding milk, a quantity of which she had placed in a deep earthern jar on the floor to cool, when the poor child fell backwards into the scalding milk, and although immediately taken out he was so much injured that he died the next morning—Verdict "Accidental death".

The Sussex Agricultural Express
26 August 1837

Christmas Day in the Workhouse

Hastings and St. Leonards
On Christmas Day the Board of Guardians gave to all the poor in our Union House a good dinner of prime roast beef and plum pudding, and a pint of porter to each man and woman. This proceeding is highly creditable of the Guardians, who were resolved, although against the rules of the Poor Law Commissioners, that the poor on this day should regale themselves, even if they paid for it out of their own pockets.

The Sussex Agricultural Express
30 December 1837

❀ *The Poor Law Commissioners were against jollifications such as this because they were of the opinion that workhouses should be 'uninviting places of wholesome restraint'. They wanted conditions to be such as would urge the inmates to do their utmost to get away from 'The Union' as quickly as possible. Naturally, they frowned on celebrations at which the paupers would get much better fare than if they were at home.*

Superlative Impudence

Udimore
On Saturday night last, some person or persons unknown killed a sheep in the field of Mr. John Woodhams, of this place, and afterwards had the superlative impudence to stick the head and skin up before his door.

The Sussex Agricultural Express
30 December 1837

Rhyming Robbers

Rotherfield

In this neighbourhood the sheep stealers have not only been bold in their depredations, but have aspired to some distinction in the production of witticism; for a few days since, Mr. Wickens found the skin of one of his stolen sheep, and within the folds, a slip of paper, on which were the following words:

> You are rich and we are poor,
> When this is gone, we'll come for more.

The Sussex Agricultural Express
30 December 1837

1838

Destruction of Young Pigs*

The disappearance of young pigs newly littered is of very common occurrence, and has generally been attributed to a propensity in the sow to devour its offspring. A circumstance came under the observations of a gentleman in this neighbourhood on Monday last, which puts a completely new and extraordinary feature on the subject. Our informant's observations were attracted to a litter of pigs in the farmyard, by seeing a young grunter outside the sty door. Soon after a large tom cat kept on the premises crept up to the pig, seized it and carried it over the roofs of two out-houses, where he killed it and returned for another victim. Watching the absence of the sow, the feline thief pounced upon another young grunter, but was prevented from carrying it off. It was discovered that the cat had carried off its prey for the purpose of feeding on it, and that he had concealed the bodies in an adjoining yard. The propensity of the feline race to destroy young animals for food is well-known, but it has never been suspected that they had made attempts of the sort on pigs.

The Cumberland Pacquet
quoted in The Cambridge Chronicle
13 January 1838

Cloaks and Coats for Huntingdon Poor

Huntingdon
The first distribution of the Donation of the late David Veasey, Esq., was made last week to two poor old men and two old women of the parish of St. Mary's in this town and at Godmanchester, the executors having provided comfortable great coats for the men and warm cloaks for the women. This acceptable present was most gratefully received. And as the same gift is to be annually bestowed, many a poor old man and woman may have the chance in future years of receiving a warm garment to protect them from the inclemency of a severe winter.

The Cambridge Chronicle
20 January 1838

Cricket Match Extraordinary on Skates*

From the regions of frost and snow, dame Winter has not infrequently provided for the amusement and health and activity of the sons of the earth, by covering with her frozen mirror the otherwise liquid lake and flowing stream, on which the gliding skate has carried its dexterous votary, sometimes in the graceful curve and anon in the rapid sweep. But seldom has the icebound water borne so enlivening a company at so novel a game as presented itself on Gosfield Lake at the mansion of E. G. Bernard, Esq., M.P., near Halstead, Essex, on the 18 th. inst. Wickets were pitched at eleven o'clock, for a match between two elevens, for one innings each, which was played on the lake by Skaters. There were among the visitors and skaters several of the neighbouring gentry, and some of the dons of the game; the fielding was highly amusing and after a well-contested match the second eleven became the conquerors, the losers having scored forty and the winners not many more. The Halstead band enlivened the day with their music on the *ground* (ice), refreshments were provided by Mr. Ardley, of the King's Head inn, by whom, after the match, an excellent dinner was served up, the musical accompaniment then being by the Gorsfield band. The falls on the ice were neither so numerous nor so severe as might have been expected, and the game proved much more within the powers of skaters than could have been at all anticipated.

The Cambridge Chronicle
27 January 1838

To Prevent Milk being Sour*

Put a spoonful of wild horseradish into a dish of milk; the milk may then be preserved sweet, either in the open air or in a cellar for several days, while such as has not been so guarded will become sour.

The Bedford Mercury
2 February 1838

Drunken Cow

Last week Mr. Castle, farmer, of Northbourne, whilst brewing some strong ale, left a portion of it in what is called the well-lodge, to cool, when one of the cows got from the farmyard into the place, and drank so plentifully of the potent beverage that she was shortly taken ill; a farrier was sent for who administered the proper remedies, but to no effect, for in a few hours the poor animal actually died in a state of intoxication, a warning to drunkards.

The Kent Chronicle
quoted in the Cambridge Chronicle
14 April 1838

Curious Case*

On the 8th. inst., an inquest was held in Fosdyke Fen, Lincolnshire, on the body of Elizabeth Wells, then lying under disinterment. The inquest was held in compliance with an application made to the Coroner, the deceased having died very suddenly and been buried in a turnip field. It appeared, however, from the evidence of Susannah Creasy, that on Saturday the 31st. ult. deceased in the evening complained of violent pain in her head, and died soon afterwards. Her husband, who is parish clerk, procured a coffin, and without further ceremony caused her to be interred in a turnip field, a proceeding which occasioned much suspicion. Mr. Coupland, surgeon of Boston, examined the body, and declared it to be in his opinion that the deceased came to her death by the visitation of God in a natural way; a verdict to that effect was returned.

The Cambridge Chronicle
14 April 1838

The Coronation*

High Wycombe
The day of her Majesty's coronation was a gay one here; the whole of the shops were closed, and business of every description entirely suspended. The morning was ushered in by the firing of several large cannon, which were kindly lent by one of our worthy members, G. H. Dashwood, Esq., of West Wycombe Park and placed on the mount, near the grotto, at Castle Hill; they were fired by two old naval veterans, one of whom had been in the battles of Trafalgar and the Nile, and the report echoing majestically among the neighbouring hills was heard many miles distant. The bells of our church rang loud and merrily, on the top of the steeple was flying a union jack, and many houses in the High Street and Queen (now called Victoria) Square were decorated with flags, bearing loyal and appropriate descriptions. About seven o'clock the business of the day began, and before eight, more than 1,100 shillings were distributed to as many poor persons and widows above 30 years of age. At 10 the teachers and children in the Sunday schools met in their several places of worship, with many excellent and tastefully made flags, banners, &c.; among the numerous inscriptions we noted the following, viz. "Long live the Queen", "Hail Victoria", "May Education Flourish" and "Victoria, may her reign be long and happy" and we were particularly struck with one very pleasing device, which was the word "Victoria", formed with heartsease, each letter being of a different colour, and beautifully enwreathed with laurel and roses—it was carried before the Wesleyan school, and was a present we hear from Mr. J. Hunt of Cressex. About 11 they all joined in one body in the High Street, making altogether about 1200, and preceded by our excellent band walked in a procession around the town, and then to Castle Hill, the delightful residence of John Rumsey, Esq., in whose romantic pleasure grounds they were regaled with cakes and wine, after which the Mayor, by design of the managing Committee, presented each with a Victoria four-penny piece; the company assembled to witness this interesting ceremony was immense and the kindness of Mr. and Mrs. Rumsey was we are sure duly appreciated. In the afternoon a variety of amusements took place in our Rye, such as donkey racing, climbing a soaped pole for a leg of mutton, jingling, running for tobacco and snuff, jumping in sacks, swimming for a duck, &c. The venerable Lord Carrington, our friend and neighbour, was a spectator of these sports from his park; his lordship was highly gratified, and we are pleased to say appeared to be in the enjoyment of good health. Shortly after nine a brilliant display of fireworks took place in the High Street, and continued until past midnight; they were distinctly seen ten miles from Wycombe. . . .

In addition to the above we have great pleasure in stating, and we feel bound to do so, that Miss M. Carter, who has recently, at a considerable expense, erected and established a school here for the free education of poor children, gave a dinner to 30 of the children attending the church school who were considered too young to join in the procession, and also a dinner at Downley, in the parish of West Wycombe, to 78 children (including teachers) of another school which her liberality has established in that village.

The Berkshire Chronicle
7 July 1838

A Foster Mother*

A person of the name of Robert Smith, of No. 1 Court, Quart Pot Lane, has at this time, three little pigs, a fortnight old, being brought up by a bitch of the mongrel breed, and she appears as much attached to them as though they were her own offspring.

The Northampton Mercury
28 July 1838

1839

A Witty Goose Stealer*

On Monday night last, fourteen geese were stolen from the premises of Mr. Thomas Smith, of Great Bramingham, Luton, leaving the gander with a bag tied round his neck, containing fourteen farthings and a piece of paper, with the following pleasing intelligence for the owner—

> Mr. Smith, you lives here and I lives yonder—
> I've bought 14 Geese
> At a farthing a piece
> And left the money with the Gander.

The Bucks. Gazette
2 February 1839

Noted Rat Catcher

A short time ago, a rat catcher of Grendon, a noted hand at his work, named Willington, was requested by Mr. Barry, of Steeple Claydon, to destroy the rats on his premises. Upwards of 400 were killed the first day. The same person is in the habit of sending great quantities to Oxford, for the collegians to worry with their curs.

The Aylesbury News
20 April 1839

Argument for the New Constabulary Force Bill

The appointments of constables furnish arguments for a total change of system. At Chesham, for instance, there is a smith appointed constable, thief-taker and peace-officer, who has been once publicly flogged in the very town of Chesham, once privately flogged at Aylesbury Gaol, once convicted of feloniously stealing lead, and once committed to hard labour for three months for assaulting and robbing a boy. The moral influence of such a *gentleman* must be truly wonderful.

The Aylesbury News
11 May 1839

❀ *The Bill referred to in this report (enacted as the County Police Act, 1839) led to the appointment of constables who served with county police forces. It was a measure introduced by Lord Melbourne's administration, ten years after the establishment of the Metropolitan Police by Sir Robert Peel.*

Opening of the Aylesbury Railway*

Monday last was indeed a gay and busy day. At an early hour inhabitants of this town were aroused by the lively strains of the Aylesbury town band, and great numbers of people were present to witness the departure of the seven o'clock (first) train. At ten o'clock the crowd of respectable inhabitants and fashionably dressed people around the station-house was very great, and the pressure to obtain the best seats was ludicrously severe. None were admitted without a shareholder's ticket, and as soon as the train (consisting of a dozen carriages) was full, the Long Credon band struck up and off went the steamer, dragging after it a long line of Aylesbury people, to the number of between 200 and 300, and to the amazement of as many thousands outside, who were regretting their ill-luck in not having obtained a ticket. The train returned from

Cheddington almost immediately, and from that time till night, the crowd beseiging the station house, clamouring for admission, was immense. We are sure that, much as Hale Leys was frequented in the old-fashioned times of bull-baiting and cock-fighting, it never had half so many people on its surface as it had on the afternoon and evening of Monday last. The whole town was crowded with country visitors, and nearly every shop was closed, but Hale Leys was the centre of attraction. Those who had travelled by the railway, or felt no desire to travel, resorted there for amusement, and it was truly laughable to witness the contention for seats which was exhibited by the anxious crowd; while it was pitiful to behold the lengthened visages of those whose exertions for the whole day had been fruitless. The directors had made every possible arrangement for the conveyance of all and the engine started backwards and forwards continually, but the train must have travelled all the week to have satisfied everybody. The day was fine and the numberless journies passed off without any accident.

The Aylesbury News
15 June 1839

❀ *The opening of the station at Aylesbury was quite early in railway history. It occurred nine years after the introduction of the first passenger service (Liverpool and Manchester Railway, 1830) and only one year after the capital's first railway service to the provinces (London to Birmingham). Queen Victoria had yet to make her first journey by rail—this took place in 1842.*

A Porcine Appetite*

About ten days ago, a man named David Kindly, who was harvesting for Mr. George Poole, of Black Notley, actually ate three pounds of fat pork raw.

The Chelmsford Chronicle
13 September 1839

1840-50

REPEAL OF THE CORN LAWS
Mr Punch's cartoon recorded the intention of the Prime Minister,
Sir Robert Peel, to repeal the Corn Laws.

1840

Early Strawberries

Ripe strawberries were gathered on Christmas-day on the hill near Axbridge.

The Bristol Journal
4 January 1840

Treasure from Window-frame

On Christmas morning last, a little boy residing at Chalford, Westbury, proceeded to take a piece of an old window frame from some ruinous premises, for the purpose of making a Christmas fire. On cutting it up, nearly 200 pieces of gold coin were discovered. They were of different sizes, of the reign of Elizabeth, and were in the most beautiful state of preservation.

The Bristol Journal
4 January 1840

A Deluge of Silver Pieces

Ilchester

On Friday se'nnight this little town was in a state of the greatest excitement, from the circumstance of a Mr. West, an innkeeper in this neighbourhood, pulling down an old house he lately bought, the workmen being nearly deluged by a shower of silver pieces of the times of Elizabeth, Charles and James II; they were contained in an ample canvas bag of dimensions large enough to contain forty pounds weight; having burst it is impossible to say how much it contained. Several hundreds have been recovered by the owner of the premises. Being considered as a God-send by the populace, a scramble took place and *non est inventus* is the return. There can be no doubt the store was large, and at that time most valuable; it was secreted in some recess of the wall, over a window. Various conjectures are afloat, but we think the most rational one is that it was placed there during the Monmouth rebellion. The time is accurately determined by the coin of James II; he ascended the throne in 1685 and the battle of Sedgemoor (not many miles from thence) was fought . . . in the course of that year; the owner in all probability died on the field of battle.

The Bristol Journal
1 February 1840

❀ *At the battle of Sedgemoor (6 July 1685), the Duke of Monmouth, illegitimate son of Charles II, led a force of 6,000; many of his soldiers were armed only with scythes. The Duke was utterly defeated, and was executed only nine days later. If he did not die in the battle, the owner of the coins could well have been one of the many followers of Monmouth who were most cruelly put to death in the weeks that followed. They were sentenced through the royal vengeance of James II, meted out on the King's behalf by Lord Chief Justice Jeffreys in his Bloody Assizes in Dorset and Somerset.*

Celebrating the Queen's Marriage

Welwyn

At the loyal and patriotic village of Welwyn, the nuptials of her Majesty with the choice of her heart was celebrated in truly festive enjoyment. The inmates of the poor-house were abundantly supplied with roast beef and plum-pudding and plenty of ale, pipes, &c., the dames with snuff, coffee and tea. In the evening they also had a supper. Mrs. Johnes Knight, the lady of the revered rector, was most happy in contributing to the happiness of the poor, and among other things sent a very liberal supply of beef and plum pudding to their houses. The children of the school, upwards of one hundred and fifty in number, were regaled with tea and buns, and presented a most pleasing scene. Sixty of the respectable inhabitants sat down to an excellent dinner at the White Hart, where the good old English fare was served up in the best style. An appropriate song, composed by that veteran patriot, Mr. Batten, was sung at the dinner, and the whole of the company joined heartily in the loyal sentiments. The same song was also sung by the children of the school.

The Hertford and Bedford Reformer
15 February 1840

❀ *Queen Victoria was married on Monday, 10 February 1840, to Prince Albert of Saxe-Coburg-Gotha. The celebrations at Welwyn would have taken place on the same day.*

Singular Circumstance*

A child of four years old, son of B. Burley, of Tregony, wandered away from his home the other day, when after some search, he was found under a sow, with a litter of young pigs, sucking away as busy as any of them. He had often made the pigs his playmates, but it was not known before that he had been so completely adopted into the family circle.

The Bristol Journal
25 April 1840

1841

The Royal Cheese*

The farmers and yeomanry of the parish of West Pennard, near Glastonbury, in Somersetshire, and about 15 miles from Cheddar, are about to present to her Majesty, an enormous cheese, made on the 28th. of June, 1839, from the united milk of 737 cows, one meal's milking, as it is called, from each cow. The immense cheese weighs nearly 11 cwt.; it is in shape an octagon; in height it is 22 inches, and measures across 3 feet 1 inch. The upper surface of the cheese is ornamented with the royal arms, deeply impressed and very well executed. The arms are surrounded with a wreath of the oak leaves and acorns and the laurel; the rose, the thistle and the shamrock are also embossed upon the surface. The cheese is now at the Egyptian-hall, Piccadilly and will, it is said, be exhibited to the public. It is one of the wonders of the dairies of Somersetshire, and perhaps the largest cheese ever yet produced from the presses. A song entitled "The Royal Cheese", in commemoration of this cheese, has been composed by Mr. T. Williams, and inscribed to the farmers of the West of England. It (the song) has been sent to the Royal Palace, and it is understood to have been approved by the Queen and her Royal Consort.

The Observer
10 January 1841

Great Skeleton found at Westbury

Last week, as some men in the employ of Mr. Jesse Greenland, Westbury, were engaged in digging clay, for the purpose of brick-making, they came to the petrified remains of some immense animal, which subsequently proved to be the skeleton of that rare creature called the ichthyosaurus. The men, being unable to distinguish the value of such a curiosity, unfortunately destroyed the greater part of it. But the circumstances becoming known to Mr. Robt. Brent (a gentleman well known in the neighbourhood for his literary attainments and scientific researches), he immediately hastened to the spot, and his experienced eye at once recognised the antediluvian properties of the huge masses of bone before him, and with the enthusiasm and zeal of a philosopher carefully gathered up what remained of these relics of antiquity. Since then there has been found near the same place amonites of the most beautiful colour, deeply impregnated with iron pyrites.

The Wilts Independent
quoted in The Observer
3 January 1841

❋ *This ichthyosaurus which the men of Westbury had dug up could have been as much as 30 feet long. It was a marine reptile which lived from 185–190 million years ago. In appearance it was something like the porpoises we know to-day, but it had a large cruel 'beak' with a row of sharp pointed teeth for catching the fish which were its prey. The first complete fossil skeleton of an ichthyosaurus had been discovered in a cliff near Lyme Regis in 1811. It was found by the celebrated Mary Anning (1799–1847).*

Female Poacher*

A fair poacher, the industrious housekeeper of a person in Barnard Castle, named Hodgson, was caught on Sunday last, at two o'clock in the morning, in the game preserves of Mr. J. B. S. Morritt, of Rokeby, near Greta Bridge, catching hares. She had been abundantly successful, and notwithstanding the inclemency of the weather, she had slipped off an under garment and converted it into a sack for her plunder. She was subsequently taken before the Magistrates and ungallantly committed to the House of Correction, Northallerton, for three months.

The County Chronicle
9 February 1841

1842

Longevity of Cats*

In our paper of the 4th. instant, we noticed the death of a cat at Rothes, at the advanced age of twenty-three years, and the paragraph concluded by remarking that this was perhaps the greatest extent of years observed to have been meted out to this class of animals. It appears, however, that this surmise was not well founded, as the neighbouring county of Nottingham affords a parallel, if not a more extraordinary case. Mrs. Ranson, who resides at Carlton in Lindric, last year had three cats (mother and two twin daughters) whose united ages amounted to more than seventy years. The mother departing this life through decay, left her ancient offspring, which are at present living not only in a good state of health, but quite confident to follow their natural avocation should a mouse come within their territories, although they are each more than twenty-three years of age.

The Doncaster Chronicle
18 February 1842

Judicious Benevolence*

We learn from a correspondent that Mr. Thomas Robinson, blacksmith, of Sessay, near Thirsk, has recently transferred into the hands of the Minister and churchwardens, for the time being, of the above place, one share in the Great North of England Railway, on which the full amount of £100 has been paid up. The wish of the donor, we are given to understand, is that the yearly profit accruing from such share shall be distributed amongst the poor of his native village at Christmas for ever. May his intention be fulfilled and his largest expectations realised. The coal-trains of the railway will not only deposit a plentiful supply of a good and cheap article at the very doors of the cottagers in question, but also to a certain extent put the purchase-money into their hands. We trust that even when the present generation shall have passed away, many a poor family rejoicing in the warmth of a cheerful Christmas fire, will point with gratitude to the forge of the humble smithy, where once toiled their warm-hearted, though unassuming benefactor. This truly liberal action we consider as one not of such everyday occurrence, as to be suffered to pass altogether unnoticed. For once the worthy blacksmith must be content to "Do good by stealth, and blush to find it fame".

The Yorkshire Gazette
19 March 1842

Singular Circumstance*

The following singular circumstance has been communicated to us by a gentleman on whose veracity we can rely; we give the account in his own words——

I was at Drakeholes, near Wiseton (Lord Spencer's) a few days ago, which Mr. Parkinson, the landlord of the Inn, was then leaving, when I observed to him—surely you have not destroyed your rookery, now you are going to leave. He said no, the old fellows have gone of their own accord. When my father came here, 32 years ago, there had never been a rook before, but a lot came that year and have remained ever since. This year I am leaving the place, and to my surprise, in the building season, some half dozen or so came and began to build; presently a large lot came—destroyed the workmanship of the others and fairly drove them away: they came afterwards for a few mornings, cawing about, to see there were no settlers, and have now entirely disappeared.

The Doncaster Chronicle
15 April 1842

A Curious Family*

Mr. William Greaves, miller of Newark, has in his mill-yard, a dog, a cat, several rabbits and pigeons, which resort together, feed out of the same trough together and lie together, and appear very happy with each other.

The Doncaster Chronicle
13 May 1842

Races and Shooting Extraordinary*

The following advertisement, after having been posted on the blacksmith's shop door, was taken down by a wag and sent to us for the express purpose, we presume, of committing it to the world, and which we give *verbatim and literatim*:

Rases and Shutins on the 14 of May 1842 At Skate beck Goge Fetherstone. Their will be prises for the following Things 2 bridles and a wip for ases or Doggs and a Splendid Man Hat for foot rasin amd 12 silk Hanchshfs and varits of waitscot pices and sum excelent truses and quantity of brases the rases and shotting to commence at 2 o'clock.

These entertainments we apprehend were to take place on Saturday last at Scatebeck, between Whitby and Gisbro'.

The Yorkshire Gazette
21 May 1842

1843

Ploughing Days*

In the northern counties one of the good old agricultural customs of our forefathers is still continued with vigour—namely a boon-ploughing day. Candlemass is the principal time when farmers change the occupation of their farms, and on their entry on their new farms, the neighbouring farmers volunteer their services by sending a draft or two each for a day to plough, to enable the in-coming tenant to plough his arable land, in order that he may sow a corn crop at the proper time in the spring, which otherwise he could not have ready with his own teams, for want of sufficient time. Nothing, it is apprehended, can afford a more pleasurable feeling than to behold fifty or sixty teams of ploughs, followed by the same number of the hardy sons of the soil, on an estate, willingly performing such valuable services gratuitously for the in-coming farmer, who, to them, in many instances, is a perfect stranger. Although it is still so early in the spring, several boon-ploughing days have taken place.

The Carlisle Patriot
18 March 1843

Easter Sports

As usual on Easter Monday and Tuesday, the fields between the castle and the river were thronged by the more youthful portion of the population, to enjoy their annual sports, amongst which the trundling of pace eggs retained a prominent place. Several of the most respectable inhabitants of the town were present to witness the amusements.

The Carlisle Patriot
22 April 1843

❀ *'Pace' or 'pasche' eggs were hard-boiled eggs which were dyed in many colours and given to the children for their Easter games. A*

*favourite among these was one in which the eggs were rolled down
a hill, the winner being the owner of the egg which made the
longest journey. At the end of the holiday the pace eggs were
eaten.*

Shoemaking Extraordinary*

We have frequently had to record extraordinary feats of the sons of
Vulcan, but the following is perhaps without parallel in the annals of the
smithy. A few days ago, Mr. W. Atkinson, of Arlecdon, blacksmith, with
the aid of a slender youth who served him in the capacity of a striker,
turned no fewer than twelve dozen horse shoes in nine hours and two
minutes—a feat which few are able to perform and none, perhaps, to
surpass.

The Carlisle Patriot
13 May 1843

Ascension Day*

At an early hour on Thursday morning, the streets were enlivened with
the cheerful tones of "the spirit-stirring drum and the ear-piercing fife",
announcing that, according to ancient custom, the freemen of Carlisle
were about to proceed to Kingsmoor, to enjoy their annual sports. They
partook of an excellent breakfast, provided for them at the Green Man
Inn, the house of Mr. John Graham, and then proceeded to the moor.
Several spirited races came off, for the various prizes announced; and the
hurdle race, in particular, excited the utmost interest.

The Carlisle Patriot
27 May 1843

Extraordinary Fact

On Tuesday last, Mr. William Moore, licenced dealer in tobacco, &c. at
Colne Bridge, caught two large rats in a trap and took them to Mr. France,
a publican, who keeps a rat-dog for the destruction of such "Varmint". On
one of them being let out in a room, the dog snapped at but missed it, and
the rat, turning round, bit the dog's tongue, which immediately swelled to
a great extent, but the dog died directly. Our Colne correspondent adds
"This is an actual fact, which can be verified, and I think will rank among
the wondrous events which happen in Yorkshire."

The Leeds Intelligencer
quoted in The Yorkshire Gazette
3 June 1843

'Dead Relatives' attend Wedding

At a wedding last week at Gainsborough, the third carriage was observed to go and return from the church apparently empty; on enquiry it was found to contain two large black crepe rosettes, to represent a brother and sister of the bride, who had been dead several years.

The Cumberland Pacquet
6 June 1843

Nest in Bottle

It is not more singular than true, that a redbreast has built its nest in an old wine bottle, which is standing, with its neck broken off, on the window-sill of a gentleman's house at Ireby. There is at present five eggs in the nest. This is the first time we ever heard of a bird's attachment to the bottle—the feathered tribe, we believe, generally carry out the principles of teetotalism with more honesty than certain bipeds of far higher pretensions, though this bird is certainly an exception. If there be any teetotalers in the village of Ireby they will probably deem it their duty to see that this feathered profligate be not allowed to bring discredit upon their order by rearing her progeny in a bottle.

The Cumberland Pacquet
13 June 1843

Hen kills Rat

One day last week, at a farm in Creed, as a hen was carefully watching over a brood of young ducks she had with her, a large rat suddenly seized and was about to make off with one of the flock, but the hen, perceiving the theft, immediately flew at the rat, which dropped the duck, and commenced an attack on her. After a severe struggle, which lasted for several minutes, the hen pecked out both the eyes of the rat, which became entirely beaten, and attempted to get away, but of course could not see, when the hen followed it up, and kept beating and pecking at the rat in a desperate and furious manner until she killed it.

The Cumberland Pacquet
13 June 1843

Remarkable Raven

A raven belonging to Mr. John Binge, of Rampton, near Retford, died a few days ago, in the 28th. year of his age. This singular bird was bred at Grove Park and could talk as plainly as any man, so far as his knowledge extended. In point of imitation, he was inimitable, and could mimic anything he ever heard. Like many others of his tribe he was often exceedingly mischievous, but generally amusing. But his masterpiece was his correct repetition of the Lord's Prayer, which for emphasis and distinct enunciation would have done no discredit to many a village schoolmaster.

The Cumberland Pacquet
1 August 1843

Stealing Stones from the Beach

Several persons were last week apprehended and brought up from the Isle of Walney, Hawcote, &c. to Ulverston, before W. Gale, Esq., under a sessions warrant, to give bail for their appearance at the next Quarter Sessions at Lancaster, to answer to an indictment preferred against them at the last sessions for illegally gathering stones upon the beach at Walney and shipping the same for different places, to be used as paving stones. The practice of stripping the beach of stones was long resorted to in different parts of the Cumberland coast, especially between Ravenglass and Millom, but the inhabitants rose en masse, and finally succeeded in driving the plunderers from the scene of their lawless depredations, after repeated, desperate and bloody conflicts with the ships's crews and their abettors.

The Cumberland Pacquet
26 September 1843

1844

A Giant Pudding*

A plum pudding, purchased by subscription, weighing 290 lb, measuring six feet in length, five feet in circumference, and which took 30 hours in boiling, was carried in procession through the pleasant village of Aughton, near Lancaster, headed by a band of music, on Tuesday last, and after having been submitted some time to the inspection of the curious, was cut up and disposed of among a host of rustic visitors, who had flocked to the village on account of its being the day when the annual sports take place.

The News of the World
14 January 1844

A stout-hearted Matron*

A person residing at Pilling, near Garstang, received a letter from her daughter in Liverpool, to the effect that her attendance was required in her family as speedily as possible, in consequence of her confinement having taken place. She immediately made ready for the journey, started from the aforesaid place at five o'clock in the evening and reached Liverpool the following morning at ten o'clock, walking the whole way, and carrying a basket on each arm. The distance is fully fifty miles, and it is a somewhat extraordinary feat for a female upwards of seventy years of age, travelling the above distance in the dark, and who declared after her arrival that she was neither foot-sore nor tired.

The News of the World
14 January 1844

Really friendly to Labourers*

In our advertising columns will be found the prospectus of a benevolent society of a sort which we hope to see spread into every county and every nook of the country. We allude to the Ombersley Labourers' Friend Society, which has been set on foot by the excellent Rector of the parish, the Hon. and Rev. W.W.C. Talbot, and which proposes to provide allotments of land to the Industrious cottagers of the district. It is so evident that the purposes of this Society are calculated to improve the conditions of the labouring population, that we need not say a word in its praise. We notice it here to engender a spirit of imitation in other quarters, and we do not think it can more effectively seek the good of the rural labourers. There is health, pecuniary profit and moral rectitude to be gained by the cottager, for the things connected with the possession of even a quarter of an acre will keep many a copper in his pocket from the huxter's shop, to be laid out on better clothes, or it may be to provide means for educating his children, and if it only enables him to do, by his own efforts, that for which he formerly depended upon charity, it must make him feel more independent, more pleased with his lot, and in many other respects a better man. With these impressions we heartily wish success to the Ombersley Labourers' Friend Society, and if we might add a suggestion for the further improvement of the scheme, it would be that the Society should encourage its tenantry to follow up the course of providential habits by joining the County Friendly Society. Indeed if the pecuniary profits of their allotments were to be solely devoted to the procuring for them the sure stay and aid of this excellent rock of defence from the evil day of sickness, or the helplessness of old age, the ability of the scheme to accommodate so great an object would stamp it as invaluable.

The Worcester Herald
24 February 1844

Ombersley
Labourers' Friend Society
Patrons
The Lord Bishop of the Diocese
and
The Lord Sandys

At a meeting of the Committee, held at the Vestry, on the 16th. February, 1844, the following rules were proposed and adopted:—

1. No allotment shall be larger than a quarter of an acre.
2. No tenant shall underlet the whole or any part of his allotment.
3. The rent shall be paid half-yearly, on the 25th. of March, and the 29th September, to the Secretary.
4. The land shall be cultivated by spade husbandry. The crop of potatoes or wheat shall not exceed half the allotment. No seed of any green crop shall be raised for sale.
5. No tenant shall work his allotment on Sunday, or during the usual hours of daily labour without the consent of his employer.
6. All occupiers, with their families, shall be expected to attend a place of worship on Sunday.
7. If any occupier, or his child or children, trespass upon the land of any other occupier, or otherwise cause damage to their crops, or enter the field in which his allotment is situated by any other way than the roads set out, he shall pay for the damage so done, and be further liable to a fine of 2s. 6d., at the discretion of the Committee.
   Any complaint of trespass by occupiers of allotments, or their children, upon the lands of any Farmer or Landowner, will, upon proof thereof, be followed by the immediate dismissal of the offender.
8. No occupier to receive parochial relief for a longer period than one week, except in cases of illness.
9. In all cases of an occupier leaving or being deprived of his allotment, he shall receive the full value of his crops, deducting the rent due, the value to be assessed by persons approved for that purpose.
10. The Committee shall select persons from amongst the occupiers to assess the value of any damage done, in company with the Surveyor to the Society. The persons so appointed shall report to the Committee any infringement of the Rules.
11. In the event of any occupier parting from the foregoing Rules, or being convicted before a Magistrate of any offence against the laws of his country, or whose general conduct meets with the disapprobation of the Committee, it shall be within their power immediately to deprive him of his allotment (See Rule 9).

12. The foregoing Rules to be entered in a book containing the names of the occupiers, and signed by each as follows:

"I, A.R., do agree to take Lot No.—subject to the foregoing Rules, at the yearly rent of ——pounds, ——shillings and——pence.

Signed this——day of——

An Annual Meeting for the distribution of Prizes, etc., to be held on the first Friday in October in each year.

Resolved,—That the foregoing Rules be adopted and printed, and that they be advertised in Berrow's Worcester Journal and the Worcester Herald.

W. C. Talbot, President.

A subscription of Five Shillings annually, or a Donation of One Pound, constitutes a member of the Society.

The Worcester Herald
24 February 1844

Severe Sentence*

At the Huntingdon Assizes on Wednesday, Gifford White, aged 18, was indicted for sending to Isaac Ilett a letter threatening to burn him and the other farmers of Bluntisham in their beds, and also to burn their property. The prisoner pleaded Guilty. One of the female servants of the prosecutor found a sealed letter inside his farm-yard, directed "To the Farmers of Bluntisham, Hunts." She took it to her master, who opened and read it; it was in these words—"TO THE FARMERS—We are determined to set fire to the whole of this place if you don't set us to work, and burn you in your beds if there is not an alteration. What do you think the young men are to do if you don't set them to work? They must do something. The fact is, we cannot go any longer. We must commit robbery and everything that is contrary to your wish.—I am, AN ENEMY."

Lord Abinger sentenced him to be transported beyond the seas for the remainder of his life.

The News of the World
24 March 1844

Shipwreck

Ilfracombe

Letters from Ilfracombe announce the loss of the brig Francis, of Whitehaven, from Balize, in the Bay of Honduras, last from the Cove of

Cork, and bound to London, which took place by the vessel running ashore in Marihoe-bay, about six miles to the westward of the coastguard station at Ilfracombe. The brig is laden with a cargo of mahogany and dyewood, and is so much embedded among the rocks that in all probability ere long she will go to pieces. At about midnight on Wednesday at least 200 wreckers of the most desperate character made their appearance on the beach to plunder the wreck; however their motives being communicated to Lieut. Coleman, the chief officer at the Ilfracombe coastguard station, he met them with a small party of men and drove them back, but not before they had a severe conflict in which the wreckers got the worst of it. The vessel is reported to be fully insured. All hands were saved.

The News of the World
21 April 1844

Black Bread*

Hampshire
Among the many clap-trap absurdities put forward by the advocates of protection, it has been constantly asserted at meetings of agriculturists that a repeal of the corn laws would reduce our peasantry to the condition of the serfs of Poland and Russia, who, they say, are compelled to eat black rye bread. We have now in our possession proof that there are Hampshire labourers who fare worse than Poles or Russians, although they work six times as hard. We have been supplied, by favour of a friend, who obtained it from the waggoner of a farmer residing in the parish of Hambledon, with a piece of bread, or rather of a nondescript article called by that name, said to have been prepared on that person's premises for the use of the portion of his labourers who board at the farm house. It is

nearly black and in appearance resembles a cinder more than anything else. We should imagine it to be composed, nearly, if not all, of bad rye. Nothing can equal the astonishment of persons here when told that it is bread and designed for human food. The man from whom it was obtained was eating a part of it for his dinner, with a small portion of coarse fat pork, and stated the bread to be quite equal to what he and his fellows were usually supplied with. We are in possession of the name of the man's employer.

The News of the World
28 April 1844

❀ *The 'advocates of protection', were the farmers and landlords, who at this time were naturally troubled at the ever-growing demand for the repeal of the Corn Laws. Since 1815 the Corn Laws had kept foreign corn out of Britain and maintained high prices for the home-grown crops. They were largely responsible for bread being so often beyond the means of the men who actually tilled the fields and harvested the crops. The writer of this report would have had every sympathy with the objects of the Anti-Corn Law League, which was formed in 1838 and was triumphant on the repeal of the Corn Laws in 1846.*

Child killed by a Ferret*

Whittlesford, Cambridge
A child about three years old, named Charles Flitton, was killed by a ferret at Whittlesford last Sunday night. The mother occupied a room in the old workhouse, and left the child asleep in bed about seven o'clock in the evening, at which time a ferret belonging to Joseph Brett was in the room in a box through the lattice of which he could pass. On her return about a quarter past nine o'clock, the mother found her child so wounded by the ferret that he died a little before three in the morning.

The News of the World
10 November 1844

The New Poor Law*

It is impossible not to be struck with the frightful mortality which appears to be the result of the administration of the New Poor Law. For the last month (we can personally testify) not a week has elapsed without the disclosure of some heartrending case, either of "death from destitution" out of the Workhouse or of gross "neglect of medical attendance" in it. Does it not sound horrible?

Yet we repeat that each week brings its two or three cases (reported in metropolitan papers alone) of human beings perishing through lack of necessities of life, or the necessary attendance in disease. An infant refused medical attention in one town, and dying in its mother's arms as she was bearing it to another. A poor labourer, living for weeks on potatoes or dry bread, sleeping in a straw loft like a dog, and dying at last rather than go to the Workhouse, which he had once entered and remembered but to dread. Another literally starving, with a starving wife and four starving children, denied relief in or out of "the house", because they should be "passed" and dying—actually (so the jury found) dying of disease and hunger in consequence. An artificer allowed to die unattended at the dead of night, in the Workhouse, while suffering from an accident. Such are a few from among the sickening cases of the last week or two only, which occur to our memory, and they are only specimens. Does the law "work well"? When will the experiments have been sufficiently tried?

The News of the World
10 November 1844

Game in Bucks*

Aylesbury
On Monday as a labourer at Quainton was crossing a field belonging to the Duke of Buckingham, he saw a great number of hares and had the curiosity to count them. In this one field he counted no less than 270 hares, which was of course much less than the number he saw, as there were many he could not count. While labourers are starving for want of food and employment, here are vermin allowed to consume and waste this food, and by their depredations to lessen the farmer's means of employing the poor.

The News of the World
15 December 1844

1845

Eighty Sheep drowned in Pond

A flock of eighty sheep were drowned in a pond at Murk Holme, in Uldale, a few days ago. The sheep being chased by a dog ran upon a sheet of water named Little Tarn, which was frozen over; but crowding together, and remaining in that position for some time, their weight caused the ice to give way, and the whole lot were precipitated into the water and drowned.

The Newcastle Journal
15 March 1845

Wedding among the Penshamites*

From time immemorial the custom has been all over Christendom to rejoice and be glad at a wedding, and in our native land—in Merry England, it has been the wont, above all things, to ring merry peals upon the church bells. So universal is this observance seen, that it is accounted little less than a sad omen of ill-luck in the matrimonial lottery if this rejoicing be not most religiously observed. But there are parishes and places where church bells never rung a peal since the first Adam, and this for a very excellent reason—their churches never had bells. Among those unhappy districts may be reckoned Pensham, Pinvin, and other places in that neighbourhood, and to make up for the want of a merry "ding dong", all the male residents, from the newly-breached urchin to the ancient sire, tottering on the grave, who could command a firelock, whether loaned, filched, or purchased, have assembled round the bridegroom's house, and kept up an irregular volley of blank cartridges. Of course little mishaps have occasionally occurred—such as setting fire to the thatch, frightening cattle and horses, and maybe burning a rick, but these were trifles our worthy rustics of "Old England" were inclined to think little of. Now, however, a new race has sprung up, and with it fearful innovation appears to be making upon the "liberty of the subject" at Pensham. For on Tuesday last, one George Gould was summoned before the magistrates of Pershore, in Petty Sessions assembled, for shooting at the wedding of Miss Bright, of Pensham, and in so doing, damaged the door of Mrs. Bright, her mother, in whose house the marriage feast was given. This serious offence was said to have been committed on Sunday evening se'nnight, and, in extenuation, George pleaded ancient usage and the custom of his forefathers. His plea did not avail him, as the right to blow holes in people's doors, although they may have been unfortunate enough to get married, was not to be found in the common, or statute law. His offence, however, did not appear to be deemed a very heinious one, as he was let off on paying a fine of 6d, with 6d damage, and 6s.6d. costs.

The Worcester Herald
22 March 1845

Free Passage to Australia

To SAIL the first week in APRIL for PORT PHILIP, an A1 VESSEL, 802 Tons burthen, with full Poop and every accommodation to secure the health and comfort of the Passengers, and will carry an experienced Surgeon.

For Terms, apply to Wm. Smith and Son, Liverpool, or Mr. George Darke, Herald Office, Worcester.

N.B. Farm Labourers, Female Domestic or Farm Servants, and Shepherds, with a few Smiths, Carpenters, Wheelwrights, Masons and Bricklayers, may obtain a free Passage by applying above.

The Worcester Herald
22 March 1845

Superstition*

The Sherborne Journal related a case of gross superstition at Weymouth. A fellow named Stone, having had a quarrel with his mother-in-law, not only beat and kicked her, but drew a prickly thorn across her face until it was covered in blood. His defence for this refinement of brutality was that his mother-in-law had bewitched him and that the only way of breaking the spell was by drawing blood from her person.

The Worcester Herald
12 April 1845

❀ *The practice of drawing blood to destroy the powers of a witch was first noticed in this book in the report of the attack on Ann Izzard as given in the* Northampton Mercury *in 1808. The Weymouth story makes it plain that in Dorset at least there was still a real fear of witches nearly forty years later. This was more than a century since prosecution of supposed witches came to an end, and only fifty-eight years before the first aeroplane got off the ground.*

Curious Fact*

At the Ledbury Petty Sessions last week, William Kendrick, of Basbury, complained against Henry Russell, Robert Cale, Richard Jones and Samuel Cope (the two former of Ledbury and latter of Bosbury) for having on Thursday, the 22nd. ult., being Bosbury Wake, placed the said William Kendrick in the stocks, without his consent or any authority to do so. It appeared that Kendrick had impounded a horse belonging to the defendant Jones, in consequence of it having strayed into Cutley Rye Meadow, and for which grave offence the defendants arraigned him before themselves at the bar of the *Bell Inn, Bosbury,* Cole acting as judge, and condemned him to the stocks for six hours! He was accordingly placed in the stocks, but liberated before the time allotted had expired. All the cases were heard separately in consequence of only one name being in each summons. Jones was fined £1.0s.6d, Russell £1.10s; Cale and Cope pleaded guilty and were fined £1.8s. each, costs included.

The Worcester Herald
7 June 1845

❁ *Stocks may yet be seen in a few of the country parishes of England. They are a source of much interest at Stow-on-the-Wold in the Cotswolds and at Docking in Norfolk. At Docking they are preserved outside The Hare inn. There are also stocks at Chapel-en-le-Frith in Derbyshire, where, incidentally, they still ring the Curfew Bell. This used to ring the evening hour from which all people had to stay indoors until the following morning.*

1846

Discovery of the Remains of the Killed in the Battle of Lewes*

On Friday night last the excavators employed in the cutting at the Priory came upon a mass of human bones, nearly 18 feet thick and 10 feet in diameter, which were deposited 18 feet below the surface, in a well of that extent. There is no doubt but these are the remains of the bodies which after the battle of Lewes were collected in the town by the Monks, whom history records as having busily occupied themselves on the occasion in burying the dead. That this was an original burial is established by the fact that when the bones were first exposed the affluvium was so obnoxious as to cause the men to desist from their work until the next day—several in fact were taken ill. The bones were conveyed away in about 13 railway waggons, and were thrown into the mass of rubbish which forms the embankment through the brooks, midway between the river and Southern corner. It is a source of deep regret that human bones should be employed for such a purpose—there is something so revolting in this appropriation that we cannot permit ourselves to speak upon the subject, lest our feelings should be excited to censure with severity the despoilers of the dead. Surely it would have been more consonant to public taste to have reburied the remains of the warriors within the walls of the Priory. The expense would have been trifling and this outrage have been prevented.

The Sussex Agricultural Express
17 January 1846

❀ *These bones had been undisturbed for nearly six hundred years. The Battle of Lewes (14 May 1264) was in the war between Henry III and his barons, who were led by Simon de Montfort. Henry, who used the Priory at Lewes as his headquarters, was defeated, and surrendered there, but not before three thousand of the rebels had been slaughtered by his son, the future Edward I.*

Death caused by 'Horse Radish'

Mr. William Farrar, of Thorp Arch, Tadcaster, was poisoned the other day by partaking of beef gravey which was impregnated with the root known as Monk's Hood, which a boy had procured from the garden in mistake for horse-radish. He died in two hours. Other members of the family were made seriously ill.

The Bedford Mercury
24 January 1846

❀ *The Monk's Hood must, of course, have been aconite.*

Accident by Fire*

A few days since, the wife of Maurice Bennett, a labouring man in this parish, while heating her oven for baking, by some means set fire to her clothes. The poor woman ran to her husband, who was working in the garden, and he immediately immersed her in the pond. She was considerably burned, but is likely soon to recover.

The Sussex Agricultural Express
4 April 1846

Rejoicings for the Repeal of the Corn Laws*

Ashton-under-Lyne

Immediately on the newspaper arriving in this town, conveying the intelligence that the fate of the Corn Laws was sealed, flags were hoisted in every part of the town and neighbourhood, bearing various mottoes, such as "Free trade for ever", "Free trade with all the world".... Amongst the number was one placed in front of a barber's shop, at Hyde, which attracted some attention, the motto being "No monopolists shaved here". Some of the millowners contemplate giving an entertainment to their workpeople, and others have already done so.

Stockport

Very great and general was the rejoicing in the borough on Friday and Saturday last, on the arrival of the news from London, that the Corn and Custom bills had virtually become the law of the land. Flags and banners, variously and appropriately inscribed, were exhibited from the principal mills and many private houses in the borough, and the roar of cannon and other fire-arms was heard on all sides, so that any stranger might have supposed that the town was almost in a state of siege. Everywhere demonstrations of rejoicing were perceptible. M. Hollins's workpeople particularly distinguished themselves in this manner; from the mill two large and handsome union jacks were seen flaunting, and the discharge of cannon which they kept up was persevering and incessant. At the mill of Messrs. Kershaw, Leese and Co., Heaton Morris, a sort of tablet was also erected, inscribed "To the memory of monopoly".

Oldham

As soon as the news of the Corn Importation Bill having received the Royal Assent reached Oldham, on Saturday afternoon, banners and flags were displayed on several of the mills and other establishments. During the evening the bells of the parish church rang joyous peals in honour of the event.

The Times
3 July 1846

A Regular Monster*

Considerable excitement prevailed in the neighbourhood of Withybrook last week, caused by the following circumstance. A labouring man in the employ of Mr. —— went into one of his master's fields on Thursday, when he was alarmed by seeing a huge body of many colours making some extraordinary motions. The man immediately ran home, and said: "Measter, there be such a dommed awful thing in t'field, as I can't make aught on". The master, upon this, accompanied the man, but was almost equally alarmed at seeing the monster jumping about in a most unaccountable manner. An alarm was made amongst the neighbours, who armed themselves with different kinds of weapons and a cart rope, for the purpose of securing the beast, the general opinion being that it was some wild beast of an unknown description. Upon approaching the spot "caution guarded the way" till one or two young men, more daring than the others, advanced to throw the rope over the beast when, upon coming near to it, they found, to their no small surprise, that it was a monster balloon—that had been sent up from Quenham Paddox, on the recent occasion of the rejoicings of the marriage of Lord Fielding, and having fallen in the field in question it had become inflated with the wind and rose a short height, progressing in a manner, and presenting such an appearance as the rural inhabitants could account for in no other way than by supposing it was "some horrid monster as had come from foreign parts".

The Leicestershire Mercury
11 July 1846

Hair-Cutting Gratis*

From a Correspondent to The Times
"I must tell you a ridiculous thing that occurred in a small village in Oxfordshire last week, and which caused a diminution in my congregation of yesterday. A man, wearing a certain badge of authority and calling at each house, informed the inhabitants that he was a Government Barber, sent from London, to cut all the poor people's hair gratis, it having been ascertained as the most effectual way of keeping off the cholera, which had already made its appearance. The fellow succeeded in carrying away with him sufficient hair to make several wigs, and the deluded people were obliged to set to and make warm caps to defend their bare heads from the cold which set in next day".

The Bucks Gazette
12 December 1846

Mortality among the Agricultural Labourers in Berkshire*

So destructive have been the ravages of fever in some parts of Berkshire that in the parish of Upton, a hamlet adjoining Bluebery, in that county, the population of which was 142 seven weeks ago, is now reduced to 73, sixty-nine having died within that short period—many through want. Among the number are four children of the minister, who, on attending the dying beds of the victims, caught the infection and conveyed it to his dwelling, whereby he lost four of his offspring. According to the opinion of the physician of the place, the only alternative appears to be for every individual to quit the village, and for every dwelling to be destroyed, there being no other means left to stay the infection; such is therefore about to be done. Respecting the cause of this awful malady, the following facts are stated: That the labourers' wages are not half sufficient for the support of their families; that the potatoes they had partly subsisted on for the last three months were poisonous and infectious; that their food was bread alone—and of that not sufficient; that meat or other substantial food they never tasted; that they could not procure firing, hence their huts were always damp and unhealthy, nor the soap necessary for common cleanliness. At length fever broke out, till none remained unvisited by the calamity.

The Bucks Gazette
19 December 1846

1847

Eccentricity*

Wimborne

On Monday last, an elderly lady at the point of death, sent to the shop of a bookseller in this town for the purchase of two Bibles at £1. 1s. each, for her two children, payment of which was made in every variety of copper coin now current, strung together in sets of 1s. value, so that about 500 pieces were rendered for this purchase. It appears that the purchaser was a shopkeeper, and had for many years past been in the habit of regarding all coins having holes therein (commonly termed by juveniles as "holy money") with great reverence, separating them entirely from the rest of her receipts over the counter, under the impression (the silliness of which could not be eradicated) that literally "holy" coin must imperatively be devoted to holy purposes.

The Poole and Dorsetshire Herald
11 February 1847

"Did you ever see a Dead Donkey?"*

This question has often been asked, and in nine hundred and ninety-nine instances out of any thousand, it has been answered in the negative. If the interrogation were put to us, we could not answer it in the affirmative, but we can record the death of a centenarian donkey, the property of Mr. Gandy, 68 Upper Bedford-street, Brighton. This ancient ass, a contemporary says, was "a great favourite with its master, and well provided for up to the time of its death", expired on Monday week at the advanced age of 100 years.

The Leeds Intelligencer
18 February 1847

Unconcerned Otter

Penzance

On Saturday evening, an otter was seen walking down Chapel-street, apparently so little apprehensive of passers-by that he nearly threw down a female, whom he ran against. A powerful bull-dog was set at him and a desperate battle took place, resulting in the death of the otter.

The Western Luminary
13 April 1847

A Living Thrashing Machine*

Last week Mr. William Rule, of Camborne, agreed with a farm laborer of Phillack, named John Carthew, to thrash a quantity of barley for him, for which he was to give 10s., six meals and four quarts of beer. Carthew commenced the following day, and in 11 hours completed the task, amounting to 921 sheaves, which is considered 6½ days regular days' work, 140 being a customary day's work. He says he will undertake for a wager, a similar task, for six successive days. He thrashed last year, in Copperhouse, 400 sheaves of wheat in 12 hours. Carthew is a tall, robust man, and 58 years old.

The Western Luminary
21 September 1847

Female Turnip-stealers

Dulverton

Mr. Henry Pulsford, of Bearnhay farm, in this parish, had lately lost some turnips at night, from a field near his house; he therefore determined to watch them, and on the night of Monday the 29th. ult., accompanied by his servant-man, he sallied forth from his house with a loaded gun; they had been on the watch but a short time when two females entered the field and proceeded to pull some turnips. Mr. Pulsford, without any warning to these poor creatures, deliberately took aim at one of them and fired, the charge lodging in her head and breast, and altogether inflicting thirty or forty wounds on her person. He then, with his servant, went away, leaving the poor creature to her fate. She, with the assistance of her companion, managed to get home, a distance of about half a mile, in a state much better to be imagined than described. The poor girl so much wounded is an orphan, by name Caroline Godby, and was employed at the silk-mills in this town, but in consequence of the bad state of trade, has been working "short time" for some months past, and without doubt sheer necessity, the cravings of hunger, goaded her to adopt this course, as her character has hitherto been irreproachable. She now lies in a very dangerous state.

The Bridgewater Times
9 December 1847

Bullock survives Cliff Fall

Mullion

On Saturday morning last, Jas. Thomas, chief boatman of the coast guard stationed at this place, whilst on duty, saw beneath a rugged cliff, a bullock standing on a rock. Not being able of himself to extracate the poor animal from its perilous position, he made known his discovery and the beast was found to be the property of Mr. W. Jose, of Mullion. It had been missing for a week. It is evident that the animal must have fallen over the cliff, into the sea, at some distance from the place where it was found, and must either have swam, or been drifted to the rock. It was free from bruises, or any other ailment, except weakness, the consequence of it having been several days without food. It was hauled up to the top of a very high cliff by ropes, drawn by a considerable number of men and, on food being presented, it ate eagerly and heartily, and promises to do well.

The Western Luminary
14 December 1847

1848

Skating Match*

A copper kettle, leg of mutton and other prizes were skated for at Cowbit Wash, on Saturday last. In this instance "the nick of time" was hit upon, as the thaw set in immediately afterwards. We think Spalding most justly famed for its skaters, for on this occasion we never saw better.

The Spalding Free Press
1 February 1848

Melancholy Occurrence—Effects of Intemperance*

On Wednesday last, a youth, about 18 years of age, named William Renton, resident at Harrogate, came to his death under the following melancholy circumstances. We understand that on Tuesday he had been working at a farm distant about a mile and a half from Harrogate, it being what is termed a "beaning" day, that is, when a person enters upon a fresh farm, the neighbouring farmers lend their teams and men for a day, for the purpose of ploughing the land. It seems that the deceased had partaken too freely of the liquor which had been distributed on the occasion, and at night, instead of proceeding home, had laid himself down in one of the fields near the farm-house, where he was discovered early the next morning, a search having been instituted. When found, though not dead, his body was stiff with the cold, and he only survived till about five o'clock in the afternoon.

The Leeds Mercury
4 March 1848

❀ *'Beaning' or boon-ploughing days have already been noted through* the Carlisle Patriot *report of 18 March 1843. This one makes it clear that the farmer who received help from his new neighbours in this way was expected to acknowledge it by providing free beer for their men at the end of the day.*

Hiring*

On Saturday last (Whit Saturday) Lancaster was crowded with young persons offering for hire, to a degree never before witnessed. The streets were in some parts almost impassable. Of course, with such a supply in the labour market hiring would not be very brisk. Able-bodied farm servants £12 to £15 per year, and women servants £6–£10.

The Lancaster Gazette
17 June 1848

❀ *This report permits a comparison of wages with those of some twenty-five years before. It will be seen by reference to the* County Chronicle *record of October 1825 that there was little change in the rate for female servants, but men's wages had risen considerably.*

Singular Combat between a Snake and a Cat*

On the 14th. instant, as a snake of the viper species was lying basking itself in the sun, in an orchard belonging to Mr. Noble Jackson, Whallenrigg, near Broughton-in-Furness, it was pounced upon by a cat. The viper, on finding himself this rudely attacked, erected himself in an attitude of defence and commenced hissing and darting its forked tongue in every direction, bidding defiance to its feline assailant. Puss, nothing daunted, returned to the charge with redoubled fury, when a fierce encounter took place, puss appearing to be perfectly aware of what kind of antagonist she had to contend with, by displaying the greatest caution and adroitness in repelling the attacks of the viper with her fore-feet. After a protracted struggle, the viper judged it prudent to retreat, on which Mrs. Puss, taking the advantage, seized the reptile by the neck with her teeth, and bore it off in triumph to a kitten which she was suckling. The viper measured 25 inches in length.

The Kendal Mercury
9 August 1848

Curious*

Mr. Thos. Frankland, butcher, of Preston, slaughtered a fat cow on Thursday week, and on opening the animal he found in the ventriculus or paunch, a pair of buckles for clogs, a halfpenny, an iron washer, a clock pinion, two or three nails, a button, and other metal articles to the number of fifteen. Mr. Frankland purchased the cow from Mr. James Fender, of Newhall-lane, in that town, in whose keeping she had been four years, and in which time she had four calves. Mr. Fender bought the cow of Mr. Spencer, Fleetwood Hall, Samlasbury ...

The Blackburn Standard
13 September 1848

A Novel Bustle*

A gander, tied in a towel, was found on Saturday week, in the bustle of a young woman, who was apprehended by the Devonshire police on suspicion of having stolen the gander in question from the fowlhouse of a farmer in the parish of Chittlehampton.

The Blackburn Standard
13 December 1848

1849

A Gold Deposit

Mr. Grange, a farmer of Whaddon Chase, in Buckinghamshire, has ploughed up a gold deposit. As he was breaking up soil that had been woodland for centuries he turned up a number of cubes of gold, to the value of £300 or more. They are claimed by the lord of the manor, and a coroner's jury is to hold an inquest of treasure-trove.

The Blackburn Standard
21 March 1849

Carnivorous Rooks at Market Drayton*

On Friday the 20th. ult., an ewe, the property of Mr. James Key, Maccleston, lost its life under the following singular circumstances.

On the morning of the accident, twelve ewes, with their lambs, were feeding in a field about sixty yards from the rectory, one of which, a Southdown, in excellent condition, unfortunately got on its back in a gutter and was unable to stir. The rooks, from a rookery close by, took advantage of the animal's situation, flew at it and lacerating it near the udder with their sharp beaks got to and dragged part of the entrails to the distance of six yards. Mr. Key himself found the ewe in this position and after driving away the rooks, hastened home for a cart, but scarcely had he gone a dozen feet before the audacious birds returned with augmented force, and carried off a portion of the poor creature's intestines.

The Staffordshire Advertiser
quoted in The Blackburn Standard
23 May 1849

1850

Frightful Journey for Mail-coach Horse

As the omnibus which runs as a mail between Sleaford and Lincoln was coming to the latter place on Sunday, one of the horses not being well shod for travelling, and the road being so very slippery, stumbled and broke its leg near the foot. Strange to say, however, the driver did not know that the leg was broken, and the poor animal was driven nearly all the way from Metheringham to Lincoln. It was found necessary to shoot the horse yesterday.

The Lincolnshire Times
1 January 1850

Careless Wassailers

On Friday morning last a rick of hay on the premises at Pilton Park was discovered to be on fire, assistance was obtained and the fire was after some time extinguished, but not before a considerable quantity of hay was destroyed. It is supposed the fire was caused by the carelessness of some men who, the previous night, were keeping up the old custom of wassailing, and some of whom were smoking when they passed the hayricks.

The Bridgewater Times
24 January 1850

✸ *'Wassailing' was part of the New Year celebrations and derived from the Old English Waes hael–'To your health'. Families toasted each other by passing round a 'wassail' bowl of spiced ale. The*

*men in this report were villagers who would have called on their
squire and the farmers with a beribboned bowl, asking for a little
money so that they too could have ale for celebrations. They would
have sung 'wassail songs' to tell of their coming.*

Fire caused by a Cat*

Belton

On the 27th. ult. a fire broke out on the premises of Mr. Thomas Maw, of
Belton Westgates, which was ascertained afterwards to have originated
thus: The cat is in the habit of sitting in the fender, and on the night in
question a cinder fell out of the fire on poor puss's back; she being unable
to get it off, rushed out of the house and into the barn, when rubbing
amongst the straw, it fell off and ignited the straw. The barn was soon in
flames, but owing to the prompt assistance of the neighbours, the fire was
got out, but not before damage to the amount of £10 was sustained. Mr.
Maw was insured.

The Lincolnshire Times
12 March 1850

Village Feast

Amcotts

The feast has been held this last week in this interesting village and a very
jolly, jovial and comfortable feast it has been, with lots of good things
stirring and a hearty welcome to all comers to partake of them. But
hospitality never sleeps at Amcotts. The inhabitants are always glad to
see their friends at their annual jubilee. It can never be said at any house
here, as it was when the miser astounded his neighbours by giving a
party—

His chimney smokes, it is an omen dire
His neighbours are alarmed and cry out FIRE.

There was a large muster of company in spite of the bad times and we fancied that some of them must be in high glee, as a voice came carolling on one's ears and then a grand chorus as we turned the corner on the Luddington road one evening—

> A glass is good, and a glass is good
> And a pipe is good in cold weather,
> The world is good and the people are good
> And we are all good fellows together.

Free trade has, at all events, neither put out their pipes, or their spirits yet, where they can sing in this strain. But on the whole we like these feasts. They bring old friends together who might otherwise seldom meet. They collect families and they lead to a general rubbing, scrubbing, cleaning up, and clearing out of all the cottages. And they afford a little variety of happiness both to the farmer and the labourer. "All work and no play" is a proverb as true of one trade as another.

The Lincolnshire Times
23 July 1850

A Remarkable Circumstance*

Westonzoyland
On the farm premises of Mr. Tice, while ricking wheat, a cat with her kitten got on the top of a wheat rick, after one load had been put on the straddles, and hid herself and the kitten between the sheaves. In the course of a few hours several more waggon loads were added to the rick. After it had been finished and thatched some weeks, persons walking near the rick fancied they heard the faint cry of a cat. At last they discovered it was in the rick, the height of one load from the straddles. They commenced drawing the sheaves in the direction whence the sound came and soon discovered the cat, from five to six feet from the outside, very feeble and pressed thin, but they found no kitten and it is supposed the old cat must have eaten it. The cat immediately drank milk when offered her, was able to walk and is now fast recovering. From the time she must have got on the rick to the time she was taken out was quite twenty-one days.

The Bridgewater Times
5 September 1850.

General Index

For the newspapers utilized, see the Index of Newspapers following.

ACORNS, for building ships, 156
Adder:
  boy killed by, 128
  milk stolen by, 72
Admirals, three from one village, 169
Advertisements:
  baths at Aldeburgh, 46
  blacksmith's, 140, 196
  coaches, 30, 74
  painting in church, 34
  racing and shooting, 286
  Robinson Cruso, of King's Lynn, 31
  runaway farm boy, 113
  'Taking of General Lee', 88
Ascension Day celebrations, 288

BALLOONS, early ascents, 112, 116, 303
Beach, stones stolen from, 290
Bear, woman killed by, 142
Bees, man's death caused by, 44
Bell-ringing for hats, 101
Birthday celebrations, 130, 211, 219
Bishop Blaize Festival, 131
Blacksmith, industrious, 288
Blenheim Palace, Royal Visit to, 114
'Blind Henry', 156
Body-snatchers, foiling of, 225
Boxing, 135, 192, 210
Bread, appeal from poor for, 59
  black, for labourers, 295
  curious loaf of, 269
  death for want of, 32
  riots, 56, 57, 77, 190
Brontë, Rev. Patrick, appointed to
    Haworth, 211
Brough Rock tragedy, 268
Bullock in public house, 153
  putrification of in thirty minutes, 154
  survives cliff fall, 307
Bull-baiting, 99, 112, 157, 170
Bull-fight in Berkshire, 169
Burial at cross-roads, 28
  hen alive five weeks after, 258

in unconsecrated ground, 104
in turnip field, 274
of man, 30 years after death, 263
Butter, mob action for cheaper, 57

CALENDAR, adoption of Gregorian, 21, 23,
    24
Cat:
  eaten by boy, 71
  fire caused by, 312
  live, eaten by shepherd, 122
  longevity of, 285
  pigs killed by, 272
  rabbits fostered by, 252
  snake killed by, 309
  survival after burial in sheaves, 313
Centenarian promises to 'rise again', 46
Charity distribution at Huntingdon, 273
Charles I, face of, 256
Cheese, Royal, 283
Chimney-sweeps, 24, 79, 123, 222
Christmas:
  gifts of coal at, 285
  hospitality, 155
  pie, 262
Christmas Day:
  in workhouse, 271
  meal for soldiers, 137
  ravens kill man on, 58
  strawberries, 281
  superstition about lights on, 267
Church:
  bell caught in fisherman's net, 183
  steeple climbed at Moulton, 183
Churches, damage to, by storms, 33, 37,
    178
Cider Act (1763):
  procession of protest, 47
  repeal of, 55
Cider for Trees, 240
Clare, John, patronage for, 215
Coach, Napoleon's, landed at Dover, 200
Cock, child attacked by, 223

Cock-fighting, death after, 51
Coffin left on rafters, 263
Coffins, stone, dug up at Acomb, 86
Coins:
  discovery of buried, 84, 105, 205, 227
  found in old houses, 86, 162, 237, 281
Corn Laws, 201, 296
  rejoicing at repeal of, 302
Coronation celebrations for Queen
  Victoria, 275
County police, unsuitable appointment to,
  277
Cow(s):
  boy killed by, 209
  contents of paunch of, 309
  felonious milking of, 105
  fire from belly of, 41
  homing instinct of, 41
  intoxicated, 274
  killed by lady's hat, 86
  suckling of other animals by, 192, 267
  wooden leg for, 226
Cricket:
  extraordinary match on Guildford
    Downs, 80
  farmer killed at, 227
  match on skates, 273
  roast sheep for winning team, 180
Crow(s):
  killed by turkey, 218
  new way of scaring, 81
Cuckoos, superstition about, 27
Cucumbers, prize exhibits, 94, 98
Curate of Patter Dale, 107
Cures (for):
  adder-bites, 164, 219
  convulsions, 144
  hoarseness, 178
  rabies, 118, 132
  rheumatism, 166
  sickness in sheep, 175
  wasp-stings, 84
  whooping cough, 259
Curious Family, 286
Customs, old:
  Lawless Court, 163
  payments in tomb, 224
  St Briavel's, Glos., 202
  St Thomas' Day, 164

DARTMOOR, child lost on, 239
Death:
  of children through farm accidents,
    105, 271
  premonition of, 73
  sentenced to, for stealing lamb, 156
  through 'horse radish' (Monk's hood),
    301
  through severe weather, 136, 174
Distress:
  among poor in Buckinghamshire, 33
  among poor in Staffordshire, 200
Dog:
  hanging of, for theft, 138
  man eaten by, 138
  man mistaken for mad, 142
  saves master numbed by cold, 138
  suckling of other animals by, 158, 276
  turnspit, 14, 147
Donkey:
  attack on sheep by, 196
  death of centenarian, 305
  on church steeple, 62
Dreams:
  of buried treasure, 205
  ominous, 236
Drowning of man cut off by tide, 117
Duck-eggs, death from eating, 166
Duel, curate kills schoolmaster in, 103

EAGLE:
  capture of on Skiddaw, 123
  ominous visit of, 185
Easter Sports, 287
Eccentrics, 81, 189, 193
Election celebrations, 60
Emigration, 219, 252, 253, 299
Enclosure Riots, 52, 53, 74
Entertainment for old people, 37
  at Huntingdon, by 'noble lord', 50
  at Windsor, by Duke of Cumberland,
    49
Eton Aquatic Excursion, 154
Execution:
  by burning, for killing husband, 66
  for murder at Tring, 18
  for rick-burning, 263
  joke at, by condemned man, 108
Exhumations, 66, 141
Explosion in blacksmith's shop, 107, 190
'Extraordinary Discovery' at Dunstable,
  266

FAIR, recruiting parties at, 88
Fairs, 21, 45, 101, 173, 228
Feat, extraordinary, at Taunton, 313

Feast, 312
Ferret, child killed by, 296
Fever, outbreaks of, 183, 254, 304
Fiddlers, 130, 175
Fires, 61, 78, 168, 172, 301, 311
Football, 52, 186
Footpads, 84, 186
Fortune-tellers, 36, 236
Foxes, 111, 113, 119, 179, 197, 209
Funerals, 105, 111, 137, 244

GAMEKEEPER, 'Walking Obelisk', 163
Game Laws informer, 223
Geese, 75, 193, 310
Giants:
    Benjamin Bower, of Dorset, 48
    Rice, of Nottinghamshire, 79
    Daniel Lambert, 179
Gibbet, new use for, 232
Gleaning, regulations for, 216
    tragedy during, 186
Gluttony, 120, 144
Gold deposit in Buckinghamshire, 310
Gooseberry, gigantic, 192
Gravediggers, 135
Graves, discovery of, 197, 262, 300
Graveside consternation, 115
Gunn, Martha, 198
Guy Fawkes' Day, 169, 255, 256

HAIR-CUTTING, free, 304
Hanging, of beggar, 20
Hare(s):
    among lawyers, 127
    motherly devotion of, 185
    prolific in Buckinghamshire, 297
    punishment for killing, 79, 230
    running on stumps, 174
    rider to hounds, 204
    superstitions about, 188, 259
Harvest, death after denying theft at, 184
    fire caused by woman's pipe, 207
    harvest home, 109, 118
    murder at, 26, 52
    veterans at, 93, 184
Hastings, Warren, acquittal celebrations
    for, 139
Hedgehog, 147, 212
Highwayman, killed by coach guard, 83
Holiday in Whitchwood Forest, 139
'Horned Visitor' at midnight, 233
Horse(s):
    death in race, 42

driven on broken leg, 311
evasion of Horse Tax, 110
'extraordinary operation of nature',
    124
kick by, curing dumbness, 226
killed by boar, 99
longevity of, 220
man killed by, 156
precautions against stealing, 90
survival after sixty foot fall, 158
Hunt:
    results of brandy at, 87
    wild-boar, 255

ICHTHYOSAURUS, dug up at Westbury, 284
Inoculation, 34
Invasion:
    alarms, 30, 159, 160, 165
    preparations against, 93, 145, 146, 159,
        161

'JUNE HARVEST', 152

'KING AND CONSTITUTION', meetings for,
    133

LABOURERS, 'independent', 209
'Labourers Friend' Society, 292, 293
Landslide, near Hereford, 134
Letters, threatening, 15, 240, 294
Liquor found in stockyard, 113
Longevity, 46, 50, 60, 89, 100, 104,
    132, 137, 144, 268

MACHINE-BREAKING, 246–49, 251
Mail Coaches, 109, 173, 225
Market, record journeys to, 92
Marriage:
    bonus for bachelors, 27
    penance in church for irregular, 124
    quick proposal of, 230
    to heiress, by mail-cart man, 265
May Day celebrations, 198
Mermaid, 190
Midwife, delivery of 10,000 women by, 60
    Man-Midwife of Bristol, 28
    veteran, 127
Milestone, punishment for altering, 25
Militia Act, opposition to, 35
Milk, prevention of sour, 274
Miserly farmer of Steeple Ashton, 140
Money, Holy, 305
Moral character, prizes for, 257

Mother(s):
of many children, 68, 98, 153
stout-hearted, from Lancashire, 291
Murder:
prevention of, 171
supposition of, 170, 195

NELSON, LORD:
death of, 166
protégé of, 167
Newt, parted with by young lady, 148
Nuts, death caused by too many, 146

OSBORNE, RUTH, drowning of, at Tring, 15, 16, 71
Otter, death of in Penzance street, 306
Oxen, prize, 97, 138

PACE (PASCHE) EGGS, 287
Paine, Tom, 133
Parish accounts, amusing, 210
Parson-soldier, 36
Pauper:
inhuman treatment of, 102, 202
killed by maggots, 189
Pears, extraordinary, 255, 257
Pigs:
child killed by, 119
child suckled by, 283
clever, 187
drunken, 206
instead of horses, 187
killed by cat, 272
suckled by cow, 192
suckled by woman, 239
Pike, watch found in, 51
Pillory sentences, 36, 135
'Pit Preacher' in Staffordshire, 129
Plough, invention of new, 49
'Ploughing Days', 287, 308
Plums, death from eating too many, 117
Poacher(s):
dedicated, 161
encounters with gamekeepers, 99, 191, 226, 231
extraordinary chase of, 261
female, 284
'Paradise' in Kent, 72
Traps for catching, 208, 210
Poor:
distress among in Buckinghamshire, 33
distress among in Staffordshire, 200
fortune for in Suffolk, 155
pull wagons to support families, 243

Poor Law Acts, 65, 261, 264, 268, 296
Poorhouse, death of family in, 63, 64, 65
Pork, appetite for raw, 278
Potatoes, need for increased crops, 151
Press Gang:
fatal clash at Weymouth, 157
female, in Cornwall, 28
holiday ruined by, 128
resistance to, 31, 92
'Priority Order', 224
Prisoners of War, 38, 145, 194
Pudding, procession of, at Aughton, 291

QUEEN CAROLINE, loyalty to, 216, 217

RABIES, 14, 73, 75
'Rags to Riches', 191
Railway, opening of, at Aylesbury, 277
Rat(s):
dog killed by, 288
drunken labourer attacked by, 178
killed by hen, 289
noted catcher of, 277
rapacious, 33, 147
roasted alive, 188
Raven(s):
fox killed by, 89
man killed by, 58
sagacious, 222, 290
Recipe:
for long life, 100
for perplexing a witch, 22
for preserving cattle, 82
Recruits, bounty for army, 90, 143
Reform Bill, passing of, 253, 254
Rick-burning, 57, 245, 246, 249, 250, 263
Riots, 56, 57, 77, 151, 152, 190, 260
Robbery:
in Keswick Market, 90
odd method of, 43
of Irish Mail postboy, 92
pigeon pie, 61
Robins, boldness of, 222, 260, 289
Rook Pie, 223
Rooks:
carnivorous, 310
departure with tenant, 286
Royal Treat, 13

SABBATH, punishment for breaking, 160, 186
Sale:
of children, 207
of man for army, 91

of wife at market, 196
Seduction, punishment for attempted, 207
Seed-drill, success of new, 106
Sermon, for benefit of animals, 209
Sextuplets at Bolsover, 78
Sheep:
  man strangled by, 45
  men's lives saved by intestines of, 174
  results of fright, 134, 298
  saved by rum, 58
  survival after burial in snow, 176
  twins wanted by, 90
Shepherd:
  for ninety years, 48
  drowned in mud, 178
Shields from battle of Shrewsbury, 221
Ship without crew, 238
Shrovetide celebrations and customs, 99, 195, 229, 233, 234
'Sir Loin' Table, 243
Skating match, 308
Skeleton, found on Durnford Downs, 25
Sky, riders in, 208, 265
Smuggling, 28, 29, 76, 83, 97, 121, 234
Soldier(s):
  exemplary conduct of, 140
  veteran, of many battles, 143
Songs, inflammatory, 261
Speenhamland System, 261
Sports and Pastimes:
  archery, 51
  backsword, 91
  chuckers, 41
  jingling, 102
  pinching matches, 227
  shooting, 75
St Thomas's Day, 164
Stag:
  captured in public house, 43
  killed in college chapel, 215
  rode with hounds, 60
  woman killed by, 162
Starlings, nest of in murderer's body, 154
Starvation, effects of, 199, 244
Stocks, illegal detention in, 300
Storm, very severe, at Littleport, 42
Sunday Schools, early, in Gloucestershire, 110
Swing, Captain, 246, 248, 250

TEA:
  death from smuggled, 14
  drinking competition at St Ives, 136

poisoned, 43
Temperance, advantages of, 270
Thieves:
  impudence of, 221, 271, 272, 276
  nest of, in Surrey, 68
Thieving, large-scale at farm, 119
Threshing:
  by 'living machine', 306
  imprisonment for poor, 188
Tithe:
  lambs, 187
  plums, 157
Toad:
  effects of venom, 43, 165
  alive after twelve months' burial, 129
Tolpuddle Martyrs, 258
Tooth-extraction, 185
Tree, giant chestnut, 35
Trees, punishment for cutting down, 175
Turnip-stealers, 204, 306

VELOCIPEDE, introduction of, 211
Vengeance, divine, 55

WAGERS, 71, 82, 97, 122, 154, 160, 177, 210, 212, 218
Wages, 228, 260, 309
Walton, Izaak, charitable bequests of, 231
Wassailers, 311
Waterloo, 199, 200
Weather, severe, 42, 85, 136, 174
Weddings, 13, 44, 59, 67, 83, 87, 118, 134, 282, 289, 298
Whippings, 25, 79, 89, 175
Widows, wood for, from Epping Forest, 63
Will, eccentric, 229
Windmills, 48, 56, 177
Witches and Witchcraft, 15, 21, 71, 176, 299
Wives:
  seven in seven years, 122
  three in seven weeks, 62
  very old man who married thirteen, 89
Woman from seashore, 148
Work, fine for refusal to, 180
Workhouses, 264, 268, 271, 296
Wounds, self-inflicted to evade Navy, 31
Wrecker(s), 17, 294
  fortune left by, 131
Wrestling, 81, 238

YORKSHIRE 'Character', 50
Yorkshire Stingo, 184

Index of Newspapers

Note: Where there is a date in brackets this records the year in which the newspaper was established. Most of these papers have long since been discontinued, or incorporated with other publications. An asterisk indicates that the newspaper is still being published under the title shown. The dagger indicates that it is suspended at the time of going to press.

ADAMS WEEKLY COURANT (1732), 55–60, 79–81, 99
Aylesbury News (1836), 277

BATH ADVERTISER (1755), 29–31
Bedford Mercury, 274, 301
Bell's Weekly Messenger, 191, 192
Berkshire Chronicle (1770), 275
Blackburn Standard, 309, 310
Bridgewater Times, 306, 311, 313
Bristol Gazette, 119, 120, 121, 122, 123
Bristol Journal, 129, 135, 281
British Chronicle, 72, 73, 75, 78, 104, 105, 107
Bucks Gazette, 276, 304
Bury and Norwich Post (1782), 153, 154, 156

CAMBRIDGE CHRONICLE (1744), 71, 135–8, 192, 202, 204, 273, 274
Carlisle Journal (1798), 193, 196, 197, 225
Carlisle Patriot (1815), 287, 288
Chelmsford Chronicle, 60–2, 77, 81, 90, 93, 260, 261, 278
*Chester Chronicle (1775), 85, 86, 130, 131, 132
Cornubian, 268
County Chronicle, 92, 122, 131, 144, 147, 148, 154, 208–12, 215–17, 228, 243, 284
Courier, 171, 173, 174
Coventry Mercury (1741), 41–3, 196, 243–50
Cumberland Chronicle, 87–91
Cumberland Pacquet, 86, 87, 289, 290

DERBY MERCURY (1732), 117, 118, 132–5, 141, 142, 144, 147

Devizes and Wiltshire Gazette (1816), 218, 219
Devonshire Chronicle, 262
Doncaster Chronicle (1836), 285, 286
Dorset County Chronicle (1821), 255–60
*Durham County Advertiser (1812), 224

EXETER WEEKLY TIMES (1827), 232–4

*FALMOUTH PACKET (1829), 238–40, 251, 268

*GLO(U)CESTER JOURNAL (1722), 44, 45, 46, 91, 92, 108–10

HAMPSHIRE COURIER, 193–9
*Harrogate Advertiser (1836), 269
Hereford Journal (1713), 219
Hertford and Bedford Reformer, 282
*Hertfordshire Mercury (1772), 227–9
Hull Packet (1787), 152, 153, 175, 179
Huntingdon Gazette, 229

IPSWICH JOURNAL (1720), 31–8, 41–3, 46, 64, 160, 221

KENDAL MERCURY, 309
Kentish Chronicle (1768), 205–7
*Kentish Gazette (1717), 63, 64, 66, 67, 68, 199, 200
*Kent(ish) Herald (1792), 157, 159, 160, 161
Kentish Post, 21–3

LANCASTER GAZETTEER (later Gazette), 154, 155, 164, 165, 168, 309
Leeds Intelligencer (1754), 35, 43, 45,

47, 49, 50, 305
Leeds Mercury (1718), 158, 159, 162–4, 210, 226, 308
*Leicester Chronicle (1810), 230, 231
Leicester Journal (1753), 256, 263
Leicestershire Mercury, 303
*Lichfield Mercury (1815), 252, 253
*Lincoln, Rutland and Stamford Mercury (1695), 110, 111, 112
Lincolnshire Times, 311, 312

Maidstone Journal (1737), 119, 129
Manchester Mercury (1752), 37, 102, 104–6
Morning Chronicle, 169

Newcastle Chronicle, 51, 92, 127, 128
Newcastle Courant, 97, 98
*Newcastle Journal (1711), 298
*News of the World (1843), 291, 294–7
Norfolk Chronicle (1761), 97–100
*Northampton Mercury (1720), 13–20, 48, 49, 52–3, 71, 73–4, 76–8, 176, 177, 276
*Norwich Mercury (1714), 82–84
Nottingham Journal (1710), 72, 105, 107, 109, 113–16, 145, 146, 207

*Observer (1791), 178–180, 189–91, 283, 284
Oxford Journal, 24–8, 51, 52, 59, 138–40, 237, 240, 244

*Poole and Dorsetshire Herald (1846), 305
Portsmouth Telegraph, 148

Reading Mercury (1723), 101, 142, 143

*Salisbury Journal (1729), 23, 24, 74, 119, 124, 172, 175
Salopian Journal, 161, 162, 220, 221
*Shrewsbury Chronicle (1772), 184–8
Spalding Free Press, 308
Staffordshire Advertiser (1795), 138, 188
Staffordshire Gazette, 254
Stamford News, 183–5
Surrey Standard, 262, 264
Sussex Agricultural Express, 270–2, 300
Sussex Advertiser (1745), 88, 90, 250, 252

*†Times (1788), 151, 152, 200, 202, 204, 224–6, 265, 266, 302

*Warwick and Warwickshire Advertiser (1806), 195
Weekly Dispatch, 155–7, 173
Weekly Register, 81, 222, 223
*West Briton (1810), 207
Western Flying Post, 28
Western Luminary, 306, 307
*Windsor and Eton Express (1812), 255
*Wolverhampton Chronicle (1789), 254
Worcester Herald, 292, 293, 298, 299, 300

York Chronicle, 210, 211, 267
York Courant, 83, 84
York Herald (1790), 140, 143, 166, 168, 169, 170, 226
*Yorkshire Gazette (1772), 222, 223, 285, 286, 288

REVIEW OF THE BRITISH CORN TRADE.

[From *The Mark Lane Express.*]

The following table, showing the arrivals of the principal kinds of grain, pulse, and flour into the port of London, during the three months ending 30th March, and the receipts in the corresponding quarter last year, may prove of interest to some of our readers.

	QUARTER ENDING MARCH	1850.	1849.
Wheat, English	qrs.	35402	31086
Ditto Scotch		100	134
Ditto Irish		—	—
Ditto Foreign		80915	312812
Total		116417	344032
Barley, English	qrs.	46501	46538
Ditto Scotch		9123	8805
Ditto Irish		—	—
Ditto Foreign		73449	130217
Total		128773	185560
Oats, English	qrs.	36539	30578
Ditto Scotch		33738	28045
Ditto Irish		11321	49724
Ditto Foreign		97607	172277
Total		184255	291124
Beans, English	qrs.	11806	9265
Ditto Scotch		180	85
Ditto Irish		75	—
Ditto Foreign		29633	12378
Total		41694	21728
Peas, English	qrs.	8024	6778
Ditto Scotch		50	10
Ditto Irish		—	—
Ditto Foreign		5772	20376
Total		13846	27164
Flour, English	sks.	59141 sks.	49740 sks.
Ditto Scotch		—	—
Ditto Irish		200	—
Ditto Foreign		54095	48726 sks. / 11103 bls.
Total		113436	89495 sks. / 11103 bls.

It will be observed that the difference in the supplies of home-grown wheat and barley is not material. In the arrivals of English oats and flour there is a considerable increase; whilst the receipts of all kinds of foreign produce have been much smaller than in the corresponding quarter last year, which no doubt, partly caused by the severity of the winter.

Though no material increase has taken place in the deliveries of wheat from our own growers, and the supplies of the article from abroad have been only moderate, the trade has last the firm tone by which it was characterized the last week or two in March; and not only has the upward movement in prices been checked, but a reaction to the extent of about 1s. per qr. has taken place at several of the leading provincial markets held since Monday. This we have no doubt been caused partly by the dull reports from Mark Lane; though we are inclined to attribute it more to the prevailing belief that the supplies from the farmers will, now that the sowing of spring corn is nearly completed, become more liberal. The change in the weather has also had more or less effect, the rise which has taken place in the temperature, and the showers which have fallen within the last few days having stimulated vegetation and imparted a spring-like appearance to the country. Indeed, there is nothing in the present position of affairs, except the lowness of prices, to encourage purchasers to take more than they require for immediate use, and there is, consequently, a general unwillingness to hold stocks. The importations from abroad may, perhaps, not be very large during the next month or two, but we are likely to have regular arrivals from one quarter or the other; and as there is now no inducement to store, all that comes to hand will probably be somewhat pressingly offered from on board ship; a very small increase in the home supplies might, therefore, have the effect of still further reducing quotations. That the character of the weather will, in a great measure, govern the actions of farmers cannot be questioned. A large proportion of the wheat remaining is, no doubt, in the hands of those who can hold; and, should anything occur to threaten injury to the crops in the ground, we should find few disposed to sell; whilst, on the other hand, a prospect of another good harvest at home and abroad would certainly lead to a desire to clear off old stocks at any sacrifice. The weather during the summer is, therefore, likely to have even greater influence than usual on prices. Hitherto the season has been remarkably propitious, and as yet there is certainly nothing to complain of.

MARKETS.

MARK LANE.—MONDAY, APRIL 8, 1850.

There was only a moderate show of wheat at this morning's market by land carriage samples from Essex, Kent, and Suffolk; and from more remote counties they was scarcely anything fresh up. The condition was scarcely so good as on this day week, and there was decidedly less inclination to buy. Factors commenced by asking former prices, and a few picked lots were placed at terms nearly equal to those current on Monday last; but before the commoner sorts could be disposed of, a decline of fully 1s. per qr. had to be submitted to.

Though the arrivals of wheat from abroad have not been particularly large of

---

17 baskets of meat have come to hand. About 500 carcasses of foreign meat have appeared on sale.

	Per 8 lb. by the carcase.			
	s. d. s. d.			s. d. s. d.
Inferior Beef	1 10 to 2 2	Middling mutton		2 8 3 0
Middling ditto	2 6 2 8	Prime ditto		3 0 3 10
Prime large ditto	2 8 2 10	Veal		2 10 3 10
Ditto small ditto	3 0 3 2	Small Pork		3 6 4 0
Large Pork	2 10 3 4	Lamb		4 8 5 10
Inferior Mutton	2 2 to 2 10			

HOP INTELLIGENCE.—BOROUGH, APRIL 8.

A very limited amount of business is doing in our market, and former rates are with difficulty obtained for inferior sorts.

WOOL.

BRITISH WOOL.—LEEDS, April 5.—There has been rather more inquiry for combing wools during the present week. Prices may be quoted about the same as last week. We have not any alteration in clothing wools to notice.

LIVERPOOL, April 6.—SCOTCH.—There continues an indisposition on the part of the trade to do much in any kind of Scotch wool at present. Stocks are, however, light, and prices well supported.

	h. d. s. d.
Import for the week	169 bags.
Previously this year	1089 ,,

	s. d. s. d.
Laid Highland Wool, per 24lbs.	8 3 to 9 0
White Highland do.	10 6 11 0
Laid Crossed do. unwashed	9 0 11 6
Do do. washed	10 0 13 6
Laid Cheviot do. unwashed	10 0 13 6
Do do. washed	11 6 18 6
White Cheviot do. do.	22 0 36 0

FOREIGN.—The recent imports find buyers on landing at full prices. The reports from the manufacturing districts are rather more favourable this week.

Imports for the week	1603 bales
Previously this year	13732 ,,

FOREIGN WOOL.—CITY, MONDAY.—The wool market continues firm, though it is quiet.

The imports of wool into London during the past week were larger, including 1,127 bales from South Australia, 1,594 from Peru, 216 from Africa, 411 from Germany, 461 from Algoa Bay, and a few bales from Madras, China, &c.

LEEDS, April 5—There has been only a limited business doing in foreign wools during the last fortnight or three weeks, many of the principal manufacturers having previously supplied themselves pretty freely to stock. Prices, however, are firmly maintained; and the manufacturing districts throughout continue in very active employment.

SEASONABLE DISH.

A **DELICIOUS and ECONOMICAL DISH of CURRY** excelling any home made preparation, is prepared with **THE INDIAN CURRY PASTE,** imported direct from Calcutta. The directions are exceedingly simple, and will prove its superior flavour and excellence.

In jars 1s. 6d., 3s., and 7s. 6d. each, to be procured, wholesale and retail, from the importers, HEARD and SON, Fore Street, Bridgewater.

TAPSCOTT'S LINE OF AMERICAN PACKETS FOR NEW YORK.

REGULAR PACKET OF THE 21st APRIL.

The Magnificent American line Packet ship "**NEW WORLD**," Captain Edward K. Knight, 3250 Tons Burthen, will positively sail as above, her regular day.

THIS splendid new Packet Ship is one of the largest and most superb Ships afloat, and is fitted up in a superior manner, to meet the wishes of all classes of Passengers, having private Rooms in Second Cabin and Poop; also, for the better accommodation of UNPROTECTED FEMALES, a large portion of the splendid Cabin has been fitted specially for their accommodation, which, with the well-known gentlemanly and kind attention of her Commander to his Passengers, should command for this noble Ship a decided preference.

For terms of passage, and to secure a preference of berths, Deposits £1 a head should be remitted by Post-office Orders, or otherwise, to W. TAPSCOTT and Co.,

St. George's Buildings, Regent Road, Clarence Dock, Liverpool.

The *New World* has made six of her Passages to and from New York within eighteen Days each Trip.

The well-known fast sailing Packet-ship "**WEST POINT**," Captain Allen, will be the succeeding Packet, and Sails 26th April.

ALSO, FOR NEW YORK.

SHIP.	CAPTAIN.	TONS BUR.	TO SAIL.
Mary Ward	Little	1800	3rd April.
Constitution	Britton	3000	9th —
James H. Shepherd	Ainsworth	1500	6th —
Roscius	Eldridge	2000	11th —
A. Z.	Chandler	1800	15th —
New World	Knight	3000	21st —
West Point	Allen	2000	26th —
E. Z.	Hartshorne	1800	28th —
Isaac Wright	Peabody	2000	1st May

And succeeding Packets weekly through the year

"Tapscott's Emigrants' Guide" can be had by remitting four postage stamps for the same.
